# Lope de Vega on Spanish Screens, 1935–2020

# Lope de Vega on Spanish Screens, 1935–2020

## The Shadow of the Phoenix

Philip Allen

LEXINGTON BOOKS

*Lanham • Boulder • New York • London*

Published by Lexington Books
An imprint of The Rowman & Littlefield Publishing Group, Inc.
4501 Forbes Boulevard, Suite 200, Lanham, Maryland 20706
www.rowman.com

86-90 Paul Street, London EC2A 4NE, United Kingdom

British Library Cataloguing in Publication Information Available

**Library of Congress Cataloging-in-Publication Data**

Names: Allen, Philip, 1989– author.
Title: Lope de Vega on Spanish screens, 1935–2020 : the shadow of the phoenix / Philip Allen.
Description: Lanham : Lexington Books, [2022] | Includes bibliographical references and index. | Summary: "In this book, Philip Allen examines the presence of Lope de Vega's adapted work on Spanish screens since the mid-twentieth century. In his analysis, Allen revisits and problematizes stereotypes present in popular and academic culture surrounding the author's life and works, which have at times been co-opted as propaganda"—Provided by publisher.
Identifiers: LCCN 2022023594 (print) | LCCN 2022023595 (ebook) | ISBN 9781666911770 (cloth) | ISBN 9781666911787 (epub)
Subjects: LCSH: Vega, Lope de, 1562–1635—Adaptations. | Motion pictures—Spain—History. | Spanish literature—Film adaptations.
Classification: LCC PQ6463 .A45 2022 (print) | LCC PQ6463 (ebook) | DDC 862.3—dc23/eng/20220602
LC record available at https://lccn.loc.gov/2022023594
LC ebook record available at https://lccn.loc.gov/2022023595

*To my dearest Emilia (Emma M.).*
*For your love of books.*

# Contents

# Acknowledgments

The journey to realize the studies contained within these pages could not have been taken alone and this book would not have materialized without the help and collaboration of many international archivists, librarians, and scholars.

An enormous debt of gratitude is owed to Yolanda Martínez Villamar and her team at the archives at Televisión Española in Prado del Rey, Madrid, who allowed me access to their offices and digital files on several occasions. Likewise, I would like to thank Emilio Rosario and the staff at the Archivo General de la Administración in Alcalá de Henares for their attention and help in locating many of the documents that have proven vital to my exploration of the censorship's reactions to many of the items included in my analyses. I must also offer my most sincere thanks to José Luis Estarrona at the Filmoteca Española in Madrid for locating and granting me access to some of the more obscure, yet very essential, audiovisual materials that have been central to my research, not to mention the various exchanges in which his advice and suggestions helped to steer my investigation in the right direction. I should also like to express my gratitude to the librarians and technical staff at the Sala de Prensa y Revistas at the Biblioteca Nacional de España in Madrid for their assistance in finding and visualizing press releases and materials from the last century. I would also like to thank María Jesús Pérez López and Noemí Pérez López for their help with the colloquial Valencian and their patience in viewing clips alongside me while they aided in the transcription of these fragments.

Finally, as this project stems from my doctoral dissertation completed at the University of Florida, I would also like to thank Dr. Hélène Huet at the George A. Smathers Libraries for helping me to acquire many of the necessary materials to complete my research. I must also express my undying gratitude to the chair of my supervisory committee, Dr. Luis Álvarez-Castro, without whose help this finished product would never have been more than an idea.

# Introduction

## *Out of the Ashes: Lope de Vega and Modern Media*

Félix Lope de Vega y Carpio (1562–1635) was a popular culture phenomenon like no other in seventeenth-century Spain, so much so that his most fanatical devotees even fashioned a version of the Apostles' Creed in his honor which stated: "I believe in Lope de Vega Almighty, poet of Heaven and Earth."[1] The blasphemous, parodical creed became so commonplace that the Inquisition had to officially prohibit it a decade after Lope's death in 1647.[2] Lope's unparalleled status in everyday early modern speech is also made evident by the fact that the expressions *es de Lope* and *parece de Lope* ("it's by Lope" and "it seems like one of Lope's"), attributed to occasions as solemn as funerals and weddings, became synonymous with excellence and perfection.[3] Known by his rivals and disciples alike as "Freak of Nature" (*Monstruo de naturaleza*) and "Phoenix of Wits" (*Fénix de los ingenios*), Lope has—as far as popular culture is concerned—certainly continued to arise, phoenix-like, from the ashes of obscurity, reentering the collective Spanish imagination sporadically in the nearly four hundred years since his death. His presence in contemporary Spanish popular culture, however, is significantly scarce, especially if we consider the posthumous fame of his compatriot and contemporary Miguel de Cervantes or his English counterpart William Shakespeare. As a matter of fact, it is interesting to note that, while scholars like Michael Andreregg (2010) have had no problems describing Shakespeare's presence in English-speaking popular culture as "too easy and too prominent" (201), the case is hardly the same for Lope. Although it is true that, like Shakespeare, Lope's plays have never ceased to be reworked as live performances throughout the ages, it is also certain that he has struggled to achieve the success that the English Bard has enjoyed on mass media outlets such as film and television.

The noticeable absence of Lope's adapted dramas on today's screens is somewhat ironic, given that his work has been credited as being a direct predecessor to both television and film. In 1943, José Luis Gómez Tello drew a parallel between Lope's trademark brand of theater and the cinematic trends of his day, writing that

> seventeenth-century theater audiences demanded the same things from the stage that current viewers of today's screens demand from filmmakers: intense action, great scene changes, [and] an intrigue that is tangled and untangled at a quick pace. [Even] with all of the magic of the exteriors captured by the agility of the camera in current cinematography . . . there is no magic comparable to that of Lope de Vega as director and developer of the filmic possibilities of the scenery of today. (3)

That same year, Miguel Herrero García (1943) made the same connection much more explicitly, arguing that "when Lope de Vega broke with the pseudoclassic canons of the three units of action, space, and time, he created the cinema" (11). More recently, Victor Dixon (2008) has attributed modern audiences' thirst for immediate gratification to Lope's accelerated speed of *comedia* production, comparing the consumption of the playwright's dramas in seventeenth-century Spain to that of television spectators today. According to Dixon, as with television today, audiences in Golden Age Spain "expected a constant stream of new works, especially three-act *comedias*, so that all imaginable subjects had to be grist to the playwright's mill, including many never thought suitable for dramatization before" (54). Naturally, the "constant stream" of new material continues to evolve in today's visual culture, evidenced by the rapidly increasing popularity of "streaming" services and trends like "binge watching" that have drastically altered television and film consumption patterns.

Such anachronistic claims about Lope's involvement in molding the film and television industries are, of course, not to be taken with complete seriousness. On one hand, it could certainly be argued that Lope's reconsideration of the Classical units of time, space, and action, as well as his habit of including two simultaneous and converging plot lines (the Italian technique of the *imbroglio*), paved the way for today's sitcoms and comedic films.[4] Furthermore, just like Lope before them, modern film and television executives are constantly pushing the limits of "acceptable" topics and imagery. On the other hand, it is much more plausible that both Lope and modern film and television producers have simply drank from the same font in order to attract and entertain audiences. It is well known, for example, that Lope de Vega's theater was greatly inspired by the Italian Renaissance, particularly the dramatic movement known as the *commedia dell'arte*.[5] Likewise, television and sitcom scholars have revealed a similar connection to the Italian theatrical trend and modern-day films and television programs.[6]

Regardless of the arguments about Lope de Vega's possible influence on the film and television industries, there is also debate on his importance within these media. Since the advent of cinema and television in Spain, there has only been a handful of Lope adaptations on film, but many more have been broadcasted on television. Although some scholars like Purificació García Mascarell (2014), to give just one example, have stated that televised manifestations of Lope's works were regular additions to Televisión Española's (TVE) programming during the Francoist dictatorship (71), the episode guides seem to reaffirm what Yolanda López (2017) had already argued, that these only consisted of merely "one or two performances per year" (47). Beyond providing us a glimpse into the total number of Lope adaptations that have reached Spanish screens since the introduction of film and public television in Spain, a review of these programming records also suggests that Lope's adapted works have tended to surface in thematic groups at specific moments in the country's recent history.

Thus, the objective of this volume is to provide a cultural-historical analysis of Lope de Vega's life and works on Spanish television and film, paying particular attention to the ideological currents found within. The purpose is to explore how his plays and his lingering legacy have been handled by the governments and/or production agencies that either produced or sponsored them. As opposed to most of the extant scholarship on these works, this book will seek to discover why they were created for and distributed to the Spanish audience of the time, rather than focusing on the more performative aspects of the productions. Although it is assumed that there will be significant changes in how these plays were used during different time periods, especially with regard to any nationalistic undertones that are certainly present in many of these adaptations, the subject has yet to be studied formally and official conclusions have not been drawn to support these suppositions. Throughout this exploration, one must remain cognizant that all of the adaptations presented within were either directly produced or subsidized with financing provided by Spain's public, government-access network, TVE. This important political aspect of the adaptations has been overlooked in much of the previous scholarship about filmed Golden Age theater adaptations, a fallacy that this book strives to correct.

Indeed, most modern Golden Age scholars have followed in Luciano García Lorenzo's (2000) footsteps by perpetuating his determination that early modern Spanish theater functioned as a "justification of the moral, patriotic, and religious values that the new regimen would put into practice to offer the world an image of the new Spain" (87–88). As such, there has been a predominant assumption that, due to the prevalent themes in Lope's dramas, which coincided with the morals and values endorsed by Franco himself, the regime gave preferential treatment to adaptations of medieval/Golden Age works. As such, many have speculated that the production of such adaptations was even incentivized by the authorities and that Spanish society shunned these works after the conclusion of Francoism because of such a close association.[7] Franco did, to some degree, conceive of Spain's medieval and early modern history as times that represented social ideals that he was eager to revive in twentieth-century society. It is also true that, like other European dictators before him, Franco implemented what Alejandro Quiroga (2014) has described as "vast programs of mass indoctrination in nationalist values" (183) to instill the ideals of the dictatorship into the popular culture of the time in order to form a more cohesive ideological bond between government and governed and the most direct means by which to influence popular culture was through the mass media outlets of the time such as newspapers, television, and film. Be that as it may, there is insufficient evidence to substantiate the notion that the dictator personally encouraged or facilitated adaptations of a particular author's works as a tool with which to disperse his ideological standards throughout Spanish popular culture. What is known, however, is that the systems of supervision that the dictator put in place to monitor which materials were permitted to air on public television did expedite the process of adapting plays like Lope's with minimal state intervention because of their inherent moral and ideological content.

Franco ensured that mass media outlets were completely under governmental control and, especially in the case of television, monopolized by the regime. It is well known that the dictator held a skeptical, if not paranoid, opinion of these new means of communication's potential influence. Franco feared that the implementation of a popular mass media could negatively impact Spanish society by undermining the societal values that his regime sought to instill in the population. He was, consequently, openly aggressive toward both, to the point that he refused to attend the inauguration of TVE in 1956, after having publicly condemned it a year prior. According to the dictator in his annual speech as Head of State in December 1955, cited in Luis Miguel Fernandez's (2014) *Escritores y televisión durante el Franquismo*, he was acutely aware of the dangers imposed

> with the facility of communication media, the power of the [broadcast] waves, film and television have breached the windows of our fortress. The debauchery of the waves and the printed word flies through space and the air with such force that they penetrate our windows, corrupting the purity of our environment. (13)

Although the obvious choice for Franco would have been to prohibit television and film altogether, this was not a viable option. Spain had been in the midst of an economic crisis since the end of the Civil War, and it soon became obvious that the expansion of these new media, whose development promised to propel his country into what Fátima Gil Gascón and Mateos-Pérez (2018) have referred to as a *Western consumption society* like those of the United States and the rest of Europe at the time (86). Instead of banning television and film altogether, Franco chose to impose a thorough scrutiny of the content broadcasted on Spanish screens, acknowledging the urgent need to organize and supervise the "informational systems within which propagandistic persuasion ended up being one of the main objectives" (Gil Gascón and Mateos-Pérez 41).[8] As a result, Franco established the Censorship Board (*Junta de Censura*), official state censorship whose main function was to review scripts prior to issuing production permits, evaluate the completed productions before public distribution, and monitor the content being displayed on screens.[9] Although there are no extant documents that show how the censors reacted to proposed or viewed television programs, the reports that these censors issued before and after film productions will prove central to the analyses of the cinematic adaptations of Lope de Vega's plays and their relationship with Francoist ideology.[10]

The criteria used on the pre-prepared forms completed by censors included a blueprint for the reviewers to consider the scripts as literary artifacts as well as to reflect on how the filmed production could affect the broader Spanish society. The criteria for a reviewed script read as follows:

(1.) Plot
(2.) Message
(3.) Cinematic Value of the Script
(4.) Literary Value
(5.) Moral and Religious Value
(6.) Social and Political Overtones
(7.) General Reader's Report
(8.) Corrections to the Pages
(9.) Artistic Point of View

No censor, of course, would have dared to question the literary value of an original Lope play; however, not even the adaptations of the Phoenix's works were immune to the scrutiny of their moral and religious value, or their sociopolitical overtones, especially in the case of dramas like *Fuenteovejuna*. Such classics, which in modern times are often still associated with the dictatorship—as Robert Bayliss (2015) reminds us, because of a "certain nostalgia for a national identity or national essence" (714)—have often been considered as immune to Francoist censorship. The simple fact that these works were subjected to such a thorough review process might be surprising to many cultural and literary scholars today. Nevertheless, the threat of liberal, republican contamination over which the regime obsessed resulted in rigorous scrutiny of (and frequent modifications to) even Spain's most treasured classics.[11]

Additionally, this volume presents the results of viewing all of the Lope adaptations in succession, which allows for an identification of differences in the ideological uses of these productions according to the sociopolitical climate in which they were released. In order to demonstrate this, the book engages with the following specific questions over the course of the present volume: How have different governments and regimes used the figure of Lope de Vega and adapted versions of his theater, or not, to promote certain agendas or ideologies? What thematic similarities exist among adaptations that are released in certain periods? What aspects of Spanish history have been highlighted by these productions and why? How are past epochs, historical figures, and nationalistic ideals presented in these adaptations and do these differ from their original presentation in Lope's theater? Where can we see traces of a perceived national Spanish identity in these adaptations? What fundamental differences exist between the adaptations released during Francoism versus after the dissolution of the state's official censorship? All of these questions require us to pause and reconsider our understanding of "national identity," especially in the case of Spain in recent decades.

## ON NATIONAL IDENTITY, NATIONALISM, AND PATRIOTISM

The phrase "national identity" is used very frequently in culture/ideology studies to refer to how inhabitants of different areas and regions in the world find a sense of belonging with their peers. Although the general concept is relatively easy to grasp, famed political scientist Benedict Anderson (1991) has been cognizant of the fact that both the adjective "national" and its accompanying noun "identity" are extremely difficult terms to define. Anderson observes that the very notion of "nation" and what constitutes "nationality" are fairly recent constructs that vary according to time, geographical location, and cultural landscapes. As such, it is virtually impossible to formulate a definition that encompasses all of the possibilities of what "nation" or its derivative "national" could mean; therefore, he uses an anthropological perspective to propose that all nations constitute an imagined political community (6).

Richard Verdugo and Andrew Milne (2016) take Anderson's thoughts on the concept of nation and nationalism as a point of departure to clarify confusions that arise from key differences in three terms they see as closely related, but not identical: *national identity, nationalism,* and *patriotism.*

Despite the fact that any attempt to define these terms could be discarded as arbitrary due to the many paradoxes and imperfections that exist within them, I find their definitions to be the most concise and consistent with the latest research on the subject. According to them, "national identity is a sense of 'belonging' to and being a member of a geopolitical entity" (3). They go on to argue that *nationalism*, on the other hand, is a strong attachment to one's country and the sense that one's country is superior to all others, whereas *patriotism* is "a strong devotion to one's country and one's behavior in support of its decisions and practices" (3). In this study, Verdugo and Milne's distinctions and clarifications are to be kept in mind when these three terms arise, while always keeping in mind the "imagined" quality that is inherent to these concepts.

One also must remain aware that the idea of Spain as a nation is also problematic, especially considering the time frames which constitute this study. Although Lope de Vega frequently referred to the Iberian territory as *España* in his literature, Simon Barton (2009) reminds us that the name used by Lope should not be interpreted as a *political unit* that nineteenth-century Western intellectuals would later define as a *nation*. Indeed, Barton argues, referring to Spain as a cohesive sociopolitical unit has always been complicated, if not entirely impossible, given that ideological discord among its citizens has always threatened to divide the country and that the specter that Spain might disintegrate has never quite disappeared. Even today, he says, "Spaniards are still trying to come to terms with that legacy; the struggle between center and periphery goes on" (121).

We see this conflict in the present-day independence movements that still threaten the unity of the nation we all know as Spain. Nevertheless, this monograph refers to Spain as a nation according to the criteria set forth by Verdugo and Milne (2016) who specify that a nation constitutes a geopolitical construct in which "being a member is based on blood, ethnicity, history, ancestry, common values, kinship, and language" (3) because these elements are all aligned with both seventeenth- and twentieth-century arguments regarding what it means to be Spanish, as demonstrated by the cultural artifacts studied in the upcoming chapters. In the pages that follow, we will study the manifestations of Lope de Vega and his works in relation to their position in the broader, national popular culture.

## ON POPULAR CULTURE

A great deal of our consideration of these adaptations and their author will center around their place in popular culture. Therefore, it is necessary to clarify what exactly the broad phrase "popular culture" means in this context.

Critical cultural studies scholars have attempted for many years, with varying degrees of success, to define popular culture and identify which cultural
products pertain to this subdivision. The adjective "popular" can be—especially for the purposes of this study—rather misleading. Derived from Latin
*populāris*, "of the people," the term has tended to bear a connotation of "low
class" or "unsophisticated" in contemporary English usage. The New American Oxford Dictionary's definition of the term continues to hint at this meaning with its entry: "(of cultural activities or products) intended for or suited to
the taste, understanding, or means of the general public rather than specialists
or intellectuals." Many scholars today continue to adhere to this literal meaning of the adjective when considering popular culture in their publications.
Dwight Macdonald (1953), for example, identifies popular culture as any art
form made readily available to the masses that attempts to counteract an elit-
ist definition of "true" art (16).[12]

An article written in the February 7, 1964 edition of the Spanish newspaper
*Arriba* offers us a glimpse into what *cultura popular* meant in Spain during
a decade in which many of the adaptations considered in this volume were
released. The description provided in this article aligns much more closely
with the colloquial use of the phrase than the modern English dictionary, saying that "popular culture tends to be the index of participation in and assimila-
tion into the cultural items that the country's population enjoys collectively"
(n.p.).[13] For the purposes of our study, the phrase "popular culture" is used
in this sense. Whereas McDonald and the New American Oxford Dictionary
frame popular culture as a separate category of products, perspectives, and
practices that depend on socioeconomic factors, I consider popular culture to
be a more inclusive entity in which members of all levels of society with a
common cultural background participate. John Street (2013) offers perhaps
the best explanation of the modern understanding of this concept, affirming
that "popular culture is a form of entertainment that is mass produced or is
made available to large numbers of people . . . no particular skills or knowledge are required; no particular status or class is barred from entry" (19).
From this point forward, this understanding of popular culture encompasses
any type of mass media, including, but not limited to, television, film, newspapers, magazines, non-academic literature, and promotional materials for all
of these products.

Obviously, socioeconomic restraints limit who can afford to participate
actively in popular culture at a given time. The understanding of "popular culture" products and byproducts in the following chapters always refers to those
materials that were readily available to significant portions of society at the
time of their introduction into Spanish culture without considering economic
exclusivity. Additionally, one must also take into account the dynamic quality of popular culture. In other words, as a certain population's sociopolitical

situation evolves and changes, so too will its sociocultural climate. These advancements affect several aspects of entertainment consumption, given that tastes and fads evolve quickly and, oftentimes, drastically over a short period of time.

## Lope in Spanish Popular Culture throughout the Ages

No other author from Spain's Golden Age has merited as much attention in the country's popular culture as Lope de Vega. Born and raised in the modest village that was Madrid during the sixteenth century, Lope's career blossomed at a time in which the literary climate was overwhelmingly active and fiercely competitive: Luis de Góngora, Francisco de Quevedo, Tirso de Molina, Pedro Calderón de la Barca, and Miguel de Cervantes, just to name a few, all lived and interacted with one another in an area comprising less than a square mile.[14] The contributions to world literature that arose from the Spanish capital during the Golden Age are unparalleled in almost any other time and place. It was here, for example, that Cervantes published both parts of his *Don Quijote de la Mancha* (1605 and 1615), a masterpiece that has been regarded as the first modern novel and has been translated into more languages than any other text in history, save the Bible. The first theatrical manifestation of the "Don Juan myth," arguably the single most influential literary figure of all time, was also conceived in Madrid during this time via a play formerly attributed to Tirso de Molina, and now to Andrés de Claramonte, *El burlador de Sevilla* (1616).[15] In spite of all of these literary accomplishments by his rivals, Lope de Vega, the most prolific author in the history of the Western world, has been the most immortalized in film and television.[16]

Once Spain's illustrious literary Golden Age had come to a close, Lope and his works quickly faded from the collective Spanish consciousness. Whereas the eighteenth century saw a popular reconfiguration of the "Don Juan myth" with Antonio de Zamora's *No hay plazo que no se cumpla ni deuda que no se pague, o convidado de piedra* (ca. 1714) and Cervantes's *Quijote* began to foster an international following in countries such as England and France, Lope was largely left out of the popular and academic literary and theatrical discourse. His decline in popularity would only be exacerbated further by the nineteenth-century Romantics, who witnessed the publication of the most influential of all the Don Juan's adaptations, José Zorrilla's *Don Juan Tenorio* (1844), again reviving the "Don Juan myth." At the same time, international intellectuals, namely August Wilhelm and Frederick Schlegel of Germany, were disseminating Cervantes's masterpiece across Europe, firmly establishing its privileged position in the Western canon. Humboldt, Sismondi, Schopenhauer, and Shelley Schlegel saw in the novel a fascinating perspective of a bygone era that was only conserved in Spain. José Álvarez Junco (2016) indicates that these early scholars of Spain's Golden Age considered the Iberian country "a medieval country, authentic and fascinating," and propelled the work and its author to the status of literary hero and indispensable artifact of European popular culture (187).

Meanwhile, Lope's plays had received virtually no international acclaim and, when they did appear in Spain, were often mutilated beyond recognition to make *refundiciones* (remakes) that failed to generate the same public enthusiasm as the originals. Enrique García Santo-Tomás (2000b) classifies his existence in popular culture during the European Romantic period as one of an "erased Lope, scratched out and rewritten," while the novel of his supposed bitter rival Cervantes was being preserved and revered as a sacred national treasure (267). In fact, scholars like Antonio Sánchez Jiménez (2008) have even argued that Cervantes's fame and popularity in Spain during this time came at Lope's expense, correctly observing that the "Cervantes's canonization has provoked the demonization of Lope," because the exaltation of the former's literature was often done by impugning the latter's (355). The memory of Lope vis-à-vis Cervantes has remained commonplace even to this day.

There was no indication that Lope would find a more prevalent place in Spanish popular culture at the onset of the twentieth century. The loss of Spain's last overseas colonies in 1898 served as a catalyst to, again, conjure the ghost of Cervantes and his *Quijote*, while Lope was largely ignored.[17] A significant shift in popular culture regarding the two authors would not be detectable until the 1940s. As the ideological forces of Franco's dictatorship penetrated ever more profoundly into Spanish society, the conceptualization of some of Spain's cultural icons, namely Cervantes and *Don Quijote*, began to change. Manuel Herranz Martín (2013) points out that the Francoist school of thought did not reject the novel, but rather offered a predominant interpretation of the *Quijote* during Francoism with the "objective of promoting its protagonist as an example of heroism in a mystical-religious sense" (16). Nevertheless, it has been argued that the central themes and motives of Cervantes's masterpiece did not fit into the Francoist ideology as neatly as Lope de Vega's plays. Amando Carlos Isasi Angulo (1973) underlines the contrast between the two authors by stating that the "conformist nature of Lope's plays is made more manifest if it is compared to the Cervantine attitude. Don Quijote's position is one of an attempt to break with the world around him" (272). Perhaps it was precisely this rebellious spirit that resulted in apprehension from television and film producers when it came to adaptations of *Don Quijote*, thus greatly reducing the amount of televised and film manifestations of the novel during this time.

On the other hand, Cervantes and his *Qujote* were still extremely present and frequent in daily Spanish life outside of television and film in the early years of Francoism. His masterpiece was still taught in public schools, his monuments were still to be found in Madrid and other Spanish cities, his 400th birth anniversary was commemorated with many public events in 1947, and his portrait even appeared on the one *peseta* bill in 1951. His absence on film and television had created a space in popular culture, however, for the emergence of none other than Lope de Vega, who, as chapter 2 will show, was the Golden Age author whose works found the steadiest presence in these new media.

Moreover, it would appear as though an interest in learning more about the author himself had been sparked in Spanish popular culture, at least in the later years of the dictatorship. Newspapers like *La Vanguardia* were attempting to convince their readers that Lope was suitable and recommendable to modern audiences, his house-turned-museum was renovated and expanded in 1965, excavations to locate his mortal remains were conducted in 1968, and *Estudio 1* produced an episode called "El mejor mozo de España" in 1970 that reenacted a day in the life of the dramatist.[18] Although it is plausible, as Manuel Herranz Martín (2013) posits, that the Spanish public had simply grown weary of the constant exaltation of Cervantes that had prevailed for centuries (19), I find it much more probable that the rediscovery of such an interesting, yet obscure historical figure had stirred an interest in popular culture to get better acquainted with Lope, the man and, especially, the myth, which this volume examines in chapter 4 alongside a consideration of the Lope *biopics* that have been produced in recent decades. Preceding an investigation into the dramaturg's place in modern popular culture, however, the adaptations of his works that have transcended the page and the stage and made their way to the big and small screens in Spain will be analyzed.

## FROM THE STAGE TO THE SCREEN: ADAPTATIONS OF THEATRICAL TEXTS

One must consider that Lope de Vega often based his plays on accounts recorded in national chronicles, local folklore, and oral historical traditions. The playwright frequently took stories from other media and transformed them into theatrical dramas, meaning that the products studied in this volume are often adaptations of adaptations. It is also necessary to remember that Spanish Golden Age plays—as opposed to modern theatrical spectatorship—invited active participation from audiences, which, in a sense, allowed viewers the opportunity to engage with their national history in a hands-on experience.

By the mid-1700s, theatergoers from all realms of the social spectrum in Spain had maintained the same behavioral habits in theaters, which included their tendency to interact with the actors who were performing on stage, much as they had done in the *corrales* for the past two centuries.[19] As the shock-waves of the European Enlightenment finally began to permeate the mindsets of Spanish intellectuals, such rowdy behavior was considered uncivilized and ill-suited to the types of dramas that were being written and performed on Spanish stages. Audience participation and instant judgment and harassment from the *mosqueteros*—groups of rowdy spectators who would loudly demonstrate their approval or rejection of a play during a live performance—had come to hinder the performances and were considered a nuisance to wealthy patrons. Riding the waves of social change, theater companies incrementally raised admission prices so as to exclude the lower classes from attending performances. Noticing a change in the quality of productions that resulted from a seated audience, such as more elaborate special effects and more complex dialogues that attendees could now hear, the Board for Theatrical Reform (*Junta de Reforma de Teatros*) officially outlawed standing in theaters and audience intervention in 1792.[20]

The interactive nature of Lope's plays had become a fundamental ingredient to their success and popularity with audiences. It is therefore not surprising that productions of his brand of *comedias* would experience a sharp decline during this period that would last for well over a century. As detrimental as these changes proved for Lope's presence on the Spanish stage, theorists of visual culture, such as Anthony Guneratne (2008), assure us that these shifts in theatrical customs facilitated and paved the way for the era of cinema that would follow (xix). Accustomed to assuming the role of passive receptor of theatrical performances, audiences found the transition from theater to cinema to be much less drastic. As the cinema began to overshadow the theater in Western cultures, European governments were painfully aware of the international implications of fostering a thriving film industry. Keith Cameron (1999) highlights that, across Europe, it had always been "natural for theater as an institution to be associated with the very identity of the nation" (80). By the mid-twentieth century, the same concept had come to be applied to cinema and, by extension, television; thus, the doors were open for a new type of adaptations of Lope de Vega's plays to be distributed across the country and, possibly, create an institution that would also be associated with the identity of the nation. Ironically, the changes in theatrical behavior that had resulted in a lack of interest in Lope's plays on the stage were precisely the innovations needed to provide them with a presence in modern mass media.

## CONTENTS AND CHAPTER OUTLINES

With the exception of chapter 4, this volume looks only at film and television adaptations of theatrical dramas that were written by or attributed to Lope de

Vega and that were created by Spanish film and television production companies for distribution within Spain.[21] The present study therefore excludes adaptations brought to life on other media, such as the theater. An anomaly in our study is *La Estrella de Sevilla*, a play that was once attributed to Lope, but whose authorship has widely been refuted by modern scholarship and is now considered to be the work of Andrés de Claramonte.[22] Another salient feature of this title is the fact that, although two feature-film screenplays were presented for review to the state censorship under Franco's regime, both were rejected and, to date, *La Estrella de Sevilla* has never been produced as a major motion picture. Chapter 1 takes an in-depth exploration into the unsuccessful attempts at converting the drama into a film and compares the screenplays side-by-side with the source text and considers the response from censors.

Additionally, as one of the primary objectives of this study is to scrutinize the treatment of Lope's plays across Spain's evolving sociopolitical landscape both during and after the Francoist dictatorship, the aim of the present volume is to arrive at more solid conclusions regarding any ideological manipulation of Lope's texts across different sociopolitical periods. To facilitate the achievement of this objective, the remaining chapters of the book are divided to correspond to two traditionally directly opposed moments in recent Spanish sociopolitical history: the dictatorship (1939–1975) and the democratic period (1975–present), which will be studied in chapters 2 and 3, respectively.

The present study is divided thematically into four core content chapters based on their subject matter:

(1.) The scripts of *La Estrella de Sevilla* that were submitted to the censors for their review and were subsequently banned.
(2.) The adaptations of rural "honor plays" centered around the common man's plight against oppressive authority figures, all of which were released only during the Francoist regime and not since.
(3.) Urban romantic comedies (*comedias de enredo*), all dealing with a leading female protagonist and her entanglement in complex love webs.
(4.) Lope as a character in *biopics* that depict his life and times.

As such, chapters 2 and 3 are divided chronologically according to their release dates in relation to the dictatorship (as stated above, chapter 2 examines those films and television episodes released during Francoism whereas chapter 3 focuses on those that have debuted since the regime's official dissolution in 1978, even though each title examined was also released at least once during the dictatorship). Although such a division may seem arbitrary due to the complexities that prevent a precise dictatorship/post-dictatorship dichotomy, the absence of Lope adaptations from 1975 to 1980, in addition to the thematic correlations described above, provides a very convenient boundary for our analysis.

The long-lasting shadow of the Phoenix of Wits, and the vast bibliography he left behind after his death, has been continually cast over academic culture in Spain and abroad. The Biblioteca Nacional de España (BNE) in Madrid, for instance, has recently offered patrons and the public an exhibition on "Lope and Golden Age Theater."[23] The event has been celebrated with lectures given by renowned Lope specialists, or *lopistas*, who, according to the BNE's official website, contribute to the library's mission of providing attendees with a "glance at and reflection of how the arrival of the digital era is affecting Golden Age theater, both in its performances and *mise-en-scene* as well as the production, diffusion, and research into this extremely rich patrimony" ("Lope y el teatro del Siglo de Oro en la BNE" n.p.). As this quote suggests, scholars are becoming increasingly intrigued by Lope's presence in modern popular culture. Chapter 4, entitled "The Phoenix Regenerated (1935–2018)" diverges from the majority of these studies by shifting the focus away from his theater in lieu of the historical figure that he has become in the collective Spanish imagination since his death. The objective of this final chapter is to attempt to include a holistic overview of the figure of Lope de Vega on Spanish film and television in order to identify what his legacy means, if anything, to today's popular culture.

## NOTES

1. All translations from Spanish to English here and throughout are my own.

2. See Menéndez y Pelayo's (1909) *Historia de las ideas* (783).

3. Profeti (*Otro Lope* II: 149, "Lope de Vega" 793), Sánchez Jiménez (*Lope Pintado* 237), and Blecua ("Más sobre" 471–473) all mention the popularity of this expression. Additionally, the Real Academia Española recently published a brief article on its importance and usage during the seventeenth century, which is available at www.rae.es/la-institucion/iii-centenario/es-lope.

4. Lope established new theatrical trends that broke with the Classical units of time, space, and action and introduced the idea of A and B plotlines in many of his dramas. He compiled those aspects of his plays that he believed made them successful and discussed them in a speech addressed to the Academy of Madrid that was later published as *The New Art of Writing Plays* (*El arte nuevo de hacer comedias*) in 1609.

5. The *commedia dell'arte*, as influential as it has been to the Western literary and media traditions, was considered a low-brow dramatic form suited only to the uneducated, lower social classes in its own day. Plays were, most often, not written down and participation from the audience was encouraged. Many studies have been

conducted regarding the influence of the *commedia dell'arte* on Lope de Vega's theater. Among the most recent include Jonathan Thacker's "Lope, the Comedian" (161–164) and Nancy D'Antuono's "The Spanish Golden Age Theatre" (240–245).

6. See, for example, Maurice Charney's *Comedy: A Geographic and Historical Guide* (2005), Brett Mills's *Television Sitcom* (2008), Marcel Danesi's *Popular Culture: Introductory Perspectives* (2008), and Martin Green and John Swan's *Triumph of Pierrot: The Commedia dell'Arte and the Modern Imagination* (2010).

7. Duncan Wheeler (2008) posits, for example, that the lack of adaptations of Lope's plays on Spanish screens—or Golden Age dramas in general—after Francoism "was most probably a consequence of the fact that, in this transitional period, Golden Age drama was often thought of as a reactionary art form that had enjoyed special treatment under Franco" (293). Veronica Ryjik (2011) concurs with this deduction, reaffirming that "durante los años de la *Transición*, la reacción a la noción de la España 'una, grande y libre,' difundida por la propaganda del régimen, llevó a un replanteamiento y subsiguiente cuestionamiento del concepto de la nación española," which, in turn, made Lope an obsolete figure in the collective Spanish imagination (7). Walther Bernecker and Sören Brinkman (2004) also attribute this indifference to the *comedia* to the fact that the traditionalist and Catholic vision of Spain, the pillars of Lope's works that the dictatorship found so appropriate for public diffusion, lost all authority and pretensions of validity after Franco's death (6–7). Robert Bayliss (2015) reaffirms these assumptions by considering the radical changes to the concept of "españolidad" during the years immediately following Franco's death as a catalyst for "un despojo de los iconos y símbolos (como Lope de Vega) propagados durante la dictadura" (717).

8. Lorenzo Díaz (1999) offers an extensive overview on the rigor with which film and television were scrutinized during the dictatorship (44–50). He reminds us, for example, that a photo of Franco was required to be displayed before and after the news broadcasts that preceded any film shown in Spanish cinemas and that any type of documentary film was nearly impossible to receive a production permit from the regime.

9. Francoist censorship also extended to monitoring the press, theater performances, and promotional materials for cinemas. See especially Manuel Abellán (1980), Justino Sinova (2001), and Bienvenido Llopis (2009). Additionally, in 1952, a systemized categorization of films was put in place to reward filmmakers whose productions were pleasing to the regime and punish those that were not. Virginia Higginbotham (1988) details these categories thusly: "The first category, 'interés nacional,' provided a state rebate of 50 percent; 1A, 40 percent; 1B, 35 percent; 2A, 30 percent; 2B, 25 percent. There was a third class, a kind of cinema Siberia, in which not only did a film receive no state funds, but it could also not be premiered in either of the country's two principle cities" (10).

10. Archivists Emilio Rosillo (Archivo General de la Administración in Alcalá de Henares) and Yolanda Martínez Villamar (Documents and Archives at RTVE) have confirmed that no official reports on Francoist television censorship exist today in their archives. The only censorship reports that remain today are housed at the Archivo General de la Administración in Alcalá de Henares and pertain exclusively to reviews of proposed and completed films.

11. As with most of the regime's policies, however, there was a stark difference between the rigor with which films and television shows were censored at the beginning of the dictatorship versus toward the end. Scholars like José Luis García Delgado (2000) have classified two stages of Francoism: the first, a strict dictatorship [*dictadura*] and the second a *dictablanda* (54). The term *dictablanda* had also been used previously to refer to the regime of Primo de Rivera. By 1962, the regime was entering this second stage and had acquired an interest in emulating its European neighbors' film industries, in an attempt to appear more democratic and end its political isolation in the West. Jose María García Escudero, director of the Departamento de Cinematografía y Teatro, even took strides to soften censorship that same year. Although he was unsuccessful in doing so, Higginbotham (1988) reminds us that his efforts were not in vain and that "he was able to establish, in 1962, a category for noncommercial, artistically valuable *cine de interés especial*, or Special Interest films. This category made it possible for young directors from the Escuela Oficial de Cinematografía (EOC), to make films in an industry that had always excluded young professionals except as apprentices" (61).

12. There is a staggering parallel between Macdonald's (1953) perspective on "true art" and those presented by Lope de Vega in his *Arte nuevo* (1609). Essentially, it would seem as though McDonald espouses an archaic perception of popular culture and that Lope was a pioneer in defining the concept in seventeenth-century Spain.

13. The description provided by the anonymous commentator in *Arriba* very closely resembles the definition offered by the latest version of Spain's Real Academia Española's definition: "Conjunto de las manifestaciones en que se expresa la vida tradicional de un pueblo" (*DRAE*).

14. This area of the "Madrid de los Austrias" is still referred to as the "barrio de las letras" and many of the streets and metro stations there are named after the Golden Age authors who either lived in or frequented this area. For more on the friendships and rivalries between these historical figures, including the so-called "literary wars" that sparked among them, see also Ziomek (204–210), Samson and Thacker (75–76), Lindsay Kerr, (10–11), and Hugo Rennert (117–120).

15. According to Armand Singer (1965), the character of Don Juan has been revived and adapted in more literature and film than any other character in history. In 1993, he calculated a total of 3,081 adaptations, categorized thusly: (1) folklore, legends, and versions; (2) certain mythological characters that represent the seducer type; (3) and themes parallel to that of Don Juan. Additionally, Juan Rof Carballo includes Don Juan—along with Faust, Hamlet, and Don Quijote—in his list of four genuine modern literary myths, clarifying that "only the last one—Don Juan—truly deserves the name of 'modern myth'" (124).

16. As I will explain in chapter 4, this phenomenon also applies to Lope's immortalization in biopics. The only two other Golden Age authors who have had feature-length biopics made about them are Santa Teresa de Jesús (Francisco Bertingola, 1929; Juan de Orduña, 1962), San Juan de la Cruz (Carlos Saura, 1989), and Miguel de Cervantes (Vincent Sherman, 1967; Alfonso Ungría, 1980). It should also be noted that Cervantes shares the spotlight with Lope de Vega in *Cervantes contra Lope* (2016), which I will examine later in the chapter.

17. According to Luis Alberto de Cuenca (2005), the defeat of Spanish forces in Cuba and the Philippines provoked a "relectura del *Quijote* por parte de los pensadores e intelectuales de la llamada Generación del 98," noticing a change in interpretation of the novel to one that expressed "los males que aquejaban a España y el despliegue de un abanico de propuestas para regenerar el país" (7). Spanish intellectuals at the time also took notice of the cathartic possibilities of *Don Quijote*; for example, Benito Pérez Galdós wrote only a few months after the loss of Cuba that the novel constituted "el principal objeto de orgullo nacional," ("Una carta" 16) while Maeztu reiterated in 1903 that Cervantes's book should always be considered "el símbolo de España" (3). It comes as no surprise then, that the early twentieth century would see such a surge of enthusiasm for Cervantes and his most famous literary work.

18. Events such as the restoration and conversion of Lope de Vega's house in downtown Madrid into a museum and the release of the proto-biopic *La musa y el fénix* in 1935 had already laid the framework for these events decades earlier; nevertheless, they certainly helped Lope to gain popularity in the 1960s and 1970s when these subjects were revisited.

19. A *corral de comedias* was an open-air theater held in a courtyard or plaza in Spain where most performances for non-royal or noble audiences took place.

20. The evolution of audience's behavior in Spanish theaters is extensively detailed in Joaquín Álvarez Barrientos (2003) (especially pp. 1395–1450).

21. A possible exception to this criterion is *Fuenteovejuna* (1972), which was a joint production between TVE and RAI (Radiotelevizione Italiana). As TVE owned 70 percent of the shares of the expenditure and RAI only held the remaining 30, it will be included in our corpus. Additionally, the production was filmed in Spain, in the Spanish language, and employed a cast of exclusively Spanish actors.

22. More than one possible author has been hypothesized, among the most likely is Andrés de Claramonte, to whom Alfredo Rodríguez López-Vázquez attributes the drama in his 2010 critical edition of the text. See also Aubrey Bell's "The Authorship of *La Estrella de Sevilla*" (97–98), Ruth Lee Kennedy's "La Estrella de Sevilla as a Mirror of the Courtly Scene—And of Its Anonymous Dramatist (Luis Vélez???)" (103–143), Jonathan Thacker's "El duque de Viseo and *La Estrella de Sevilla*" (152–155), and Frederick de Armas's *Heavenly Bodies* (1996).

23. The exposition took place from November 28, 2018, until March 17, 2019.

# Chapter 1

# Unlucky Stars

## *The Dictatorship's Forbidden Films*

The persisting debate as to whether or not Francisco Franco's authoritarian regime favored and/or gave special permissions for adaptations of Lope de Vega's dramas to be produced throughout the realm should have been settled in the middle of the twentieth century. Nevertheless, most scholarship in the last half of a century overlooks or omits the most salient evidence that the dictator's censors gave no preference to any particular author or time period when it came to deciding which scripts were green-lit and which were shelved. Indeed, two film scripts labeled as adaptations of original plays by none other than Lope de Vega were prohibited by the censorship and never achieved a theatrical release.

The drama in question, *La Estrella de Sevilla*, has been problematic for a plethora of reasons. Little is known about the play's early years, as its oldest textual witnesses are far from reliable. They were printed during a time in which the Board for Reform,[1] established by King Philip IV in 1621, was already beginning to increase scrutiny and discourage the publication of dramatic works for general distribution, fearing that they would contribute to the corruption of the nation's youth.[2] The only two known seventeenth-century versions of the play have come down to us as an independently printed edition (*suelta*) and a longer *desglosada*—that is, a play originally printed as part of a volume and then extracted from it.[3] According to Ramón Foulché-Delbosc (1920), the *suelta* was published between 1624 and 1635 and the longer *desglosada* between 1630 and 1635 (506).[4] Whatever the case may be, both extant witnesses are extremely problematic. As Alfredo Rodríguez López-Vázquez (2010) reiterates in his critical edition of the text, both of them likely derive from a common previous edition of the play—quite possibly a manuscript—that was probably composed around 1623, but has been lost for centuries (73).[5] To make matters worse, there are no documented contemporary performances of the play, which reinforces James Pyle Wickersham Crawford's (1930) assertion that *La Estrella de Sevilla* "attained no degree of popularity during the lifetime of its author" (495).

The drama's lack of popularity in its own time is perhaps not surprising when we take into account its subject matter. The play revolves around the triumphant arrival of King Sancho IV of Castile (1258–1295)—known to history as *Sancho el Bravo*, or Sancho the Brave—in the newly conquered city of Seville in a civil war waged against his own father and, subsequently, his nephew Alfonso de la Cerda.[6] The second son of the beloved King Alfonso X the Wise and Queen Violante, Sancho was never considered heir apparent to the throne of Castile due to his older brother, Fernando de la Cerda, having provided two male heirs prior to his untimely death in 1275. Unhappy with his position as the "spare" and not the "heir," especially after the death of his elder brother, Sancho had broken with his father in 1282 and, although he was initially unsuccessful in securing the crown for himself, assumed royal authority in Valladolid later that same year. He would, consequently, be crowned King of Castile upon the death of his father in 1284. The conflict resulted in Sancho's excommunication and his issue being declared illegitimate.[7] The strained relationship between Sancho and the legitimate members of the royal succession caused him to be a highly disliked historical figure during the Medieval and Early Modern eras.

In the seventeenth-century drama, King Sancho arrives in Seville after triumphantly winning the city in battle, an episode which is not shown or referenced much in the text. As he is getting acquainted with his new subjects, he becomes infatuated with Estrella Tavera, the sister of Seville's *Corregidor*, Busto Tavera.[8] Despite the fact that Estrella has been betrothed to her brother's best friend, Sancho Ortiz de las Roelas, the king makes inappropriate advances on her in public, stalks her, and manipulates her house slave into letting him into her chambers late at night after ensuring that her brother would be away until morning. The house slave, Natilde, is promised a handsome sum of money and her freedom in exchange for her participation in the conspiracy. Unbeknownst to the sinister king, Busto had been made suspicious that someone at court might attempt something lewd on his property and catches the sovereign in the act, having returned home earlier than expected to protect his household. Unaware that the assailant was none other than the newly arrived King of Castile, Busto unsheathes his sword and threatens to take the intruder's life. King Sancho, humiliated and offended by his new subject, finds himself unable to publicly denounce Busto's behavior lest he uncover his own impropriety and thus initiates a cryptic quid pro quo with Estrella's fiancé and Busto's best friend, Sancho Ortiz, to kill Busto in exchange for clemency and a coveted position as a royal border guard.

Sancho Ortiz's strong sense of loyalty to the crown and obsession with honor drives him to comply with his agreement with the king—which he makes before being made aware that his target is his best friend and future brother-in-law—and goes temporarily mad with grief, hallucinating that he has descended into Hell. In spite of his lamentations and the realization that the zeal to please his king has caused him to be the author of his own downfall, he refuses to confess the true motive behind the murder and implicate the king in the crime, before being relieved to hear that he will face capital punishment for the homicide. In an attempt to convince the warden to spare his hitman's life, King Sancho eventually confesses to ordering the murder. Naturally, the monarch is never in any danger of being held accountable for his conduct due to the understanding that his sovereign will constitute law; as such, it is his subjects who are left to face the consequences of his conspiracy. Estrella, tainted by the scandal and unable to give herself as Sancho Ortiz's lawfully wedded wife, resigns herself to a convent while the latter is perpetually banished from Castilian territory for the murder.[9]

*La Estrella de Sevilla* is unique among Golden Age plays in its placement of a monarch in the role of antagonist. It is even more distinctive in its conclusion, which does not serve justice against the villain, apart from the fact that he expresses momentary regret at the catastrophe he has caused. The impression of King Sancho IV that audiences and readers of the original play are left with is that of an immoral, homicidal, and capricious monarch who, unlike other despotic characters of the day, is never put to justice, either by a higher secular authority or by divine intervention. English bibliographer and scholar Sir Henry Thomas (1923) astutely observes that an element of the play that might explain its poor contemporary reception was the fact that the medieval storyline would also have reminded contemporary audiences of uncomfortable episodes in their own recent history. Readers and viewers in seventeenth-century Spain could all too easily have made a connection between the plot and when King Philip II instigated the murder of Juan Escobedo in 1578 and/or when his grandson, King Philip IV, encouraged the assassination of the Conde de Villamediana in 1622 (xiv).[10] Whatever the case may be, and in spite of the drama's negative depiction of the monarch, placing him in a central role, even as an antagonist, clearly did not convince contemporary theater companies to debut the play on stage.

In addition to the drama's tumultuous textual transmission and potentially problematic subject matter, the play has also caused fierce debate among scholars regarding its authorship. Throughout the first three hundred years of its existence, *La Estrella de Sevilla* was unquestionably considered to have been written by Lope. There are many reasons as to why this confusion has loomed throughout the centuries. Primarily, as Rodríguez López-Vázquez (2010) reminds us, printing presses in the 1730s had already developed the habit of stamping Lope de Vega's name on any and every printed drama in hopes of boosting sales, leading to many works being equivocally attributed to the dramaturg (43). It is likely for this very reason that *La Estrella de Sevilla* has continued to be published as a Lope play, even though scholarly consensus since the 1920s has almost entirely discarded him as a plausible author. The economic interests of early modern printers and modern film and theater producers notwithstanding, one does not have to leave the confines of seventeenth-century literature to find clues as to whether or not Lope likely penned the drama in question. Lope took any opportunity to boast of his vast collection of original *comedias*, at times even publishing lists of dramas that he had written up until the publication of his newest work of literature.[11] Not once did he claim one titled *La Estrella de Sevilla*.[12]

The overwhelming opinion of scholars since the 1920s has been that Andrés de Claramonte is the author of this title, although the influence of Lope de Vega on the dramaturg is so noticeable that the confusion is understandable.[13] The twentieth-century film and television adaptors of the drama, however, did not want to miss out on the potential cultural and economic capital that the name of the latter could bring to their productions, so they conveniently marketed their versions as adaptations of an original Lope de Vega play.

Regardless of who composed the *comedia*, the negative reception of *La Estrella de Sevilla* in seventeenth-century Spain caused it to remain dormant and virtually unknown in its native country for the following two centuries. Only on January 22, 1800, would Spanish poet Cándido María Trigueros's theatrical adaptation of the play, titled *Sancho Ortiz de las Roelas*, rescue the Golden Age text from oblivion when it was performed at Madrid's Teatro de la Cruz.[14] As some scholars have indicated, this remake of the drama drastically reduced the action of the earlier text to maintain a higher degree of unity of action, despite spreading it out across five acts as opposed to the original three. As aptly suggested by the title, the adaptation places the secondary character of Sancho Ortiz de las Roelas in the starring role. Moreover, in keeping with the increased patriotic cultural currents of the time, Trigueros's drama minimizes the severity of King Sancho's crimes in order to create a more palatable villain for his audience.[15] The adaptation's transcendence from page to stage was not, however, realized without certain difficulties.

Almost prophetically, Trigueros's rendition of the play only managed to obtain approval from the ecclesiastical censors in 1788, but failed to receive a green light from the government of Madrid, which had taken somewhat drastic measures to suppress performances of Golden Age plays in the late eighteenth century.[16] The Board of Directors for Theater Reform,[17] ironically, considered any rendition of these classical dramas—as René Andioc (1998) reminds us—"morally and aesthetically inappropriate for the new circumstances" (145) of a country whose government was becoming increasingly obsessed with decency and overcoming the long shadow of the *black legend.*[18] According to the censorship report of Santos Díez González, his objection to the play being performed on stage stemmed from his disapproval of the character of King Sancho IV, whom he characterized as a "Nero chasing after an innocent woman to satisfy a silly passion" (Andioc, 1998, 147). Nevertheless, the drama was given a license to be performed on the Madrilenian stage 12 years later and, according to the editions of the *Diario de Madrid* from January 22, 1800, to January 29, 1801, *Sancho Ortiz de las Roelas* enjoyed a healthy eight-day run that was received positively by critics and performed well at the box office. Later that same year, on Thursday, December 4, the *Diario de Madrid* announced that printed copies were available for sale at various locations across Madrid.

Unlike its predecessor *La Estrella de Sevilla*, Trigueros's *Sancho Ortiz de las Roelas* made an immediate (and significant) literary impact not only in Spain but throughout all of Europe and even in the United States.[19] The play, along with the original *La Estrella de Sevilla*, was known in England as early as 1806 upon the publication of Lord Holland's *Some Accounts of the Lives and Writings of Lope Félix de Vega Carpio and Guillen de Castro*, which was reprinted with additional matter in 1817. Furthermore, barely over two decades had passed since the play's revival in Madrid when the Baron von der Malsburg published a translation of the play in Germany in 1824, which was modified and rereleased in the same country by the Baron von Zedlitz in 1829.[20] Curiously, the adaptations of a play that had experienced such a problematic trajectory in its home country had little problem being disseminated and popularized abroad, considering that an English-language translation of *La Estrella de Sevilla*, titled *The Star of Seville*, was printed in Boston in 1828, which was so positively received that a second edition was reprinted in 1840, followed by a third in 1844. Meanwhile, back in Europe, Lord Holland's translation had inspired French dramatist Pierre Lebrun to adapt the play for Parisian audiences; his version, titled *Le Cid d'Andalousie* debuted in the French capital on March 1, 1825.[21] The drama's reception in France differed greatly from that in England, Germany, and the United States; the critics were extremely harsh and the production only managed to be performed four times before being removed from the marquee.[22]

Henry Thomas (1923) posits the very likely possibility that *Le Cid d'Andalousie* failed on the French stage due to authorities intervening to prevent societal tensions between audiences and the government at a time when the country was still reeling from the aftershock of the Napoleonic dictatorship and the ensuing political instability (xiv). Pierre Lebrun offered an alternative explanation, according to an 1875 article in *Le Figaro* in which the adaptor states that the reasons for the play's failure "are found in the severity of the censors' criticisms, the ill will of certain actors, and in the bias of defenders of a classical school of thought [that were] eager to take their revenge on him" for his previous theatrical blockbusters.[23] Regardless of the reasons for its failure to impress critics and audiences, the play was never again performed in France, although the following decade would see the birth of English actress Fanny Kemble's adaptation, *The Star of Seville*, which debuted at the Walnut Street Theatre in Philadelphia on August 7, 1837.[24] Again, the subject matter of the drama was the root of controversy, this time in nineteenth-century New England society. As recorded by American Hispanist James Pyle Wickersham Crawford (1930), the play was dedicated to Lady Dacre, despite her initial objections to having her name associated with a play that included an "objectionable" scene in a bedchamber that she deemed unbecoming of a young lady (498).[25] Despite the changes made to the original script to make it more suitable for a New England audience, the play is widely considered a creative and commercial failure.

With the exception of a short-lived opera titled *La Estrella de Sevilla* that ran in Paris in 1845, the drama and its adaptations would again remain dormant for the better part of a century. When an adaptation of the drama, entitled *L'Étoile de Seville*, arrived in France in 1941, the sociopolitical climate, as well as the reception from audiences, could not have been more different than a century earlier. As Harvey Johnson (1945) has explained, the themes and subject matter that had made audiences and authorities uncomfortable in the nineteenth century (namely the protest and condemnation against injustices perpetrated by ruthless tyrants) were now applicable to and enthusiastically welcomed by audiences in mid-twentieth-century German-occupied France (223). Reviewer Marc Beigbeder (1941) highlighted the relevance of the plot when he wrote in *Esprit* that the spectacle was "most admirable, undoubtedly full of style, [which is] both powerful and clear [and] carries the dialogue constantly with great ease towards our concerns, our problems, and towards the current times" (426). *L'Étoile de Seville* was in such high demand in the non-occupied areas of France that it went on to enjoy a successful tour in many French cities, as well as in Tunisia and Algeria. The success of the drama in the twentieth century would, nonetheless, be short lived and limited only to France, given that the seventeenth-century piece would go on to face insurmountable obstacles back in its native Spain at the end of that very same decade.

## THE FILM THAT NEVER WAS (TWICE)

On June 14, 1949, the first screenplay adaptation of *La Estrella de Sevilla* arrived to the censorship office. Its author, a former newspaper journalist and would-be filmmaker by the name of Juan Perales Perpiñá, could not have known at the time he dispatched his script that it would be dead on arrival.[26] The 215-page document submitted to censors for review was a complete blueprint for a full-length feature-film adaptation of the seventeenth-century drama. Although there is no evidence to suggest that the script was commissioned by a professional production agency, the document in question does not appear to have been prepared by a complete amateur or novice screenwriter. It contains speaking parts, stage and camera directions, instructions on the location for each scene, and outlines for 428 distinct shots spread out across seven sequences, complete with indications of when the cameramen and editors should fade-in or fade-out, close-up, zoom in and out, and so on.[27] The screenplay, it would appear, was ready to be distributed to set and wardrobe designers, cameramen, and actors once it received the required seal of approval from an initial reading by censors. For reasons that will be examined moving forward, the script never received that authorization and the project was permanently shelved.

Perpiñá's industrious screenplay indicates that the majority of scenes would be shot on location at the Alcázar of Seville, a stunning royal palace formed from Gothic and Romanesque renovations made to a Muslim residential fortress for King Peter of Castile in the mid-fourteenth century. The Alcázar continues to be an important tourism destination in the city, as the palace represents an iconic example of Andalusian Mudejar architecture. Such an awe-inspiring setting would provide for a degree of realism and authenticity that would always be lacking from a staged theater performance of the drama. Apparently wishing to provide spectators with a visual experience unlike that of the stage, the screenwriter also included many scenes that depict a gathering and/or movement of masses of people, a strategy that was very much in vogue at the time of the script's composition.[28] Despite the efforts made to surpass the visual limitations of the theater, Perpiñá did not forsake all aspects of the source text's theatrical genesis. He made the artistic decision to respect the original drama's dialogues almost in their entirety, making fewer alterations to the play and leaving the speaking parts in verse. Such an editorial judgment clashes quite strikingly with the aforementioned innovations; chiefly, it is perplexing that such ambitious plans were made to provide viewers with an authentic seventeenth-century visual experience while maintaining artificial—albeit often eloquent—speech patterns that presumably do not reflect the manner in which people actually communicated with one another. Given the sociopolitical climate of the time, however, one can understand the potential benefits of preserving the original lines of dialogue from a text marketed as a Lope de Vega drama, especially considering that appeasing censors was a top priority at every stage of the process. A novice filmmaker's manipulation of a text penned by a canonical

Spanish author might have been thought a gross overreach. Be that as it may, none of the censors were impressed with Perpiñá's screenplay. The document remains a mostly forgotten artifact, stored in a box at the General Archive of the Administration in Alcalá de Henares.

A new script bearing the same title as Perpiñá's ill-fated screenplay arrived on the desk of the censorship office seven months later. This time, the text had not been prepared by an obscure novice, but rather by veteran novelist and university professor, Gonzalo Torrente Ballester.[29] Having moved to Madrid to teach history at the *Escuela de Guerra Naval* three years earlier, Torrente Ballester teamed up with fellow journalist and up-and-coming Spanish filmmaker José Antonio Nieves Conde to compose the screenplay that was sent to the censorship office in 1950. The intended production company, *Productores Cinematográficos Asociados*, headquartered in Valencia, was an enterprise founded and administered by none other than Juan Perales Perpiñá, the same journalist-turned-screenwriter whose adaptation of the play had been prohibited by the censors a year earlier. The name and owner of the production company were, logically, not explicitly given credits on the copy of the script sent for review or on the petition for filming permissions.

The team had no reason to believe that their adaptation of *La Estrella de Sevilla* would face any opposition from censors. After all, their screenplay shared the excitement of Perpiñá's movement of masses and maintained the overall story arc of the early modern drama, but it did not make the mistake of preserving the original verse in the dialogues. To avoid any possibility of being accused of attempting to improve upon a work written by such an esteemed historical dramaturg, the adaptors were careful to include the caveat "according to Lope de Vega's drama" to the title page of their work. So confident were Torrente Ballester, Nieves Conde, and Perales Perpiñá in receiving the approval of censors that they had even gone so far as to hire actors and announce the release of the film in the magazine *Primer Plano,* which even included a full-page spread of a teaser poster promoting the film.[30] Nieves Conde was prepared to direct an all-star cast comprising celebrated Spanish film stars such as Ana Mariscal, Carmen Sevilla, Mary Delgado, Fernando Rey, and Jesús Tordesillas once the 63-page screenplay had passed the first stage of the censors' scrutiny. The anonymous interviewer of the article in *Primer Plano* recorded the hopeful atmosphere in Torrente Ballester's home office thusly: "The atmosphere of the whole [interview], in this cozy and confidential office, is thick with the highest hopes for the best of successes" (21).

Nevertheless, despite all of the planning, preparation, and publicity that the creative team had put into the production before submitting the document to authorities, the censors' initial observations were far from favorable. Again, the dream of adapting *La Estrella de Sevilla* to the big screen was extinguished.

In spite of the damning reports submitted by the censors, Torrente Ballester was not willing to surrender the project without a fight. His objections reveal a great deal about how sacred the name Lope de Vega should have been to the national authorities. In a letter written on March 15, 1950, to Gabriel García Espina, the general director of Cinematography and Theater, Torrente Ballester wrote:

There are many reasons why I am as interested as I am in this matter. You, as well as I, must understand that even the most insignificant trifle can reach extreme importance. The Official Censorship Office cannot not authorize the filming of a film based on *La Estrella de Sevilla*, which, whether correctly or not, is reputed as one of the best of our historical dramas (see Menéndez y Pelayo), because, correctly or not, it could pass for a Lope de Vega play.[31] Perhaps the priests who have judged the script are absolutely unaware of these circumstances and, therefore, could not possibly foresee that prohibiting its filming or vetoing it once the film was made could give cause for a very unpleasant case against us overseas. Can you imagine the headlines? "Franco's Censorship Forbids a Drama by Lope de Vega." Keep in mind that regarding this matter, Nieves Conde and myself, as well as the producer (who has yet to be made aware of these facts due to his being in Valencia) could keep quiet.[32] (1)

Torrente Ballester reveals several important insights regarding some of the editorial decisions made in drafting the script; primarily, that he seems to have been fully aware that *La Estrella de Sevilla* was not, in fact, an original Lope de Vega play. Instead, his initial argument is that the play *could pass for* a drama by the renowned playwright. In doing so, the adaptor seemingly admits to attempting to defraud the censors by enticing them with the name of Lope de Vega, fully expecting this invocation of the seventeenth-century dramaturg to cut through any red tape that might otherwise have inhibited the screenplay from advancing throughout the bureaucratic process of making it to the filming stage. The academic doubles-down on this claim, suggesting a compromise that might persuade the censors to change their minds:

send the script to Mr. Juan Fernández,[33] not just the script, but also Lope's original *comedia* (which is why I'm sending you this copy now); show him how conveniently he can compare the script with the drama; don't hesitate to draw his attention to the fact that it's a famous classical work; also tell him, please, to carefully point out which corrections that he sees fit. Because I am willing, if he is agreeable, to soften, change, smooth it over, as long as the fundamental theme is preserved, since without it the film would fall apart: that is, this well-known, unfortunate, and especially unusual case of a king wanting to take a young damsel to bed and committing a crime invoking the divine right of kings. (2)

This fragment of his letter suggests that Torrente Ballester was willing to make concessions and changes to the text in order to please the censors. Although his (slightly desperate) determination is felt strongly in the letter, his willingness to cooperate with the authorities in any way to guarantee the required filming permissions was not enough to convince them to take any further action or to continue to review the proposal.

Second, and perhaps more consequential, Torrente Ballester includes a thinly veiled threat to the priests in charge of producing the initial report on the screenplay; he alludes to the idea that the international press would use the censors' prohibition of the film as propaganda against the dictator, given that it was Franco's censorship office that halted production. Reading between the lines of the letter, it is tempting to believe that the academic-turned-screenwriter was expressing his intention to make sure that the debacle reached printing presses outside Spain. In order to reiterate this claim and also to proactively exculpate himself in the event that the issue was raised by foreign journalists, he continued his letter by writing that

> this very afternoon I've heard ranting, and I have no doubt that the day after your all's report is issued, all of the Madrid cinema community will have heard about it thanks to foreign press correspondents. I insist that it would be a hot topic for some people. I give you my word of honor that I deeply regret my involvement in this issue, but, once I've been put in the middle of it (and I could never have foreseen what is happening; I never imagined a couple of priests conjuring the agenda of the Inquisition and the political censors of [King] Philip III), I believe, like Gracián, that one can try to make the best out of any bad situation. I am not defending my own interests, much less those of the producer (as you will see below), and even more less my own personal project: you can believe me that, in my opinion as a writer and literary scholar, even the best film script is sloppy, and if I have taken on such a project it is only to make a living. (2)

Regardless of his warnings on the dangers of word-of-mouth transmission of the events throughout Madrid's cinematic circles and, coincidentally, the world, the general director was not convinced and the restrictions placed on the screenplay were never lifted. Having twice failed to earn the approval from censors, no film adaptation of *La Estrella de Sevilla* ever made it past the initial screenplay. There would be no filmed version of this title at all until a 1964 episode of *Estudio 1* aired a made-for-television adaptation of the drama and, to date, no feature-film rendition of it has ever made it to the silver screen.

## APPROACHES TO THE ADAPTATION

Curiously, both of the screenplays submitted to the Censorship Office were strikingly different in their approaches to the adaptation of the drama. As the next chapters will show, there is no "one size fits all" formula for converting a seventeenth-century text into a screenplay that would convince the censors to grant it approval to begin filming. Essentially, both scripts aim to tell the exact same story as the source text, although slight alterations are made to the denouement to accommodate modern tastes. This process has been deemed by José Luis Sánchez Noriega (2000) as creating "integral adaptations" (72–75).

Both Perpiñá and Torrente Ballester chose very different narrative routes when it came to how they told the story of *La Estrella de Sevilla*. Perpiñá, for example, took a risk in making a film that would complement the seventeenth-century verse with visual cues and stunning outdoor scenery, a technique for adapting Golden Age plays that would not prove successful on the big screen in Spain until Pilar Miró's *El perro del hortelano* (1996). Torrente Ballester, on the other hand, opted for an adaptation style in keeping with the vast majority of the Lope scripts that would successfully pass the initial review of the censorship and make it to cinemas during the dictatorship. This style of producing "recreated performances," as Sánchez Noriega (2000) categorizes them, involves taking a much higher degree of liberty in terms of altering dialogues, introducing new speaking parts and, occasionally, characters that are not present in the source texts, making efforts to camouflage the story's theatrical roots (45). Moving forward, the two unsuccessful scripts will be analyzed before a study of the reactions documented by the censors to justify their objections is presented to supplement these findings.

It is suitable to review the screenplays in the same order as Franco's censors did in the mid-twentieth century, beginning with Perpiñá's proposed adaptation of *La Estrella de Sevilla* (1949), which he aptly subtitles "Cinematic Transcription." At first glance, it is easy to assume that the adaptor took an edition of the Golden Age text and simply transcribed the dialogues into a previously prepared template with outlines of the scenery and other technical aspects included. A closer look at the text, however, reveals that much more editing went into the preparation of the screenplay than meets the eye. Whereas the play begins, for example, with King Sancho proclaiming his gratitude to the city of Seville to his trusted councilor Don Arias, the film adaptation was going to begin with several shots—including a bird's-eye view—of an outdoor party taking place in front of the Alcázar of Seville in the early afternoon. The scene in question was to include a significant amount of extras dressed as noblemen, foot soldiers and soldiers on horseback, commoners, heralds, and members of the clergy in order to create a scene of people gathered en masse to greet the new ruler of the city. Only after viewers are treated to such a spectacle would the camera pan to an interior shot of the palace and focus on the king and Don Arias. The first 10 verses recited by the king in the play were to be left entirely unaltered, although they were to be uttered off camera, as the following shots return the attention to the masses awaiting the king outside the palace.

The following scenes omit any dialogue, opting to introduce audiences to the central conflict of the story by showing it as opposed to telling them directly. Shots of the people of Seville waving from their balconies to greet the king as he emerges from the palace introduce a female character—which the script informs us is the titular Estrella—with whom King Sancho, without uttering a word, is clearly enchanted at first sight. When the opening dialogues resume, a careful reading reveals the suppression of all classical references—such as the mention of Phaeton (v. 70) and Jupiter (v. 138)—from the source text. The practice of removing all classical Greco-Roman references from the film and television adaptations is commonplace in all of the film and television adaptations of Golden Age dramas produced and released in Spain. Although one might assume that the rigid *nacionalcatolicismo* of the day could explain the omissions of pagan gods in these early adaptations, the fact that this practice continues even into the modern day, well beyond the death of the dictator and the dissolution of his censorship, eliminates this possibility. It is much more likely that the adaptors were thinking solely of their future audiences, especially those who might consider an adaptation of a historical literary text full of such allusions as too high-brow a form of entertainment for them to enjoy, or the vast majority who simply lacked the necessary education to understand the lines in question.[34] In lieu of some of the verses that were suppressed, the eleventh scene of the adaptation introduces a troubadour who sings eight verses in hendecasyllables that are completely absent from the source text:

> He who can say that, setting eyes upon you, / is not in love with you, if that could be, / did not deserve to love or look upon you, / for he could look at you and yet be free. / Unworthy of you, I was worthy to see you, / a thousand souls I pledged and, in a sense, / that is the price I had to pay to love you, / take them to compensate for my offence.[35]

Apart from breaking with the rhyme and meter of the rest of the drama's verses, which are almost all octosyllabic and boast a wide range of rhyme schemes, this intervention is also strange in that it contributes little to nothing to the action of the plot. The unnecessary adulation contained in the above verses appears to serve little purpose other than to add a festive atmosphere to a moment in the film that was set on-site in the Gardens of Charles V, located outside the Royal Alcázar of Seville.

In the example of the added troubadour we see one of the most salient features of this screenplay. Many of the elements included provide an impressive audiovisual experience of one of Spain's most treasured buildings in one of its most famous and important cities. Many scenes in the document are explicitly labeled as "in mere transit," indicating that the action and/or any suppressed dialogue is of no importance to the narrative. As is made particularly evident in the case of 1950's *La moza de cántaro* in upcoming chapters, including elements of *españoladas*—iconic visuals or practices considered emblematic of traditional Spanish culture—was looked upon very favorably by the authorities and could even earn a script the distinction of being awarded the superlative of "beneficial to national interest."[36] As such, a reader of the script is left with the sensation that the dialogues, indeed the entire story, were secondary to all of the ambitious audiovisual aspects included in the screenplay. The interpolation of festive, visually stunning scenes would not be the only editorial decision made by Perpiñá with the apparent objective of merely appeasing the censors.

Although many moments in the script, such as the one discussed above, are not present in any existing editions of the source text, other instances that are found in the original are clearly suppressed due to the sociopolitical climate of the time. An episode that closes the first act of the seventeenth-century drama is moved to an earlier, more prominent position in the screenplay, halfway through the second sequence, and omits two verses spoken by the character Natilde—styled in both cinematographic adaptations as Matilde— that underscore the gravity of Don Arias's plan and the king's true intentions. The lines in question are delivered at the precise moment in which the slave girl and the king's councilor are discussing the betrayal of Estrella and Natilde confirms, "so, I will put you, sir, into the same / bed as Estrella tonight" (vv. 848–849).[37] The suppression of these verses is not at all surprising, given that the mention of putting the king in Estrella's bed explicitly defines the sexual nature of the conspiracy, which would have been considered entirely indecent in mid-twentieth-century Francoist Spain.

The lines spoken by the slave girl were not, curiously enough, the only aspects of her characterization that were suppressed in the screenplay. A thorough reading of the filmic text reveals that her condition as a slave in the Tabera household was only ever mentioned once, whereas it is reiterated many times in the source text.[38] Of course, any references to Spain's slaveholding, imperial past were to be treated with great care to prevent viewers from being reminded of a dark chapter in the country's history, especially foreign spectators who could use facts like these to portray a negative image of Spain abroad. Nevertheless, the fact that Matilde is a slave in the original is vital to understanding her participation in the conspiracy, as one of the conditions of her aiding the king in his sinister mission is that she is to be given her freedom after it is accomplished. The screenplay handles this complicated matter very delicately without eliminating her social position altogether. Whereas her seventeenth-century counterpart blatantly tells Don Arias, "because I am a slave girl / without my sacred liberties / locked in death and a perpetual prison" (vv. 829–831),[39] Perpiñá's character would only utter, "because I am a slave girl." In subsequent scenes, the term "little slave girl" (vv. 906, 1161, 1240) is substituted with "dear maid," or "little woman," so as to soften the harsh truth of her slavery.[40] Regardless of the adaptor's desire to rhetorically camouflage the unfortunate reality of the character's life, the same kid gloves were not used when it came to portraying her gruesome death.

In both the source text and Perpiñá's adaptation, Natilde—Matilde—is publicly hanged by the neck outside the palace by Busto to demonstrate to the king that (a.) Busto had figured out King Sancho's plan against his sister, and (b.) he would not tolerate such an affront on his household's honor without exacting severe consequences on the offending parties, no matter what social standing he or she might have had. In the seventeenth-century original, the horrifying discovery is naturally not to be shown on stage, as this would have been a nearly impossible visual effect to safely portray.[41] Instead, the dialogue informs spectators of what has become of the Tavera's treacherous slave:

> DON ARIAS: There, in the Alcázar, I see / a shape swaying in the wind. / REY: A shape? Oh, what could it be? / DON ARIAS: Something important, I think. / REY: Get closer, Arias, to see / what it could be. DON ARIAS: It's a woman! / REY: A woman, you say? DON ARIAS: A woman. / REY: A woman? DON ARIAS: Already dead, / so she's not one anymore. / REY: See who it is. DON ARIAS: It's the slave girl; / in her hands, a piece of paper. (vv. 1231–1241)[42]

The camera's ability to show more advanced visual effects was to be taken full advantage of for this episode in the film, as indicated by the directions in the script: "Don Arias, in the background, looking out the window. Framed within it, Matilde hung by the neck from a rope. She will wear the letter from the King stuck to her chest" (shot 272). As we can appreciate from this example, while even the slightest mention of sexual impropriety was to be completely avoided in the screenplay, Perpiñá considered that a visual depiction of a woman hanging dead by the neck was not a problem to receive approval from the censors. Curiously enough, he was correct in this assumption, at least to some degree, given that none of the censors' reports mention any opposition to this scene in their review of the script.

As the above example indicates, Perpiñá fully intended to use the advantages of the film camera to show and not tell his audience about pivotal moments in the story of *La Estrella de Sevilla*. Just as in the source text, letters (such as the letter that is found on Natilde's person when she is hanged) and other written communications are exchanged frequently by the characters. Each time this happens in the screenplay, the camera is instructed to zoom in on the document as opposed to having it read aloud. Perpiñá extends this creative license for the adaptation by showing a character who neither appears nor is even mentioned in the source text: the Queen. Although the historical King Sancho IV was indeed married to Queen María de Molina, not a word is spoken about her by any of the characters in the original drama.[43] By omitting this aspect of the King's life, his crimes in the play are somewhat diminished. His character may very well be a homicidal sexual deviant, but he is not an adulterer per se. Therefore, the decision to include the Queen as a character in the script makes his advances on Estrella more than a simple offense against an engaged woman. The character of King Sancho in the proposed film actively attempts to betray the Christian institution of marriage.[44] The sudden appearance of Queen María in the fifth scene of the seventh and final sequence of the script serves as a convenient deus ex machina technique to resolve the central conflict of the plot and allow for an implausible happy ending.

The insertion of the character of the Queen presents a minor plot-hole that is not present in the source text, given that she somehow knows exactly what the king had been up to in her absence. This is evident when she sits beside her husband while Estrella and Sancho Ortiz present their cases to the authorities. The majority of Don Arias's verses are transferred to the character of Queen María, with the exception of an added one that insinuates that she has recently given birth.[45] It is not Don Arias then, who urges King Sancho to confess to ordering Busto's Murder, but Queen María. Unlike the seventeenth-century original, however, Sancho and Estrella are to be seen embracing from a bird's-eye view while the king is heard laughing off camera. The Queen is heard saying "you were blinded" to the King, to which he simply responds "fruit from another field . . . when mine is better" (VII.10).[46] The screen was to fade to black while a loud kiss was heard, also off camera. As opposed to the original denouement, Perpiñá's King Sancho expresses that he has learned his lesson at the film's close and realizes how happy he is with his wife. The adaptor logically considered this to be a more appropriate ending, given that it underscores the importance and predominance of the traditional family lifestyle. Instead of forcing Estrella into a nunnery and effectively banishing Sancho Ortiz from the kingdom, the two are brought together and two presumably happy marriages result from the climax. Coincidentally, the three lives are not ruined by the extreme act of tyranny brought about by King Sancho.

The screenplay submitted for review by Perpiñá outlines a very expensive production whose entertainment value is highly questionable. Although it is true that the adaptor cut many of the soliloquies and expressions of adoration between characters that slow down the action of the original drama, he failed to replace them with any meaningful content. Moreover, he completely removes one of the more consequential scenes of the third act in which Sancho Ortiz is literally driven mad from guilt and hallucinates that he is in Hell for killing Busto after being interrogated by Don Pedro and Don Arias. The scene from the original play illustrates the consequences of the blind loyalty to the king that the character of Sancho Ortiz experiences and explains his desire to be executed and unwillingness to accept Estrella's plea for clemency. The scene would have added a significant amount of time to the film's run if kept as it was in the original, but Perpiñá demonstrates his ability to compact lengthy dialogues into shorter sequences with a bit of movie magic in many other moments of his script. Therefore, one must consider whether the omission was strictly for the benefit of the censors: perhaps the adaptor thought that Sancho Ortiz's ordeal might be considered a call to disobedience to authorities, which would not have been acceptable to the censorship. What is left in the script, however, is a great deal of proposed scenes that are merely shots of impressive masses of people or of beautiful buildings that do not serve much purpose with regard to advancing the action of the plot. The resulting script details plans for a film that would have been costly, lengthy, tedious to view, and void of any perceivable moral or cultural commentary.

The same cannot be said, however, for Torrente Ballester's screenplay from 1950, which is much less technical and much more literary in nature than the one submitted by Perpiñá a year earlier. Although both adaptors effectively desired to tell similar stories, the latter script takes an entirely different approach to adapting *La Estrella de Sevilla* than the former. First of all, Torrente Ballester's proposed film did not maintain the original seventeenth-century verse at all. Moreover, this script wastes no time in capturing readers' attention by opening in medias res in the middle of a battle scene between King Sancho's troops and the opposing forces of the Infante de la Cerda. The document outlines a series of different, yet honorable, modes of combat, "within the norms of knightly combat": one-on-one combat among foot soldiers, knights on horseback, and other noblemen fighting against more noblemen (1). The character of Sancho Ortiz is given a higher degree of protagonism in this rendition by having him appear as a soldier on the battlefield who is thrown to the ground and is about to be killed by another combatant. A principal nobleman—who is shortly thereafter revealed to be King Sancho himself—rides over on his horse and saves Sancho Ortiz. As opposed to the scenes depicting masses of people in Perpiñá's script that add little to nothing to the content of the proposed motion picture, this episode contributes a great deal to the characterization of one of the story's central characters in that it helps to explain Sancho Ortiz's devotion to his king and his honorable obligation to serve him as loyally as possible.

In addition to the battle scene that was to open the film, the second script also goes beyond the confines of the content provided in the source text by providing more historical context for viewers, so that they would better understand the underlying political motives behind some of King Sancho's actions. In the second scene, for example, an instigator, referred to as the

*Agitador*, is speaking to a large audience of Sevillian citizens, pledging the city's allegiance to the king's brother, Alfonso de la Cerda. Upon hearing reports of Seville's insubordination to King Sancho, Don Arias threatens to put the city under siege. Busto Tabera comes onto the scene in opposition to the *Agitador* and serves as a peacemaker striving to prevent further combat and tragedy by subduing the citizens. Although he is called a traitor by the *Agitador*, the latter is silenced by the crowd as they overwhelmingly support Busto. This episode, though completely absent from the source text, also contributes to the characterization of one of the film's protagonists, as the reader is aware of the political friction developed between Busto, who is beloved by the city, and King Sancho, who faces some resistance and suspicion from the people. The script does, however, criminalize Busto somewhat by having him provide sanctuary to the Ulloa family, who outwardly decry King Sancho as a usurper and outright refuse to accept him as King of Seville.

The script does not treat the figure of the King any more sympathetically than it does Busto in the early pages. In several instances following the opening battle sequence, Don Arias is forced to remind the king to give proper thanks to God for His role in the victory and to sing the *Te Deum* before he enters the city (2–3). The fact that his advisor had to remind him to give the proper praise and acknowledgment to God merely introduces the inherent lack of Christian instincts possessed by the king that would become increasingly evident as the screenplay continues, thus nullifying any genuine attempts at appeasing the censors by inserting the hymn or acknowledging divine intervention in the outcome of the battle. More striking, however, are moments of the script that appear to be even sacrilegious in nature. An episode in which Don Arias awaits Estrella after mass to inform her of the King's indecent proposition, for instance, includes an unfriendly greeting by Estrella, who asks the advisor, "What is the devil doing in church?" to which he simply retorts, "devilry" (22). The most sacrilegious event, however, occurs when King Sancho enters the Tabera household to realize his diabolical plan with Estrella, passes in front of a statue of the Virgin Mary, and blesses himself before continuing toward his intended rape (28). As important as these moments are to demonizing the sordid king's character, one can understand how they would have been considered far from appropriate by the censorship.

From a Francoist perspective, the most inappropriate moments of the script, however, derive from scenes and dialogues from the source text that Perpiñá had judged too risqué to include in his rendition of the drama. Torrente Ballester, on the other hand, takes an entirely different approach by letting his characters blatantly express some of the most taboo and scandalous sentiments imaginable for the time. While discussing his plan to seduce/rape Estrella, the King explains his urges to Don Arias thusly: "It's no longer an obsession, Arias. It's my dignity as king. What more could that *hidalgo* want than a royal bastard in his family!" (21) As if his plan wasn't sinister enough in the first place, his admission of the possibility of fathering an illegitimate child with the innocent woman in such crude terms and defending his desire to do so as part of his dignity as a king is a surprising inversion of the prescribed social order. Arias agrees with and echoes these sentiments in a subsequent scene when he demonstrates perplexity at Busto's offense upon discovering the king's intentions, exclaiming, "What more could that *hidalgo* ask for than your love for Estrella. There are great families in Castile that would give anything so that their women could be the king's lover!" (36)[47] In this instance, Don Arias's claim is even more severe and damaging to the image of Spain's noble history as it suggests that kings having extramarital affairs with women of great Spanish families was not only commonplace but something that was aspired to. Even these utterances, however, still do not exemplify the most egregious use of indecent language in Torrente Ballester's text.

The episode in which Estrella's slave—also named Matilde instead of Natilde and never once referred to as a slave in this manifestation—concocts the treacherous conspiracy with Don Arias does not handle the conversation discretely, as is the case in Perpiñá's screenplay. Instead, the conversation is even more explicit than in the source text. Matilde says to the advisor, "I will take the king to Estrella's bed. And if she screams, I will cover [the bed] with tapestries so that no one can hear [her]" (24).[48] The willingness to drown out Estrella's screams in the event it is needed elevates the gravity of the conversation from merely indecent to explicitly violent in nature. What was to be spoken, however, pales in comparison to what was supposed to be displayed when the King made his move on Estrella shortly thereafter. Torrente Ballester intended to film a brutal interaction between King Sancho and Estrella in the latter's bedroom. Estrella does her best to escape from the King, running around the bed, but he catches her by the arm and disarms her from the dagger she was carrying to defend herself. Immediately following her capture, the stage directions indicate that the King "throws her over the bed. Estrella, increasingly agitated, manages to defend herself and escape for a moment. The King follows behind her. Estrella, running, arrives next to a window and attempts to open it. The King grabs her again, gripping her, and doesn't defend himself against her strikes and scratches, but rather kisses her passionately" (30). Although modern readers, accustomed to seeing even more violent physical abuse on screens, may not consider this episode to be overtly inappropriate, one must keep in mind that the same would not have been true for an ecclesiastical censor in the 1950s. Moreover, the fact that the aggressor is a king of Castile would have been extremely disconcerting for any reader or viewer of the time. This likely explains why a line with an "X" is drawn in the margin of the entire scene on the copy of the script that is conserved in the archives today; it was a source of great concern for the first readers of the document.

The violence in Torrente Ballester's screenplay is not limited to the interactions between King Sancho and his victim, the titular Estrella. As mentioned earlier, her brother Busto's characterization is made more complex in this rendition of the drama by having him harbor the rebellious Ulloa family in his home until he can help them to escape Seville. They are caught, thanks in part to Matilde's cooperation with Don Arias, and the family patriarch is subjected to various types of torture, which were to be filmed and included in the finished product. Even worse, Don Arias brings Ulloa's wife into the dungeon in order to watch him being racked, screaming as she realizes what is taking place before her and hears his groans and protests. One might expect that showing a dissident being punished by an authoritarian state for his disobedience might have been welcomed on the big screen during the dictatorship, but the historical context in which this script was presented to censors allows us to appreciate why this might have been problematic. Spanish popular culture at the time was still attempting to combat elements of the *black legend* that had resurfaced as a result of the atrocities committed before, during, and after the Spanish Civil War; therefore, reminding audiences of medieval torture devices and tactics would have been counterproductive to this aim.[49]

Furthermore, the violent fate of Matilde in this version of the drama mirrors that of her end in Perpiñá's script almost exactly. Immediately following the torture scene in the dungeon of the palace, Don Arias runs into the king's chambers completely flustered and, despite King Sancho's orders to leave him alone, opens the curtains to allow the King to see, according to the stage directions, "Matilde's cadaver, hanging from a rope, with a knife stuck into her chest pinning the paper that the king has given her and the pouch [full of] gold" (35).[50] Again, the adaptor opted to show and not tell readers and viewers the grisly fate of the poor servant girl. As this rendition of the drama never refers to her as a slave, but rather as a "daughter of Allah" (25),[51] meaning Muslim, her freedom was never a condition of her participation in the betrayal of Estrella. Torrente Ballester's Matilde volunteers to help, even demonstrating her awareness of the dire consequences of her involvement should she get caught, for spiteful reasons, expressing that she hates her mistress and would celebrate her downfall (23). All she asked for in return was to be married to a man of high station and given the money for a respectable dowry. She was guaranteed both by Don Arias and again by an official letter and pouch from the King, thus explaining the items found stabbed into the chest of her dead body. Although certainly an exciting series of events, one cannot overlook the increased level of violence and bloodshed in this adaptation when compared to the previous screenplay and the source text.

Despite the heightened violence in this rendition, Torrente Ballester, like Perpiñá before him, had outlined plans for his own *españoladas* to be included in the film, which, in addition to making such a tragic saga more palatable to censors, would have contributed a great deal to the overall entertainment value to the production. To celebrate King Sancho having won the war and his annexing of Seville to the Crown of Castile, the city throws a party in his honor, complete with a bullfighting spectacle. The description of the event as described in the screenplay was to show early modern Spain in its entire splendor:

> The bullfight is celebrated in a plaza in Seville, surrounded by houses, such as those in small towns. The architecture, between Gothic and Moorish, with wide shots intertwined. . . . The windows and balconies appear decorated with people peering out of them. In the actual plaza there is a wooden barrier that surrounds the thing (we'll just call it that). Between the houses and the barrier the populace is crowded together. . . . The scene begins with the King's entrance, on horse-back, and his entourage. Trumpets blast and the masses move, making way for the king and the entourage in suite underneath one of the archways that connect the plaza to the streets. (I.32–33)

Clearly, the scene was designed with the intention of showing Seville as a vibrant, densely populated, wealthy metropolis, united in their cultural practices and loyalty to their king. Even the specifications of the architecture were to pay homage to the nation's multicultural past. The contrast between this festive scene and the darker, more daunting scenes of attempted rape, torture, and murder-for-hire could not be illustrated more starkly. More telling still, however, is the role that the film's eventual protagonist, Sancho Ortiz, would play in the scene. In shot 37, the indication is given that "Sancho Ortiz bull-fights," and that Estrella, watching him from a balcony, "drops one of her favors, which Sancho Ortiz picks up. He kisses it, waves, and returns to the bull" (11). In addition to proactively characterizing Sancho as a valiant and faithful soldier, as had been done earlier in the screenplay, this scene depicts him as the archetypal courtly gentleman and pure-blooded *macho ibérico* whose bullfighting skills are enough to impress the women of Seville.

Essentially, Torrente Ballester used very similar techniques as Perpiñá to attempt to win over the opinion of the censors and create a film that would be a cultural and commercial success. The adaptor even went above and beyond the previous script by including scenes that involved movements of masses that would rival even the most ambitious Hollywood production of the day, molded the character of the king into an odious and larger-than-life villain, made Matilde more deserving of her gruesome fate, and centered the spotlight on Sancho Ortiz, whom he transformed into the archetypal Sevillian and, by extension, Spanish gentleman. The screenplay, however, diverges from its predecessor in the manner in which it handles the denouement and conclusion of the narration. This time, instead of a queen appearing to restore the natural sociopolitical order of the court, King Sancho is forced to admit to his crimes in a similar way to his literary counterpart; the only way to prevent Sancho Ortiz from being executed, resulting in an inversion of any true justice, is for him to announce to the mayors—*Alcaldes*—of Seville that he ordered Busto Tavera's death because his loyal subject and namesake refuses to name him as his homicidal employer. Also in keeping with the source text is King Sancho's attempt to pardon Sancho Ortiz by royal decree, which is rejected by the city's mayors in the screenplay by having one of them retort to the monarch that the laws and customs of the people of Seville carry the same weight as the King's pleasure, arguing that, "if you represent God, so do the people. They are also right" (60). As a result of his inability to override the pre-established laws and pardon Sancho, he confesses to his crimes and, as opposed to all of the previous manifestations of the drama, the King faces the consequences of his actions by being forced to forfeit his claim on Seville and flee the city with his troops and entourage in tow. The screenplay ends with a final shot of King Sancho looking melancholically at Estrella's closed window as he abandons Seville forever.

Torrente Ballester's bold approach to adapting the ending of the drama was likely to have been considered by himself and fellow producers as a conclusion that would save the screenplay from being discarded by censors. He had taken all measures necessary to earn their seal of approval and had gone so far as to hire actors and announce the project to the press. Besides the more satisfying ending, he had modified the dialogues by composing them in prose (as opposed to Perpiñá's verse) and had planned to include stunning visual effects, of which he gave ample details, and ample *españoladas*, techniques that had proven successful to contemporaneous adaptations of titles bearing the name of Lope de Vega.[52] Unfortunately, his attempts at wooing the censors were all in vain and his screenplay received vetoes and harsh critiques from the censors that matched their hostile reception of the screenplay submitted a year earlier by Perpiñá. In the following section, the explanations they offered for their objections to the screenplays will be examined in order to draw definitive conclusions as to why a drama attributed to the famed Phoenix was deemed unadaptable to Spanish screens on two consecutive occasions.

## CENSORING THE ESTRELLA

The reports submitted by the censors offer a great deal of insights into not only what they thought of the drama itself and its possible adaptations for mass distribution, but also their beliefs about cinema and its role in (inter) national society. Their objections to the screenplays of *La Estrella de Sevilla* exhibit a wide array of concerns. Primarily, the censors demonstrate a great awareness of the fact that the proposed films would be consumed by Spaniards and non-Spaniards alike. Therefore, they were particularly worried about how the country as a whole might be reflected by the scripts.

In the early days of Spanish cinema, the censors' job was rather straightforward. Their duty involved a thorough reading of the proposed screenplay, followed by the completion a form provided in a template designed by the Department of Education.[53] Here they were to provide a synopsis of the plot of the screenplay, its thesis, the cinematographic value of the script, the literary value of the document, the moral and religious value of the proposal, a statement on any political and social overtones, and finally, their overall impression of the play. There was also space allotted at the very bottom of the form for reviewers to include any corrections they deemed necessary. In the case of both screenplays, critics were unanimous in their opposition to the characterization of King Sancho IV. This was due not only to the fact that his multiple indecent acts and homicidal conspiracies might not set the best example for Spanish viewers, but also because of the ramifications that the character's portrayal might have on the image of Spain and Spanish history as a whole.

Reviewer Fermín del Amo gave a thorough synopsis of Perpiñá's screenplay in his report dated June 20, 1949. He observed that the proposed adaptation's thesis was simply "a king and a vassal are true to their word," which would not have been any cause for the film's dismissal (1). Del Amo's most vehement objection to the proposed film, however, stemmed from the portrayal of the king. He expressed his concern that the political and social overtone was not "very exemplary, due to how badly the figure of the whimsical King is portrayed, murderous on various occasions" (1). He reiterated this claim at the end, writing about his overall impression of the screenplay. Although he chose not to make any specific judgments, he certainly implied that the depiction of the king was inappropriate: "About the political opportunity to present some reproachable acts committed by a king (which are hardly justified by the public confession of the crime), we remit to the superior criteria of the [Board's] director" (2).

In an undated report, Francisco Fernández González, a reviewer of Torrente Ballester's script, similarly expressed his disapproval of the treatment of the King, his advisors, and his victims. He noted that the King was a professional rapist, "the characters are all vilified beings, and the only two figures donned with a certain degree of nobility are persecuted, tormented, and killed" (1). The most scandalized of all the reviewers of both scripts, however, was an anonymous reviewer of Torrente Ballester's screenplay, who opposed the production because of the predominance of "a shameless king . . . and dumb! A [royal] favorite . . . without a conscience. To what end? Even, at times, with blasphemous dialogues. Totally unacceptable" (1).

Clearly, making a flawed monarch the antagonist of the film was, in the opinion of these censors, an irredeemable error of the screenwriters (and, by extension, of Lope's original play). Despite the fact that the historical figure in question is—and always has been—infamous for his misconduct and general recklessness, immortalizing him on the big screen did not cast an image of Spain, its people, its history, or its culture, that the regime considered apposite to broadcast to the world. Nevertheless, in the case of Perpiñá's attempt, the negative portrayal of a king of Spain was not the issue to which censors were most opposed. For all of the reviewers whose reports have been conserved in the archives, the biggest problem with the first screenplay of *La Estrella de Sevilla* was the wording. All censors vehemently and unequivocally opposed the decision to leave the dialogues in verse instead of rewriting them in prose.

Considering that Perpiñá was acutely aware of the fact that the fate of his project depended entirely on the initial reading by the regime's censors, he likely believed that maintaining the lines from the source text would spare him any criticisms. After all, what modern reader would dare impugn the work of Lope de Vega? Fermín del Amo's report seemed to agree with the quality of the original play, but not with that of the adaptation: "We are not judging Lope de Vega's work (that's not our mission); its adaptation to film, conserving the verse, we consider barely less than impossible" (1). Del Amo goes on to elaborate further in his overall impression of the screenplay, stating that he feared that the recitation of the verses would reduce the credibility of the film and, even if it didn't, it would only be understood by specialists in historical Spanish literature: "We reject a film in verse, since the realism of the cinema requires clear, prose language, adapted to current times. Otherwise, only a small part of the audience familiar with our classical theater would understand the expressions from Golden Age Spanish" (2).

As expected, Del Amo gave Perpiñá's screenplay an unfavorable rating, although he saw some compensating qualities that could justify a reworking, as long, of course, as it is "rewritten in prose" (2). These objections were echoed by another censor, José Luis García Velasco, who commented on no other aspects of the screenplay, saying only that the proposed film was inappropriate in every way: "Suffice it to say that it's a transcription—in verse and everything—of a work arguably attributed to Lope. We believe that, in order to make it into a film, it is not enough to transcribe it, but rather to adapt it" (1).

It is difficult to believe that Torrente Ballester, working alongside Perpiñá as the producer of the film, would not be familiar with these censors' observations and he most likely took them into consideration when he prepared his own version of the source text, given that none of the seventeenth-century verse is conserved in his screenplay. As a result of this editorial decision, his version of *La Estrella de Sevilla* fared slightly better with the censors. In his report dated March 3, 1950, reviewer Juan Esplandín gave a very favorable valuation of the script, especially with regard to the cinematic potential of the planned scenes, indicating that it was visually appealing as a period piece and that it had moments of great cinematographic and dramatic interest (1). This particular comment allows for an appreciation of how Torrente Ballester's intentions of using scenes including multitudes of people—a technique that tended to please the censors—managed to impress at least one of the reviewers enough to recommend its approval and production of the film. I daresay the screenwriter was counting on the other censors to have a very similar reaction. Again, he was improving upon an aspect of Perpiñá's screenplay that had fallen flat at the censorship office. As discussed above, the first script of *La Estrella de Sevilla* to be submitted in 1949 did indeed include conglomerations of extras, but these were clearly devices inserted by the screenwriter to either impress censors or, in a best case scenario, treat viewers to a contrasting visual spectacle that differed from the rest of the scenes in a process that has come to be known by Sánchez Noriega (2000) as "airing out the work"; in other words, moving, amplifying, or adding scenes in exterior spaces to increase the verisimilitude of the adaptation and make it more visually enjoyable (73). Unfortunately, in the case of Perpiñá's script, the added movements of masses do little to nothing to advance the plot or contribute to a more impressive ambiance in the proposed film. The gratuitousness of such shots did not go unnoticed by the censors, who used this weakness of the screenplay as yet another reason to reject it. Fermín del Amo gave a particularly poignant criticism of this element of Perpiñá's script, recording his opinion that "the movement is scarce from a cinematic point of view and the shots including masses are mere inserts" (2). The lesson Torrente Ballester learned from his predecessor's mistake is easily identifiable: inserting scenes with masses can be an effective strategy for some films, but they must be done well and a screenwriter must ensure that they contribute more to a film than a fleeting glance at a large group of people. Despite his efforts at avoiding the Perpiñá's pitfalls, the reviewers provided many other reasons to prohibit the production of his proposed film.

Francisco Fernández González was entirely opposed to how Torrente Ballester's film portrayed Spanish history, reducing the screenplay to a film that would be an exhibition of the "horrendous moral and human poverty that exists in the history of Spain" (1). He goes on to defend his claim by writing that just as there are scenes of disheveled democratism, there are actions and scenes of criminal and monstrous tyranny. It all gets confused and tries to have dramatic strength—and wishes to have a humorous impulse at other times—and it just comes off as absurd and contradictory. The issue of the battles lacks interest, originality, and plausibility; [these] are aspects that place this script completely out of place among the serious and worthy ones that Spanish cinema should consist of. And all of this with Seville as the background. (2)

The censor, as demonstrated from this reflection on the script, was not at all impressed with the way in which the screenwriter attempted to maintain the tragicomic essence of the source text. He found the attempt absurd and contradictory and felt that it would leave an indelible stain on Spanish cinema, all the while defaming one of the nation's most important cities. Fernández González was not alone in his opinion of the screenplay. An anonymous colleague of his wrote that the play's thesis was absurd, its cinematographic value scarce, its moral and religious value negative, and its political and social overtone destructive (1). What these observations reveal to us is that it was not enough for a film to "check-off the boxes" when it came to incorporating elements that would impress the censors. Even if one or two reviewers were convinced of a production's potential, a film that was proposed to the administration could pose no risk of damaging the national image or reputation in any way if it was to be approved by the censorship. Who the author of a source text was, be he even a national treasure to the caliber of Lope de Vega, did not matter if the screenplay in question painted any part of Spain, its people, its culture, or its history in anything even resembling a negative light.

Herein we have our first piece of evidence that problematizes the notion that adaptations of Lope de Vega's works were promoted or given special concessions by Francisco Franco's regime. Instead of his dramas serving as an ideological vehicle to promote the dictatorship's sociopolitical and cultural interests within Spain, the censors considered mass media to be an instrument by which to manipulate the population's ideas of the nation and its history, both inside the Iberian country and abroad. Far from promoting any particular author or time period, the authorities were much more preoccupied with halting the production of any project that could possibly tarnish the image of Spain on the (inter)national stage. In the following chapters, I will examine film adaptations that did manage to secure the required filming and distribution permissions from Francoist censors. As made evident by the reactions of the reviewers of the scripts and finalized productions, one common thread among all of the films that were appraised favorably by censors is that they were considered to be beneficial in creating a positive image of the nation both domestically and abroad.

## NOTES

1. *Junta de Reformación.*
2. See Claudia Demattè's (2003) "Mélanges et littérature mêlée: De *La Dorotea* de Lope de Vega (1632) au *Para todos* de Juan Pérez de Montalbán (1632)" and Anne Cayuela's (1993) "La prosa de ficción entre 1625 y 1634: Balance de diez años sin licencias para imprimir novelas en los Reinos de Castilla."
3. Famed Spanish literary scholar Marcelino Menéndez y Pelayo (1921) suggests that the *suelta* must come from a lengthier publication that has been lost (175).
4. The *deglosada* pertains to Foulché-Delbosc's private library (cit. Claramonte 123).
5. Tracing the textual transmission of the play is complicated further by the fact that the *suelta* is missing two entire folios.
6. Juan Batista González (2007) provides us with an ample description of King Sancho's military tactics that led to his victory in this conflict (180–192).
7. The royal family's infighting against Sancho el Bravo has recently been discussed in great detail in Joseph O'Callaghan's (2011) *The Gibraltar Crusade* (296–311). A more concise, though still quite thorough, synopsis is provided in Richard Emmerson's (2011) *Key Figures in Medieval Europe: An Encyclopedia* (592–594).
8. In medieval and early modern Spain, a *Corregidor* was a type of royally appointed mayor of a city or district who was charged with a wide array of administrative and gubernatorial duties.
9. There are many fascinating interpretations of the role of the monarch in this drama and the lack of justice presented at the denouement. See especially Irene Coromina (2001) and Máximo González-Marcos (1982). For an intriguing parallel between the figure of King Sancho IV and Zeus that helps to better understand the seemingly ambiguous conclusion of the play and the importance of the character of the king throughout, see Frederick A. de Armas's (1994) "Splitting Gemini."
10. Harry Sieber (1994) even goes so far as to posit that *La Estrella de Sevilla* in fact conceals an "indictment of both Philip IV and the Count-Duke of Olivares . . . [revealing] a profound discontent with both government policy and the practice of kingship in the early 1620s" (133).
11. The most extensive list provided by Lope of his corpus of *comedias* is found at the end of the prologue of *El peregrino en su patria* (1604).
12. Many scholars assume that these lists would have been embellished by the author; as such, it seems unlikely that he would omit any of his *comedias* in these compilations of titles.
13. The topic of the authorship of *La Estrella de Sevilla* has been thoroughly researched and argued since Sturgis A. Leavitt's (1930) *La Estrella de Sevilla and Claramonte*, in Rodríguez López-Vázquez (43–56) and in Joan Oleza's (1999) "La traza y los textos. A propósito del autor de La estrella de Sevilla." An exploration into the topic is also revisited and referenced by many contributors to *Heavenly Bodies: The Realms of La Estrella de Sevilla* (1996). Although today's scholars still disagree on certain aspects of the research into this issue, the important conclusion for our study is that no one can sustain the claim that it was written by Lope.

14. For a thorough synopsis of the contents of this adaptation, see Julián Jesús Pérez Fernández (165–186).

15. See Pérez Fernández (167), Wickersham Crawford (499), Charles Qualia (337), and Andioc (144).

16. Censorship of performances of dramas had been intensifying since the mid-eighteenth century, a process that culminated in the establishment of the Junta de Dirección de Reforma de los Teatros which, in 1801 published a new series of laws regarding the types of dramas that could be performed in public theaters, required them all to be in the Spanish language, and instituted a formal process of legal censorship before the works could be performed, printed, or sold. Within lies a clause that allows censors to prohibit performances or publications based on a consideration that they were "perjudical a las buenas costumbres y su conjunto compuesto de personas corrumpidas, llenas de miseria o vicios, en descrédito de la profesión cómica" (670). See the *Novísima recopilación de las leyes de España*, Ley XII (669–671).

17. *Junta de Dirección de Reforma de los Teatros.*

18. For more on the theatrical climate in Spain during this time and the implications on popular culture, consult, José Romero Castillo's (2015) volume on Spanish theater over the centuries.

19. Charles Qualia (1993) documents at least five reprints of the play in Spain in its debut year, as well as new editions in 1802, 1813, and 1818 (338). Juan Eugenio Hartzenbush also included his edition of *La Estrella de Sevilla* in the *Biblioteca de Autores Españoles* in 1853.

20. Sir Henry Thomas (1923) thoroughly outlines the trajectory of the adaptations of *La Estrella de Sevilla* throughout Europe in the introduction to his English-language edition of the play (xix–xxii).

21. The title, though seemingly very different from its Spanish source text, indirectly references a verse from the seventeenth-century original in which one of the pretenders for the position of Capitán General de las Fronteras de Archidona, a distinction that is eventually bestowed upon Sancho Ortiz de las Roelas, is referred to as "cordobés Cid" (v. 390). Later in the play, Don Arias refers to Sancho Ortiz de las Roelas as "el Cid andaluz" (v. 1219).

22. An article printed in the February 12, 1875, written half a century after the play's Paris debut, offers us some of the only available data on the play's performance on the stage (1–2).

23. My translation.

24. Due to the objection of the censorship, the drama would not be published until 1844 (Thomas xx; Wickersham Crawford 196).

25. Barbarina Brand, better known by her title Lady Dacre, was an English aristocrat, turned poet and playwright in her later years, who fostered relationships with members of the English and American literary intelligentsia.

26. Juan Perales Perpiñá is not documented in any film credits that could be found at the time this volume was published. Curiously, the only information about this adaptor's personal or professional life that is available for consideration comes from a March 25, 1950, edition of *Primer Plano* in which his career as a journalist is briefly mentioned (20). The article credits him as the technical script writer for an

upcoming film titled *La dama de Elche* (1952), that is not documented or conserved in any current databases, which suggests the project never came to fruition.

27. According to the article in *Primer Plano*, Perales Perpiñá had spent the majority of his journalistic career dedicated to writing about films and was a founder member of the *cineclub* of Valencia before putting his periodical writings on hold to produce films in the hope of achieving a "cine interesante e inteligente" (21). His dedication and study of films is likely what equipped him with the skills to write such a technical script.

28. François Albera (2009) provides a great deal of insight into how techniques of showing large agglomerations of people were used to compete with big-budget North American productions in the early years of Spanish cinema (125–131).

29. Torrente Ballester (1910–1999) began his literary career as a journalist in Oviedo, Spain before moving around various parts of Spain and France to complete his post-graduate education. He published his first novel, *Javier Mariño*, in 1942 and would go on to enjoy a prolific literary production of novels, theater dramas, essays, and film and television scripts. He would be granted the most prestigious literary accolades in Spain in the later years of his career: The National Literature Award for Narrative (1981), the Prince of Asturias Award for Literature (1982), and the Miguel de Cervantes Prize (1986), among others (Garrido Ardila 46–52).

30. *Primer Plano* n. 470, October 16, 1949, p. 33.

31. Torrente Ballester is almost certainly referring to Marcelino Menéndez y Pelayo's (1921) seminal study on the theatrical works of Lope de Vega, *Estudios sobre el teatro de Lope de Vega*, in which the esteemed Spanish literary scholar posits that *La Estrella de Sevilla* is indeed an original Lope *comedia* that was re-written by Andrés de Claramonte. In the section dedicated to the work in question, Menéndez y Pelayo refers to the drama as "one of Lope's masterpieces" (176).

32. It is worth noting that while Torrente Ballester has no qualms about naming his partner Nieves Conde in the letter, he avoids referencing the producer, Juan Perales Perpiñá, by name, perhaps in an attempt to avoid reminding the Censorship Office of their prohibition of the previous script. On the preliminary film poster, however, the producer's name is listed as Juan Perales.

33. The man cited here, Don Juan Fernández, is likely none other than Don Juan Fernández Figueroa, a left-swinging censor who, a year after the publication of this letter, would go on to become the editor-in-chief of the journal *Índice*, which advocated for more open criteria of the censorship and, in time, would go on to publish materials that were prohibited by the regime (Diego González 18–19). Apparently, Torrente Ballester saw in him a potential ally and someone who might be able to convince the other censors to overturn their verdict on his screenplay.

34. As Louie Dean Valencia-García (2018) reminds us, public education in Spain during the early years of the dictatorship was severely deficient and, as a result, illiteracy remained a significant social problem in the subsequent decades (43).

35. Original: "Quien se pudo alabar, después de veros, / si puede ser, que se libró de amaros, / ni mereció quereros ni miraros, / pues que pudo miraros sin quereros. / Yo, que le merecí sin mereceros, / mil almas, cuando os vi, quisiera daros / si lo que me ha costado el desearos / a cuenta recibís del ofenderos."

36. The term *españolada* was applied to films that portrayed regional folkloric elements (characters, settings, music, etc.), especially those of Andalusia, and created an idyllic, stereotypical image of the country. In the late 1950s and 1960s, the term became a cautionary adjective that suggested an antiquated filmic subgenre that was best avoided. As I will discuss in chapter 3, by the late 1970s and early 1980s, the term was applied to films that overzealously exaggerated the trends of the *Destape* era with excesses of erotic and/or grotesque elements that had been prohibited taboos during Francoism and defined Spanish cinema during the *Transición*. See José Luis Borau (560–584).

37. Original: "pues yo le pondré en la mesma / cama de Estrella esta noche"

38. The family's surname, Tabera, is written interchangeable with Tavera in the earliest textual witnesses of the source text, but both screenwriters change the spelling to Tabera in their scripts. As the spelling does not alter the pronunciation of the name in Spanish, the editorial decision is rather arbitrary. In this volume, I will use the Tavera spelling to refer to the characters in the source text while using the alternative Tabera spelling to refer to their filmic counterparts.

39. Original: "que soy esclava . . . y sujeta, / sin la santa libertad, / a muerte y prisión perpetua"

40. Original: "esclavilla," "criadilla," and "mujercilla," respectively.

41. We should also keep in mind that it was common practice in seventeenth-century Spanish theater for characters to be killed off stage, often making noises or exclamations to inform the audience of the action that they were unable to see.

42. Original: "DON ARIAS: En el Alcázar está / un bulto pendiente al viento. REY: ¿Bulto, dices? ¿Qué será? / DON ARIAS: No será sin fundamento. / REY: Llega. Llega, Arias, a ver / lo que es. DON ARIAS: Es mujer colgada. / REY: ¿Mujer, dices? DON ARIAS: Es mujer. / REY: ¿Mujer? DON ARIAS: Y está ahorcada, / con que no lo viene a ser. / REY: Mira quién es. DON ARIAS: La esclavilla / con el papel en las manos."

43. A recent publication, *María de Molina, Queen and Regent: Life and Rule in Castile-León, 1259–1321* by Paulette Pepin (2016), provides one of the most extensive biographies available on the queen in question.

44. Tyrannical authorities attempting to bed the fiancés of their subordinates in the Middle Ages was a common trope in the central argument of many of Lope's dramas such as *Peribáñez, Fuenteovejuna*, and *El mejor alcalde, el rey*. In those cases, however, the offender's marital status, exactly as in the source text of *La Estrella de Sevilla* is always concealed.

45. Queen María, upon seeing the king for the first time, simple utters "Mi rey y señor . . . tan solo por deciros . . ." to which he responds "¿Varón?" and she shakes her head affirmatively (shots 392–393).

46. Original: "fruta de campo ajeno . . . cuando la mía es mejor."

47. Original: "¿qué más podía pedir ese hidalgo que vuestro amor por Estrella? ¡Grandes familias hay en Castilla que lo darían todo porque [*sic*] una de sus mujeres fuese la amante del rey!"

48. Original: "Yo llevaré al rey hasta la cama de Estrella. Y si ella grita, cerraré con tapices para que nadie se entere."

49. Steven Marsh (2005) thoroughly addresses the issue of the Francoist regime and its struggles to diffuse the negative image that the *black legend* was still casting over the country and popular culture's participation in helping with this objective during the dictatorship in *Spanish Popular Film Under Franco* (95–100).

50. The imagery in this scene is strikingly reminiscent of the gruesome end that Judas meets in Matthew 27:1–10.

51. Original: "hija de Alah."

52. Specifically, *Fuenteovejuna* (1947) and *La moza de cántaro* (1950), which we will study in depth in the coming chapters.

53. *Ministerio de Educación Nacional: Subsecretaría de Educación Popular.*

# Chapter 2

# Despots and Dictators

## Lope on TV and Film during the Dictatorship (1949–1975)

In this period, no other playwright from the Golden Age had a greater presence on television and film than Lope de Vega, not even by far. In the years that spanned Francisco Franco's dictatorship (1939–1975), Lope's plays were adapted to major motion pictures on four separate occasions. On the big screen, he only had to compete in popularity with Pedro Calderón de la Barca, whose theatrical works were adapted to three major motion pictures.[1] Compared to other seventeenth-century Spanish playwrights, Lope indisputably reigned supreme on television. Of the 46 Golden Age plays adapted to the small screen after TVE debuted *Primera fila*, its first program that specialized in televised theatrical works in 1964, over half (51 percent) were either Lope's or attributed to him. Compared to his 29 adaptations, Calderón came in second place with 13, followed by a wide margin by Tirso de Molina with five, Agustín Moreto with three, Juan Ruiz de Alarcón and María de Zayas with two each, and finally Guillén de Castro, Francisco de Rojas Zorrilla, and Luis Vélez de Guevara with only one. Taking into consideration the total number of adaptations of Golden Age plays produced during Francoism, it is clear that Lope de Vega had more works adapted as all the other authors combined.

While the studies by Bayliss (2015, 717) and Julio Montero and María Antonia Paz (2014, 782) have provided crucial information to situating Lope's works within contemporary Spanish popular culture, these scholars have misconstrued this predominance of Lope's presence in comparison to his contemporary rivals. For example, both have perpetuated the assumption that Francoists actively promoted television and film adaptations of the playwright's dramas as to instill his conservative seventeenth-century values into the twentieth-century collective consciousness. What these scholars overlook, however, is that the amount of adapted works from the Golden

49

# Total Broadcasts of Spanish Golden Age
# Adaptations on TVE (1959-1977)

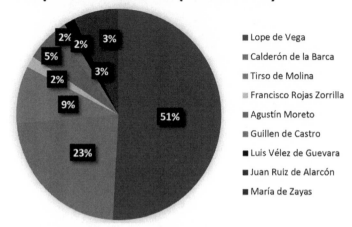

Figure 2.1. **Graphic Depiction of Golden Age Authors' Adapted Works on Primera fila, Estudio 1,** Teatro de siempre, and El teatro During the Years in Which Francoist Censorship of Film and Television Was Active. *Source: Original graph from episode guides provided by TVE archivists.*

Age—including those attributed to Lope—constituted a very small fraction of TVE's overall programming. While Lope's works' relative popularity on Spanish television sets and cinema screens may appear to be a remarkable accomplishment, one must keep in mind that, although televised theater was somewhat popular during the Francoist dictatorship, Golden Age plays were not especially frequent additions to TVE's programming. For example, of the 102 episodes of *Primera fila*, only 5 (a mere 4.9 percent) were adaptations of Golden Age plays, and such data is echoed by *Estudio 1*, which only dedicated 16 (roughly 4.3 percent) of its impressive 371 episodes to classical Spanish theater. Even programs like *Teatro de siempre*, which boasts the highest percentage of Golden Age plays, only broadcasted 23 adaptations of classical Spanish theater during its 150-episode run (slightly above 15 percent). If one considers the total amount of episodes of all programs specializing in televised theater, it becomes evident that adaptations of plays from Spain's Golden Age did not occupy more than a mere 7 percent of total broadcasts with only 46 episodes out of 651.

Adaptations of more recent Spanish plays, especially those based on works from the twentieth century, were significantly more common on these programs during the early years of TVE. Translations or dubbed re-broadcasts of foreign dramas—such as Shakespeare's *Romeo and Juliet* (1966), *Macbeth* (1966), and *The Merchant of Venice* (1967)—and popular North American plays such as Arthur Miller's *Death of a Salesman* (1972) and Reginald

# Categories of Televised Theater During Francoist Censorship (1964-1977)

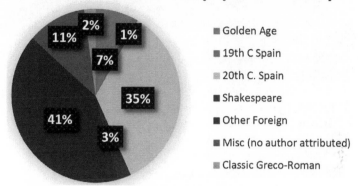

- Golden Age
- 19th C Spain
- 20th C. Spain
- Shakespeare
- Other Foreign
- Misc (no author attributed)
- Classic Greco-Roman

Figure 2.2.  Totals of the Percentages of All Categories of Televised Theater (Grouped by Time Period or Geographic Region). *Source: Original graph of episode lists for Primera fila, Estudio 1, Teatro de siempre, and El teatro provided by TVE archivists.*

Rose's *Twelve Angry Men* (1973) also eclipsed the amount of Spanish classical dramas that were adapted for these programs in later decades.

As this chapter will demonstrate, adaptations of Lope's dramas held no particular prevalence in popular culture and those productions that were carried out still underwent a thorough degree of censorship. Accordingly, despite the fact that Lope's plays lent themselves well to productions that were deemed suitable for public consumption by the censors, this chapter also analyzes the complex relationship between Francoism and Lope de Vega that challenges the general conception of the dramatist's role as an intentional ideological weapon in the regime's audiovisual artillery.

The following is a list of all of Lope de Vega's plays that were adapted to film and television during this period:

## Motion Pictures

1. *Fuenteovejuna*, Dir. Antonio Román, 1947
2. *La moza de cántaro*, Dir. Florián Rey, 1954
3. *Fuenteovejuna*, Dir. Juan Guerrero Zamora, 1972
4. *El mejor alcalde, el rey*, Dir. Rafael Gil, 1974.

## Television

5. "La Estrella de Sevilla" (*Primera fila*, 1964; *Teatro de siempre*, 1969)
6. "El perro del hortelano" (*Estudio 1*, 1966)

7. "Peribáñez y el comendador de Ocaña" (*Primera fila*, 1964; *Teatro de siempre*, 1967; *Estudio 1*, 1970)
8. "El castigo sin venganza" (*Teatro de siempre*, 1967)
9. "Fuenteovejuna" (*Teatro de siempre*, 1967; *El teatro*, 1975)
10. "El nuevo mundo descubierto por Cristóbal Colón" (*Teatro de siempre*, 1968)
11. "El caballero de Olmedo" (*Estudio 1*, 1968, *Cuentos y leyendas* 1975)
12. "La dama boba" (*Estudio 1*, 1969)
13. "El villano en su rincón" (*Estudio 1*, 1970)
14. "El mejor alcalde, el rey" (*Estudio 1*, 1970)
15. "La discreta enamorada" (*Teatro de siempre*, 1970)
16. "La prudente venganza" (*Hora 11*, 1971)
17. "El bastardo Mudarra" (*Teatro de siempre*, 1971)
18. "La malcasada" (*Estudio 1*, 1973)
19. "La viuda valenciana" (*Estudio 1*, 1975)
20. "Los milagros del desprecio" (*Teatro de siempre*, 1967; *Estudio 1*, 1972)
21. "Por la puente, Juana" (*Teatro de siempre*, 1970)

Moving forward, this chapter explores in detail the adaptations of Lope's plays that were released during the dictatorship, excluding from the main analysis those which were only brought to the screen once and those that were recreated after Francisco Franco's death in 1975, the latter being reserved for examination in chapter 3. As such, this chapter will be concerned primarily with the study and analysis of the adaptations of the most canonical works on this list, which, coincidently, were the titles adapted the highest number of times; namely, *Fuenteovejuna* (1947, 1967, 1962, 1975), *La Estrella de Sevilla* (1964, 1969), *Peribáñez y el comendador de Ocaña* (1964, 1967, 1970), *El mejor alcalde, el rey* (1970, 1974), *El caballero de Olmedo* (1968, 1975), and *Los milagros del desprecio* (1967, 1972).

In addition to the fact that all of these plays were adapted on multiple occasions, it is worth considering that they all have essential traits in common.[2] For example, they all take place during the Middle Ages and pertain to a subgenre of Golden Age plays referred to by Felipe Pedraza Jiménez (2009) as *comedias villanescas*, which deal with topics that were also important to Francoist ideology such as honor, the importance of popular traditions, the political struggles of the lower class, and upholding the established sociopolitical order.[3] Using Pedraza Jiménez's (2009) subcategorization of these plays and my own observations as a foundation for my analysis, I have narrowed down three characteristics shared by all of these adaptations that demonstrate why these particular plays were best suited for Spanish airways during the dictatorship: (1) Power and Authority, (2) the unifying concept of an inherent "Spanishness," and (3) treatment—or lack thereof—of the "Other."

## ON POWER, AUTHORITY, SPANISHNESS, NATIONAL IDENTITY, AND ESTABLISHED SOCIAL ORDER

In the earliest stage of his regime, Franco recognized the need for a strong nationalistic impulse that would rally the Spanish population behind his political platform under the guise of a modern, integrative, and socially beneficial renovation of Spain's former glory. This would not be an easy task, given that, as Stanley Payne (2018) reminds us, he was "neither eloquent nor impressive in physical appearance" (123). Franco and his sympathizers would, in turn, have to rely on a technique practiced by Primo de Rivera before him and win Spaniards over to his side of the ideological debate by exalting what they believed were the shared traits of all Spanish people, namely a collective history, common *lingua franca*, and a strong Catholic devotion.[4] Franco and his followers looked to Spain's distant past as a model for sociopolitical perfection and invoked the names of Catholic Monarchs Ferdinand and Isabel to rally his base behind the cause. As Carolyn Boyd (1997) reminds us, "Catholics and Falangists constantly invoked the imperial age, Catholics spoke as if the intervening passage of time could be disregarded; the sixteenth century was not just a source of inspiration and rededication, as it seemed to be for the Falangists, but a still viable model for contemporary social and political life" (236).

Given that the Lope adaptations studied in this chapter take place during the Middle Ages in Spain and depict this period as an example of proper political and societal conduct while employing melodic Castilian verse, the temptation to believe that the regime favored these works and were directly involved in producing adaptations of them is understandable. On the contrary, as the data examined earlier in this chapter demonstrate, the regime appears to have maintained a rather indifferent attitude toward adaptations of classical literature, including that of Lope. In any case, whereas the censorship monitored and controlled what *should not* to be displayed on Spanish screens and awarded productions that best abided by these constraints, there was no political entity that promoted the creation and distribution of certain films and television programs that *should* be publicly broadcasted. It is therefore impossible to label the adaptations of Lope de Vega's plays as intentional weapons of mass indoctrination used by the Francoist regime. Nevertheless, the adaptations that were produced and distributed during the dictatorship take full advantage of the themes and representations of the Spanish population in the Middle Ages to portray a sense of Hispanic identity that was reminiscent to that of medieval and early modern Spaniards.

The concept of a naturally established order between centralized governing authorities and the populations over which they rule, exemplified during the Middle Ages, is arguably the most important ideological topic on which

Francoist objectives and Lope de Vega's plays converge. Naturally, Franco's totalitarian regime depended heavily on his population being obedient to his sociopolitical hierarchy, which he considered not only a natural part of any government but as a divinely sanctioned rule ordained by God and upheld by the Catholic Church.[5] Determined not to make the same mistakes as Primo de Rivera before him, Franco consolidated his power and had the "Fundamental Laws" drafted between 1945 and 1947 that granted him absolute legislative, executive, and judicial authority.[6] Nevertheless, Franco was aware of his— and, quite likely, his dictatorship's—mortality and the fact that his regime was not a proper model for his idea of a unified Spain under one legitimate crown.[7] As such, realizing he had no reasonable alternative, he began to show an interest in restoring the traditional Spanish monarchy of days past, thus converting the concept of his dictatorship as a type of interim government that would, in time, come to a conclusion and ensure Spain remained structured in its previously established sociopolitical, religious order.

In spite of his brief ambition to maintain a republican system early in his military career, Francisco Franco was a lifelong conservative and monarchical sympathizer.[8] In line with this personal ideology and vision for the nation, the dictator fashioned a twofold philosophy of Spanish nationalism that combined Spaniards' common history with their shared Catholic faith. Supported by nationalists and monarchists who saw the emerging figure of Franco as a unifier of Spain and protector of traditional culture, this new definition of Spanishness became the battle cry of his official political party, *La Falange Española Tradicionalista*, formed in April 1937. The party quickly grew in numbers and influence until, two years later, the final Republican strongholds in Madrid and Valencia fell to his new regime.

Franco was extremely familiar with his predecessors' mistakes and thus saw an immediate need for his regime to convert the Falange's nationalist philosophy into a doctrine and a functional political system. He did so by contaminating symbols of the nation with totalitarian meanings that implicitly camouflaged Spanish nationalism in various disguises that permeated cultural and political discourses. As Sebastian Balfour and Alejandro Quiroga (2014) have observed, nationalism under Franco took on a chameleonic nature and resurfaced as

> patriotism, constitutionalism, solidarity, or as the expression of an immemorial and universal principle. . . . Most of its implicit manifestations attribute a common identity and destiny to the inhabitants of Spain, embracing all those who share a cultural heritage passed on through generations since the early Middle Ages, if not since Roman times. (1–2)

In order for Franco to achieve this objective, however, he would have to select his historical role models carefully. Unlike Benito Mussolini, who had managed to fashion himself as a new Caesar Augustus and leader of an Italy that would regain the former imperial glories of Ancient Rome, Spain's imperial legacy was far more recent and more firmly rooted in the national consciousness than the Roman Empire of antiquity.[9] Franco did not need to revert to Spain's Ancient Roman past, for Spanish monarchs, especially after the discovery of America, had always fashioned themselves as successors to the Roman Caesars, thus legitimizing their claims to the New World as a form of *translatio imperii*.

Instead, Franco relied on a Castilian-centered perspective of Spanish history and did so by conjuring several ghosts of Spain's past, chiefly the Catholic Monarchs, Isabel I of Castile and Fernando II of Aragon. Moreover, the dictator contaminated their national symbols for his own self-fashioning. This was most evident in his appropriation of the "eagle of San Juan," a symbol of the Reconquest of Spain that was a prominent feature on the crest of the Catholic Monarchs, whom he admired for their strict adherence to and enforcement of Catholicism on an international scale.[10] In fact, as early as 1942, in his address to the Youth Front, Franco had already evoked the figures of Fernando and Isabel to declare that the "national unity that our Catholic Monarchs forge is closely united to the spiritual unity and the expansion of our faith" (Díaz-Plaja, 1972, 116).[11] Some might be tempted, then, to consider this the reason why, a mere five years later, the first of Lope's plays to be successfully adapted to film would be none other than *Fuenteovejuna* (1947), a play with a denouement that centers around the intervention of the Catholic Monarchs.

Naturally, the topic of power and authority was considered by the Francoist regime to be a delicate subject that must be handled with utmost care. In the case of Lope de Vega's plays, Francoist authorities were wary about how some of the abusive political figures of Spanish Golden Age literature could be interpreted by audiences who were inclined to perceive a revolutionary undertone in these works, most of all in *Fuenteovejuna*. Let us not forget, for example, that Federico García Lorca had written and produced a theatrical adaptation of this play with La Barraca in 1933 that encouraged an uprising of the masses against anti-republican leaders.[12] García Lorca eliminated a third of Lope's text—including the entire subplot of the Commander's betrayal and intervention of the Catholic Monarchs—in order to focus on the inherent social drama and inspire a sense of urgency in his audience to act against oppressive tyranny by demonstrating the persistence of past problems in the present. His version demonstrates only one specific example of the interpretation of a democratic and revolutionary subtext in *Fuenteovejuna*.[13]

The Board of Censors was apparently aware of some of the concepts defined and systemized decades later by the proponents of reader-response theory, specifically that institutions (religion, society, schooling, among others) affect the way readers perceive and interpret texts, and that people are often inclined to follow interpretations supported by the culture of their time. In other words, the censors ascribed to an interpretive community whose understanding of classical literature was to be disseminated throughout popular culture, lest "incorrect" readings threaten to undermine the ideology propagated by the regime. Accordingly, the dictatorship, through its censors, meticulously read and scrutinized scripts of even the most canonical Spanish literary masterpieces to make sure that the "correct" understanding of the text, according to their perception, was adapted.[14]

## "ALL FOR ONE AND ONE FOR ALL": FRANCO'S *FUENTEOVEJUNA*

The regime's approach to adaptations of *Fuenteovejuna*, therefore, is by far the best example of how the censors attempted to control the interpretations of a work whose central theme of power and authority could easily be manipulated by leftist screenwriters and directors. As such, only adaptors deemed worthy of upholding the ideology and values of the regime would be allowed to even consider producing an adaptation of such a potentially problematic text. In fact, before Antonio Román successfully produced and distributed his adaptation of *Fuenteovejuna* (1947), another director, Carlos Arévalo, had already set his sights on bringing the play to life on the big screen in 1942 and had even gone so far so as to secure a production permit for the adaptation, only to have the project halted before it could even begin filming.

Although the exact reasons for the film eventually being discarded are unknown, Pepe Coira suggests that Arévalo's previous fiasco with the film *Rojo y negro* (1942)—which led to the premature withdrawal of the movie from cinemas—caused the authorities of the time to mistrust the director with such sensitive material. This explanation is especially probable if we consider that Spanish cinema had, from then until the end of the Second World War, shied away from making authoritarian-themed films (118).[15] Antonio Román, on the other hand, despite having directed some of La Barraca's productions in the 1930s, had become a highly regarded cinematographer during the regime due to his work on nationalistic films such as *Los últimos de Filipinas* (1945) and the film adaptation of Franco's idyllic autobiography *Raza* (1941).[16] By teaming up with screenwriter José María Pemán, to whom Wheeler (2008) refers as a "stalwart" of the Francoist regime (287), the pair presented their script to the Office of the Under-Secretary of Public Education of the Ministry of National Education. On August 20, 1946, they were given official permission to begin production on what would be the first adaptation of *Fuenteovejuna* to make it to Spanish screens.[17]

The Secretary General of the Cinema Division was generally impressed by the initial reading of the screenplay. His official report praised the proposed film, regarding the "cinematographic vision of the drama [as] magnificent and the script excellent" ("Informes" n.p.). He specifically addressed the previous republican "misinterpretations" of the play in his report to the General Director of Cinema and Theater (*Dirección General de Cinematografía y Teatro*) submitted on September 17, 1946, in which he summarized the censors' opinions of the script:

> I believe it interesting to call the film director's attention to the danger of leaving a demagogic or morbid interpretation to the final picture, which revolutionary propaganda has made their flag and anthem, whether or not this is the director's intention at all. Therefore I must caution him to be very careful in order to avoid these two dangers by not accentuating nor allowing them to be recreated in the most precarious passages like those twisted interventions. (González Álvarez n.p.)

The report clearly demonstrates the censorship's preoccupation with the sociopolitical representation of the film and its potential to inspire a revolutionary attitude in viewers, especially with regard to how power and authority would be depicted in the final version of the film. The tone of the remarks made is strikingly similar to the reasons provided for not authorizing the production of either script of *La Estrella de Sevilla* three years later. Unlike in *Fuenteovejuna*, in which the denouement of the play relies on the appearance of the honorable Catholic Monarchs who arrive at the small Cordovan village to restore the established order, the treacherous Rey Sancho of *La Estrella de Sevilla*—as has been established in chapter 1—is a rapist, murderer, and liar upon whom justice is not served. In other words, the intervention of the legitimate rulers of all Castile is what allowed the former title to be adapted to films whereas the latter fell short.

As such, Román and Pemán, like every adaptor of *Fuenteovejuna* since, were sure to include and highlight the intervention of the Catholic Monarchs in their film. Although all of the scenes that take place in the sovereigns' chambers in Acts I (I.8) and III (III.10) are omitted—likely for time and possibly to conceal their intervention until the very end for increased dramatic impact—and the characters' total on-screen time is only around three minutes (01:09:51—01:13:03), they are given special treatment in the opening credits. A title card that reads "and the prestigious collaboration of Lina Yegros and Julio Peña in the roles of the Catholic Monarchs" is shown immediately before the onset of the action. No other characters are given a similar introduction. Although most censors and journalists seemed unbothered by the lack of monarchical presence in the film, upon viewing the finished product, the Provincial Delegate of Logroño noted in his report that this was a shortcoming, especially in comparison with the care with which the other characters had been developed. The censor complained that most of the characters were carefully constructed, "with the slight exception of those who represent Fernando and Isabel, which do not satisfactorily show the majesty that History attributes to the Catholic Monarchs" ("Informes" n.p.). While he does not specifically mention the scarce screen time given to these characters, it is notable that he is the only censor who expressed a desire for them to be developed in more detail.

Perhaps the reason behind the other censors' silence on the brevity of the Catholic Monarchs' presence in the film has to do with the fact that Pemán introduced a completely original scene into the film that clearly delimited "legitimate" versus "illegitimate" power and authority. His version contrasts the monarchs with an even more sinister Commander than Lope's original. The added scene in question takes place at church during mass (00:11:51). Intercalated wide-angle shots of the altar and close-ups of the Commander's facial expressions are manipulated to show how he looks angrily toward the abbot during the homily, in which the latter discusses how God will humble the powerful and exalt the lowly, reminding the congregation of the Biblical prophecy that "[the powerful] will be thrown from their seats [of power] if they don't use their power as an instrument of mercy" (00:12:50).[18] In addition to offering a satisfying foreshadowing to the Commander's downfall, the added scene clearly underscores the adaptation's message for its implied audience in the event that the forthcoming action does not successfully transmit this interpretation of the plot's essence to spectators.

Immediately afterward, the abbot and the Commander speak in private and the latter scolds the former for his words and threatens to squeeze the life out of him. As if this were not a grave enough sin for the Commander to commit, he goes on to blaspheme against the blood of Christ, calling the communal wine "your wine from Hell" and referring to it as poison (00:13:00). The abbot's reaction is one of patience and kindness. He beseeches the Commander to be a just ruler, to act with love and mercy toward his vassals, and to "love your men more . . . and their wives less" (00:13:40). The Commander defends his actions by arguing that Castilian men are, by nature, excessively flirtatious, to which the holy man responds that he should heed his advice sooner than later, as he is not exactly a young man and that his day of judgment is impending.[19] Feigning humility at the thought of being eternally punished for his transgressions, the Commander finally concedes that the abbot is "somewhat right" before agreeing to try to do better and exiting (00:14:22).

Although the scenes described above are relatively short (coming in at a combined total of just under three minutes), they are overwhelmingly significant. On one hand, they underscore the importance of Catholicism in relation to political power. The juxtaposition of the violent, blasphemous Commander and the patient, kind, forgiving abbot clearly demarcate the divisive line between "good" versus "evil" management of power in the film. The religious leader whose authority outranks that of the Commander in Catholic doctrine controls and limits his power by being gentle and amiable instead of imposing his will forcefully upon others as the Commander does later. On the other hand, this scene also distances the Commander from legitimate, Catholic rulers who—like monarchs—are granted their authority by God, according to tradition. As such, Lope's version more subtly suggests that the Commander's legitimacy as ruler is nullified by his moral transgressions, whereas Pemán's adaptation uses this original scene to communicate the idea much more explicitly. Moreover, in emphasizing the Commander's sacrilegious behavior, any comparison between the tyrant and Franco would be almost impossible to make, thus removing any potential negative associations between the villain of *Fuenteovejuna* and the devout, God-fearing Franco.

Although it may seem paradoxical that a dictatorship would want to disseminate a positive image of the monarchy—which is essentially a competing form of government—one must consider the political advantages that doing so was assumed to have for Franco and his regime. First of all, the monarchical tradition in Spain was tightly linked to the periods of Spain's past that the dictator was eager to evoke in order to encourage cultural and political unity in the country. His desire to define the nation as a single political unit was especially echoed in the "Law of Succession" of 1947—the same year that Román's *Fuenteovejuna* began to circulate in Spanish cinemas—that clearly states in its first article that Spain "as a political unit, is a social and representative Catholic State that, according to tradition, is declared a Kingdom" ("BOE 160," 3272). In this same piece of legislation, Franco also explicitly outlined his plans to restore Spain to a proper monarchy whenever his regime came to an end. He did so without specifying an expiration date for the dictatorship and without naming a specific successor, claiming only in the ninth article that the next sovereign must be Spanish, Catholic, at least 30 years of age, and loyal to the principles of the "National Mission" (3273).[20] Second, in restoring the monarchy on his own terms, Franco not only paved the way for his particular brand of governance to prevail after he was no longer dictator, but he did so in a way that would appease his most loyal supporters. It is well known that sympathizers of the monarchy had sided with the rebellion military and Franco since the early days of the Spanish Civil War in opposition to the Second Republic and continued to be some of the dictator's most influential supporters during his regime. The Francoist definition of "power" and "authority," therefore, was always approached exclusively from a pro-monarchical perspective.

After Torrente Ballester's failure to turn his vision of *La Estrella de Sevilla* into cinematic reality in 1950, no *comedia villanesca* would be adapted to the big screen until the Juan Guerrero Zamora remade *Fuenteovejuna* in 1972. Meanwhile, despite this absence in cinemas, these *comedias* found a reasonably stable home on television, especially between 1964 and 1975. As Eduardo Rodríguez Merchán (2014) indicates in his research on the origins of theatrical adaptations on Spanish theater, "dramatic programs (and especially theater) [have] an outstanding and even preeminent position in this primitive television" (269). By 1959, TVE had launched one of its first original series, *Fila cero*, that staged and broadcasted live performances of a variety of Spanish plays. The show's name was changed to *Primera fila* in 1962, but the content and format were essentially the same as before (272). Given that the vast majority of plays broadcasted were performances of more contemporary Spanish and foreign dramas, Golden Age *comedias*, two attributed to Lope de Vega, were the subject of only five episodes of the series.[21] The two recorded performances of plays attributed to Lope de Vega, *La Estrella de Sevilla* and *Peribáñez*, both aired in 1964, were not recorded for re-broadcasting or syndication and therefore are not conserved or accessible for viewing in the TVE archives.

Although it is impossible to access the broadcasts of *Peribáñez* and *La Estrella de Sevilla* from *Primera fila* in 1964, the adaptations of these dramas that were aired on *Estudio 1* (1967) and *Teatro de siempre* (1969), respectively, are conserved in TVE's archives.[22] It is also worth noting that *Fuenteovejuna* would also be adapted to the small screen on *Teatro de siempre* in 1967. Let us consider the reasons why, after a nearly 20-year absence from Spanish screens, the *comedia villanesca* would resurface, this time on national television. As I have mentioned above, Franco publicly declared his intentions to restore the monarchy upon his death from a very early stage of his dictatorship, but he had done so in vague terms and had not yet named who his royal successor would be; he only made clear that as "Head of State," it would be he who hand-picked the new monarch. Meanwhile, the relationship between Franco and the royal family fluctuated between hostility and adoration. Although he publicly ridiculed Prince Juan Carlos and his father Don Juan, his only daughter married the grandson of Alfonso XIII and potential heir to the Spanish throne Alfonso, Duke of Anjou and Cádiz.[23]

Nevertheless, the dictator was not getting any younger and, as many historians indicate, he was becoming increasingly obsessed with his legacy in the 1960s as the biological fact of his mortality became imminent.[24] In July 1969, pressured by entities such as the *Opus Dei* to follow the traditional lines of royal inheritance as closely as possible, Franco officially named Prince Juan Carlos as his successor. Time was of the essence and, as the early years of the century had demonstrated, the question of a reigning monarch in Spain was problematic for many Spaniards, even some of Franco's most loyal followers. He had a great task ahead of him: the regime must convince the Spanish population that, beyond having always been a part of national history and identity, the monarchs of Spain were always working in the interests of the people and crucial to the country's stability and well-being. Starting in the mid-1960s, popular culture outlets served as an ideological vehicle to try to accustom the population to the idea of a restored monarchy and cement this concept into the collective Spanish imagination.

Naturally, the manifestations of Spanish royalty in Lope de Vega's plays were well-suited to demonstrate the time-honored, solid bond between subjects and crown that had always existed in Spain, as the regime would have people believe. Indeed, a July 1967 article in *ABC Sevilla* titled "Monarquía popular," written by José María Villar y Romero, explained this sacred connection to his readers very clearly. Taking inspiration from the national myths of Visigoth Spain, from whom he insists the current royal line of monarchs descends, Villar y Romero relies on literary examples to substantiate his claims that the Spanish monarchy had always strived to maintain the well-being of its citizens by working closely with them, arguing that

> the literature of our Golden Age demonstrates to us and corroborates such a state of things: Lope, Calderón, Tirso, Rojas, Moreto, etc. in immortal dramas like *Fuenteovejuna, El alcalde de Zalamea, Del rey abajo, ninguno, Peribáñez y el comendador de Ocaña* . . . and many, many others eliminate any possible doubt surrounding the intimate rapport, the binomial, perfect and indestructible King-people equation. (3)

It is likely not a coincidence that this article was printed the same year that both of the Lope plays he cites were adapted to television. In any case, as opposed to Román's adaptation in 1947, the version of *Fuenteovejuna* that was filmed for *Teatro de siempre* in 1967 hardly touches Lope's original text at all.[25] It would appear as though the regime was permitting the production of these adaptations in conformity with its political objectives depending on the administrative priorities of the moment; in other words, when it was convenient to clearly demarcate the difference of "legitimate" versus "illegitimate" power and authority, the text could be added to or suppressed accordingly. As the importance of emphasizing this political distinction faded into the background of Franco's ideological agenda, Lope's original verses were deemed worthy of speaking for themselves and required little intervention from screenwriters.

As previously stated, the dilemma of power and authority would again come to the forefront when Juan Guerrero Zamora presented his adaptation of *Fuenteovejuna* in 1970 to the dictatorial censorship, whose members collectively disagreed with the director's depiction of the monarchy and the population. In their opinion, as expressed by a note sent to the Board of Censorship and Film Rating (*Junta de Censura y Apreciación de Películas*) by the General Director of Popular Culture and Spectacles, General Subdirection of

Cinematography on September 17, 1971, the film's violence overshadowed its message of royal justice and contributed to the "black legend" of a barbaric citizenry and unruly sociopolitical climate in Spain ("Carta a la Junta de Censura" n.p.). Their advice was for Guerrero Zamora to consider discarding his adaptation and making an entirely new production, suggesting he give a "reconsideration and new setting to the movie in question, in such a way so as to eliminate, in all ways possible, the unfortunate and excessive exaggeration given to the film and making it better suited, as much as possible, to the spirit of exaltation of justice [that is] predominant in the work of Lope de Vega" (n.p.). These comments, when compared to those made by the censorship about Antonio Román's 1947 adaptation of the same text, demonstrate that the regime's apprehensions to improper interpretations had subsided. Their objections were now rooted on strictly aesthetic considerations.

Despite his insistence that the adaptation be released first in cinemas, Guerrero Zamora's film was scheduled to be released on TVE in 1972, but its broadcast was postponed indefinitely after the censors reviewed the finished product. The director did not take the censors' criticisms and treatment of his project lightly; an undated letter written to the General Director of Popular Culture and Spectacles, General Subdirection of Cinematography (*Director General de Cultura Popular y Espectáculos, Subdirección General de Cinematografía*) by Guerrero Zamora details his interpretation of power and authority in Lope's play and defends the artistic decisions that were made during the process of creating the adaptation. The director argued that the

> most profound and exceptionable liability of tyranny lies not in the concrete fact of his scandals, but rather in that he corrupts the very nature of the oppressed. The people of Fuenteovejuna, hardworking and peaceful, incubate a resentment that degenerates them. And it is this degeneration, this corruption, this almost second nature that is imposed upon them that becomes manifest in their consequently ferocious vengeance. The forgiveness of the Monarchs is a grace that purifies those vindictive people and, as a result, they will become aware of the state to which they were reduced against their will. Returned to their authentic selves, they understand that a bloody, inexcusable act weighs on them, since violence is never the answer. When they return to their village, they do so not [feeling] regretful, but certainly sorry, wishing—as a meaningful song goes—to transform their bitter legacy into a fruitful present. ("Carta a la Junta de Censura" 2)

As demonstrated by this letter, Guerrero Zamora was aware of the importance of the Catholic Monarchs' intervention, an opinion he later reiterates by contrasting his adaptation to that of the Soviet Union in which, as he indicates that the "intervention of the Monarchs is suppressed, meaning that the State's power shifts to be represented by the Commander; in other words, it becomes associated with oppression" (2). According to the director's interpretation, the monarchs cured the inhabitants of Fuenteovejuna of their insanity that was brought on by the abuses of the Commander, which, despite being one of the most important functions of power and authority in the play, he considered it "one of the text's weakest scenes" (1).

As a result of this perceived literary weakness in Lope's original, the director saw himself obligated to compensate for this narrative shortcoming, forcing him to

> modify or amplify the scene, composing only three-quarters of it originally, and showing the uncertainty of the Monarchs not only in facing the dilemma, but also in facing another political [figure] that advises them to forgive, as a warning to their feudal peers and to attract the people to their cause of unifying Spain. Their pardon is, therefore, in the interest of the State and proof of their good governance. (2)

In other words, Guerrero Zamora argued that the ideological undercurrent of his adaptation was indeed in line with that of the regime, and that "exactly what my version is going for is a semantic equilibrium that is compatible with the reactivation of the original" (2). Nevertheless, his argument was not enough to convince television producers or the press. An article in *Fotogramas* from September 25, 1975, argued that the director's vision went in direct opposition to "the post-romantic and classical [vision] of an evil Commander [versus] the excellent people and just Catholic Monarchs" (6).[26] Despite the presence of the Catholic Monarchs in the film, the journalist goes on to compare the adaptation more to "the Russian one, in which Fuenteovejuna is a town that rises up against the tyranny of the oppressor" (6–7). The film was released in cinemas on November 17, 1972, rated as suitable only for spectators 18 years and above and with 47 sequences removed from the adaptation by the censors in order to reduce the amount of violence shown on screen. Guerrero Zamora was so outraged by the censors' involvement in the film that he refused to attend the premiere or speak of the film to most media outlets at the time.[27]

Unfortunately, the film did not have much better luck with the press of the time than it did with the censors. Whereas Román's adaptation in 1947 was advertised extensively in newspapers and film magazines with full-page ads and small images of the official film poster mentioning its release date and cinemas where the public could view it, complete with phrases like "it's an honor for Spain and Spanish cinema" months before its premiere ("Fuenteovejuna" 4), Guerrero Zamora's film received much less hype prior to its release.[28] Although some reviews released in the press following its debut were very positive, most journalists painted a dismal picture of the film in its reflections of the production, but mainly due to cinematic aspects that do not take into consideration how the ideological undercurrents are presented in the adaptation.[29] Despite the press's silence on the issue, it should, however, be noted that the film does indeed illustrate Lope de Vega's views on power and authority in a unique, artistic way.

For example, Guerrero Zamora's adaptation highlights abuses and tyranny of the Commander from the very first sequence, in which horror-movie inspired, anxiety-inducing music is played while images of Laurencia screaming and being tortured are shown. The proleptic scene goes on to show more images of others going through similar punishments while they are asked "Who killed the Commander?" and frightening echoes are heard in the background. In order to highlight the Commander's cruelty beyond that of the original play, an additional scene in which he captures, restrains, and holds women captive in his cave-like lair while laughing maniacally and ridiculing them as they beg for help is also inserted into the film adaptation. Dialogues that are not present in Lope's original are also added to further develop the character of the Commander as a ruthless—quasi-psychopathic— authority figure. The exchange that best illustrates this strategy is when the Commander enters a set that is designed to look like a dungeon and a woman is restrained, crying for help. The Commander is not fazed and the following original dialogue is included:

*COMMANDER:* Innkeeper! A bottle of wine with no glass! And you, prepare a bed for me! Let Fame crown that fool!
*WOMAN:* Help, for the love of God, help!
*FLORES:* I doubt anyone will help you, unless they hear cowbells. Check out how startled she looks!
*WOMAN:* Help! I'm a married woman!
*FLORES:* If you let me borrow her, I'm not the one stealing her from you!
*COMMANDER:* And, therefore, so that no one can say that I mistreated something I borrowed, he who sees this can say otherwise. Let them agree that this woman is willingly tempting me to satisfy her passion. And if commanders are the cure for passion, I will pay no heed to her fury, being a Commander. (00:08:35–00:09:50)[30]

Although this added scene certainly underscores the traumatic effects of such political abuses that Guerrero Zamora uses as evidence to the fact that the village was driven to madness by the despot's cruelty, the fact that they are completely original to this adaptation makes it is tempting to wonder if the director was trying to deliberately incorporate an element of "horror" into the film to attract audiences.[31] At any case, it is clear that, by introducing these scenes so early in the film, Guerrero Zamora certainly kept the topic of power and authority as a central element to his adaptation.

Moreover, the scenes of the Catholic Monarchs in their chambers, which were entirely omitted in Román's adaptation, are not only included but expanded upon in Guerrero Zamora's. For example, Queen Isabel's monologue in I.9 is extended. Whereas her proclamation in the text reads "and it is well to win by hand / before we see the damage done / if we do not manage to mend / and clearly be a simple one" ["y es bien ganar por la mano / antes que el daño veamos / que si no lo remediamos / el ser muy cierto está llano"] (vv. 639–642), her speaking part in the film alters these last three verses and adds to them:

*ISABEL:* It would be good to get ahead of Juana's claims to the crown, for those who do not sit idle have much to win. If Juana the *Beltraneja* were to make a nest here with her husband, she would be a wasp rather than a bee. The crown of Castile is not for those who wish it ill, because Alfonso of Portugal wishes it to be a village humiliated to the neighboring kingdom, not a sovereign state. But the kingdom of Castile is not water for such wine. (00:23:49)[32]

These added lines emphasize the profound love Queen Isabel felt for her kingdom and help to establish the historical context of the plot by reminding spectators of the conflict between Portugal and Castile. The character development of a loving, yet firm queen further contributes to the triumph of monarchical power over the tyrannical Commander in the film's denouement. The juxtaposition of these two authority figures, somewhat implicit in Lope's original, becomes visually and verbally evident in Guerrero Zamora's adaptation. No matter the possible influences of other popular film genres like horror or the reiteration of themes once applauded by censors and journalists, the film failed to captivate audiences and has been considered a commercial catastrophe given the amount of financial and artistic resources that went into its production.[33]

## VIRTUOUS VILLAGERS AND
## TROUBLESOME TYRANTS

While Guerrero Zamora was in the process of preparing his adaptation of *Fuenteovejuna*, another of Lope's *comedias villanescas* with a central theme of royal power and authority was also being adapted for television. *Estudio 1* released its version of *El mejor alcalde, el rey* in May 1970. Like the adaptation of *Peribáñez* three years earlier, the episode opened with a narration that placed the work into its historical context. A man dressed in typical early modern fashion comes into the shot and introduces the play by saying:

Alfonso VII was proclaimed nothing less than Emperor of Spain in Leon in the year 1135. In that peninsula divided amongst Christian kingdoms and Arabic kingdoms, Alfonso's will to see national unity would not be fulfilled until 400 years later with the Catholic Monarchs. The theme of *El mejor alcalde, el rey* seems rigorously historic, and Lope was inspired by the fourth part of the *General Chronicle of Spain*. (00:00:20)

Although the topic of the monarch's supreme power, authority, and just rule is certainly central to both the original text and the televised adaptation, it is curious that the narrator does not highlight this in his introduction. It would appear as though, at least in this example, there was more motivation to revert to previously held preoccupations of the regime: those of fostering a sense of national unity through historical literary works.

With very few exceptions, the adaptation again includes virtually all of the original text. The passages that were removed are very justifiable considering the play had to be formatted for a television show with a limited duration. Most of these omissions were likely the result of needing to modernize the language or remove comical moments that, although enjoyable to spectators, do little to advance the plot. For example, verses containing archaic language such as "talega" and "trebejos" (vv. 1235–1238)—as I will clarify moving forward—were completely omitted, as well as several puns uttered by the buffoon Pelayo. What is highlighted by the film, however, are the lines that best emphasize the regime's opinion of the monarchy. In v. 1776, for instance, which is left textually unaltered, the King Alfonso VII character stands and exclaims "the best judge, the king!" as the camera zooms in on the authoritative look on his face as he promises justice to Sancho (01:00:32). The adaptation also underscores the approachability of the monarchy to the common man. From the onset of the episode, visual emphasis is placed on Sancho's lowly social stature with the camera focusing on his humble abode (which is a stereotypical Galician farmhouse or *pazo*) and his worn clothing. Nevertheless, he and Pelayo are welcomed to an audience with the king when they arrive at court, despite not being of sufficient social stature to warrant such an encounter. In this instance, implicit as it may seem, the producers create a sensation of a welcoming Spanish monarchy that is willing to attend to the needs of even the lowliest Spaniard in order to assure justice and fair treatment that transcend social status.

The last adaptation of a Lope play to be adapted during the life of the dictator was *El mejor alcalde, el rey* that was brought to the big screen in 1974 by director Rafael Gil. As opposed to the 1970 episode of *Esudio 1,* the 1974 recreation was a freer adaptation of Lope's original that, in addition to adapting the verse to a modernized prose, it included many cinematographic elements that would foreshadow the aesthetics of the films released during

Spain's period of transition from dictatorship to democracy in the 1980s.[34] For example, the opening scenes of Sancho pursuing a ferocious wolf—with close-ups on the wolf growling, barking, and showing its teeth—and wide-angle views of the countryside and traveling interior shots of the Count's palace offer a more modern perspective of the play than any of the Lope adaptations released in Spain beforehand. Furthermore, nudity is included in the film in the scene in which Feliciana—who has been renamed Felicia in this adaptation—appears on screen for the first time (00:06:00). Although she is only shown from behind, her entire body is visible in the frame and spectators can see how Sancho smiles as he watches her from afar. Notably, the same censorship that was so appalled at the violence in Guerrero Zamora's *Fuenteovejuna* had no objections to the nude scene.

One of the most noticeable consequences of the increased degree of openness to international organisms was the emergence of a trend referred to in hindsight as an uncovering.[35] The "uncovering" trend began during the second stage of the dictatorship (1950–1960) and continued to allow more progressive elements on film and television until the final years of the dictatorship. By the early 1970s, more risqué visual and verbal content was beginning to make its way onto Spanish screens and in the press. Far from being a reactionary movement rebelling against the previous repression during the more rigorous censorship of early Francoism, it was sanctioned by the regime as a way of integrating Spanish popular culture into the European mainstream. The motivation behind this increased tolerance was both political and financial. The only hope Spain had for fostering better international relations—not to mention establishing and nurturing diplomatic and economic alliances with the rest of Europe and the United States—was showing the world that it was taking strides toward providing their citizens with the types of freedoms that the inhabitants in those countries enjoyed. It is imperative to consider the sociopolitical climate of Spain during these years in order to understand how the nude scene in *El mejor alcalde el rey* (1974) was permitted.

As the censors' reports demonstrate, the positive portrayal and praise of the monarchy, as demonstrated by the trumpets that play every time the king is on screen and his final, regal exit on horseback at the end of the film, must have completely overshadowed any fear that showing the backside of a nude woman might compromise the regime's moral standards.[36] According to the contemporary press, they were successful in this venture. A review of the film published in *Arriba* on May 5, 1974, praised the affinity between the king and his people and the depiction of the monarchy by describing the theme of the film thusly:

> the feudal aristocrat, ambitious and a traitor, despotic and cruel, is the com-
> mon enemy of kings and countrymen; the protection of the humble and the

punishment of the powerfuls' outrages binds the king with his people with the ties of faithful solidarity . . . [Rafael Gil] has specialized in the adaptation of literary works of the past . . . in all of Rafael Gil's adaptations you can appreciate the respect, not only to the spirit, but also to the words of the original; diligence and dignity in the recreation of the characters and settings and, of course, the correctness of the technical aspects. (20)

In any case, it is clear that the drive to make an aesthetically impressive movie took precedence over the careful insertion of the regime's ideological values. Unfortunately for Gil, his aesthetic progressivism did little to impress the government. For reasons undisclosed, a report from the Secretary of the Board for Rating and Qualification of Films from 1973 reveals that Gil's request to have the film characterized as "special interest" was declined (n.p.).[37] Four years after the dictator's death, Gil would reappeal this decision on grounds of his film's "exaltation of the Spanish Monarchy, made precisely during the days leading up to the current political transition" (n.p.). As Gil correctly indicates in this last comment, Spain's political situation had changed significantly since his film's debut. A year earlier, the democratic constitution—a topic that will be revisited in chapter 3—had been drafted and approved and Spanish society was taking strides to modernize popular culture, especially with respect to film and television. The fact that his appeal was also declined on grounds that it did not "meet in any way the requirements or grounds for the revision of a firm and decided administrative act" (n.p.) is a testament to how the ideological undercurrents highlighted by Gil did little to impress the authorities of the new political era. It would appear as though the appreciation for power and authority as defined by Lope de Vega faded quickly after the fall of the regime.

Many connoisseurs of Lope de Vega's works would be tempted to analyze *El caballero de Olmedo* as yet another example of a drama that highlights the themes of "power and authority," given that the denouement of the original play relies on the figure of King Don Juan making a personal appearance in the final scene. Upon being informed of Don Rodrigo and Don Fernando's role in the murder of Don Alonso, the King enacts justice upon them by ordering their beheadings. Although Lope's drama certainly shows the proximity of the Castilian king to his population and emphasizes his just moral supremacy over corrupt nobles, this aspect is virtually always entirely omitted by the televised adaptations. The 1968 episode of *Estudio 1* that adapts the play makes only fleeting references to the king and he is not presented as a character. Furthermore, the episode offers no justice to the ill-fated gentleman as neither Don Rodrigo nor Don Fernando are shown or implied to have faced any consequences for the homicide. The 1975 adaptation of *La leyenda del caballero de Olmedo*, despite making some attempt to satisfy the spectators' sense of justice by showing Don Rodrigo laying his head on a chopping block and panning to a shot of an executioner swinging an axe, does little more to highlight royal power and authority than the 1968 adaptation does. Although it is true that an off-screen voice can be heard saying "thus is the justice that his Majesty the King and the governors in his name order to be served against this gentleman by ordering his decapitation for [being] a murderer" (00:55:17), it is notable that the figure of the King does not take the hands-on approach to serving justice that he does in the Lope's play. The scene in the adaptation is presented as more of a standard legal consequence for any murder as opposed to the original, which shows the honorable King taking a personal interest in serving justice.

What the televised adaptations of *El caballero de Olmedo* lack in reinforcing a sense of national identity by highlighting the monarch's supreme authority, they make up for in their representations of Spain's past that demonstrate a prosperous, tradition-oriented society that thrived under the established sociopolitical order of the time. In addition to maintaining the festive "Medina fair" backdrop that serves as the original play's setting, the 1968 adaptation reiterates the fact that the entire concept of the drama was derived from a folkloric Castilian song.[38] Host Ángel Losada opens the episode by reminding us that the song relayed the death of a gentleman from Olmedo during a duel. As such, spectators are given a glimpse into the rich early modern popular culture from which the original play was derived before the episode even begins. Both adaptations, in addition to making sure to include a character who sings the song in their respective episodes, attempt to portray a vibrant, jubilant culture with the insertion of festive scenes that contribute virtually nothing to the action of the plot or the play's overall message. Such imagery and depictions of Spain's rich cultural heritage act as a cinematic device employed by all of the adaptations analyzed in this chapter to forge a historical sense of Spanishness. They do so, however, by emphasizing elements of the play that are already present in the original. In other words, the interventions cannot be conceived of as a deliberate attempt at ideological manipulation.

The backdrop of festive events such as fairs (*ferias*), weddings, jousts, and banquets was commonplace in seventeenth-century dramas. In fact, nearly every one of the plays under examination has at least one example of such an energetic scene accompanying the action and dialogues therein. For example, *Peribáñez* begins at a peasant's wedding (I.1), the second act of *Fuenteovejuna* leads to the plot's climax during the wedding scene that concludes the second act (II.12), Elvira is abducted by Don Tello during the celebration of her wedding in *El mejor alcalde, el rey* (I.10), *La Estrella de Sevilla* opens with a celebration in honor of the king having reconquered the city (I.1), and, as indicated above, *El caballero de Olmedo* takes place during the city's *feria*.

Again, Lope's original version of *Los milagros del desprecio* is an exception to this trend, but it will be included in this section of our analysis as the adaptations of the work incorporate festive dance sequences as well.

Lope did not leave a great deal of stage directions to guide adaptors in making their versions of the festive sequences. For example, the opening scene of *Peribáñez* simply indicates the setting as taking place "at a small-town wedding." Although there is a choir of musicians who sing many of the verses that comprise the scene, there is nothing in the text that indicates tempo, melody, or accompanying instruments. Likewise, the few stage directions provided are also quite vague, simply indicating dancing, singing, gaiety, and shouting.[39] The dialogues from the main characters that are interspersed throughout the singing and dancing are essential because they prepare the plot by providing much-needed background information, so it would be destructive to the storyline to remove this scene from the televised adaptations altogether. Leaving the performative aspects of the episodes aside, it is significant that both adaptations took great care to make the sequences very elaborate, relied on the participation of a great deal of extras and are extremely lengthy, especially considering the financial and time constraints involved in producing television programs in the 1960s and 1970s. Evidently, the notion of spectacle was considered of superior importance to the content.

The 1968 episode of *Estudio 1* dedicates an entire seven minutes of choreographed dancing, singing, and drinking, often shown using a wide-angle lens that, although providing a pleasing vantage point of the celebration, does not permit dialogues to take place while the festivity unfolds (00:05:20–00:12:11). In the case of the 1970 adaptation, the initial dance sequence lasts a total of three minutes with no interspersed dialogue at all (00:00:00–00:03:02). Extras continue to drink, laugh, and dance in the background for an additional six minutes after the first toast is given by the priest and the dialogues between Casilda and Peribáñez are spoken. Considering that the total duration of the first adaptation in 1968 was one hour and ten minutes and the 1970 version lasted an hour and sixteen minutes, it is worth noting that, in addition to all of the financial and artistic resources required to include these scenes, they occupy around 10 percent of each adaptation. This is especially significant if one considers the fact that other moments from the original—including entire scenes—were discarded completely, assumedly to reduce the total run time.

Incorporating cheerful singing and dancing had, of course, been a common practice in the adaptation of Lope's plays since their earliest appearances on Spanish film and television, albeit none dedicated such an overall large percentage of the total run time to these elements as the two adaptations of *Peribáñez*. Antonio Román's 1947 *Fuenteovejuna*, for example, includes two such scenes; the first shows musicians playing instruments while the villagers joke around, laugh, and smile during their daily chores (00:07:30–00:08:42), and the second one is an extremely elaborate musical sequence that takes place during Laurencia and Frondoso's wedding scene and incorporates singing (with verses taken from the original text) and a choreographed dancing shot from an impressive variety of camera angles that often include wide-angle shots in which multitudes of townsfolk can be seen celebrating.

These moments of the film were met with great enthusiasm by censors and the press; journalists reiterated their appreciation of these scenes with comments like "[we] welcome this film that will arrive to our screens with the unmistakable aroma of our greatest traditions" ("Estreno de *Fuenteovejuna*" n.p.). The 1967 televised adaptation of the play also includes an elaborately choreographed dance during the wedding scene, but its duration is, naturally, significantly shorter than in the major motion picture adaptations (00:41:23–00:43:12). Guerrero Zamora's 1972 adaptation of the film also includes an astounding choreographed dance sequence, complete with musical accompaniment and dancers using castanets. The wedding scene that corresponds to II.12–13 in Lope's original, including the merriment and festive tone, is interrupted by the arrival of the Commander after nearly four minutes (00:58:30–01:01:52).[40]

Some adaptations, however, treat the singing and dancing quite differently on film and television than they do in Lope's original. The 1969 adaptation of *La Estrella de Sevilla*, for instance, incorporates a brief choreographed dance sequence to begin the episode. Despite the fact that the first scene is festive in the textual witnesses of the drama, the cheerful moment is not incorporated into the festive action of the episode. As it is a recorded live performance, the dancers simply process off the stage and the actors with speaking parts enter the scene to deliver their lines. Given the lack of cinematographic technology at their disposal at the *corral de comedias* in Almagro, there is no festive action at all in the background while the actors speak. Conversely, the 1970 adaptation of *Los milagros del desprecio* adds an elaborate courtly dance sequence at the beginning of Act I that the text does not indicate at all. Although this festive event is absent from the text, it could arguably be conceived that the dance, in addition to announcing the commencement of the performance, contextualizes the play, given that—as opposed to the vast majority of Lope adaptations that were being broadcast on television during the 1970s—*Los milagros del desprecio* takes place in a palace and the main characters are members of the high nobility. Thus, the courtly dance appropriately introduces spectators to the setting.

Likewise, the 1974 adaptation of *El mejor alcalde, el rey*, which completely diminishes the tragic wedding scene by having it interrupted before any singing, dancing, or music can begin, adds a banquet scene in which the Conde is seen gluttonously devouring entire roasted pigs while he admires the dancers and enjoys the music performed in his palace. Although the dialogue is more or less consistent with the source text in this scene, it is clear that the adaptors wished to highlight the privileges of the corrupt nobility compared to the common population, thus intensifying the dramatic effect of the king's justice in the denouement. Though some modern spectators could find this addition frivolous, the visual aid graphically enhances the class divides that twentieth-century audiences might not have grasped if presented solely verbally, as opposed to seventeenth-century theatergoers that were more accustomed to hearing dialogues in verse.

Clearly, a significant amount of financial and artistic resources went into inserting these festive sequences into the adaptations. The insistence of the producers to include these moments could be for a variety of reasons. On the one hand, they do create a very aesthetically pleasing and awe-inspiring spectacle for audiences to enjoy that gives them repose from attending to such dialogue-heavy plays. Keeping these scenes and elaborating on them in the adaptations could therefore simply be conceived of as a marketing technique to lure audiences to watch these programs even if they weren't interested in the stories they told. Furthermore, one could consider these sequences as homage to seventeenth-century staging procedures who, Henry Ziomek (2014) indicates, used music to serve a variety of functions in Spanish Golden Age drama, ranging from keeping the audience quiet at the beginning, end, and intermissions of the play to welcoming the audience as they arrived (32–33). However, it seems much more likely that directors and screenwriters would go to such lengths to include these scenes because they directly enhanced the plot or message of the adaptation in some way, precisely as was customary in early modernity. As Elena García-Martín (2017) notes, Golden Age *corrales* often added rhythmic elements such as music and dance because they "intensified the tragic effects of ritual scenes with mathematical precision" (138). The Francoist adaptors certainly seem to be following this seventeenth-century technique in the adaptations of *Peribáñez* and *Fuenteovejuna*, in which the joyful wedding scenes are juxtaposed to the ensuing tragedy of the brides' abductions.

While the latter possibility certainly applies to some of the productions being studied, I propose an interpretation of these sequences that explains their contribution to all of the television and film adaptations of the plays. Reflecting on the paradigmatic postmodern concept of creating historicity in art, Fredric Jameson (1991) argues in *Postmodernism, or the Cultural Logic of Late Capitalism* that the past is approached in modern popular culture through a process he coins "stylistic connotation," or "conveying 'pastness' by the glossy qualities of the image" (19). In other words, we are most capable of recognizing and understanding adaptations of history and/ or historical literature when it is presented to us in ways that correspond to what we believe it should look and sound like. Therein lies the function of the music, singing, and dancing in the adaptations of Lope de Vega's plays. Despite their contributions—or lack thereof—to the action or message of the film or television program, the dances allow filmmakers and television crews to introduce the image of Spain's past that they desired into the collective Spanish imagination. By extension, these scenes foster a sense of nostalgia in audiences for the idyllic past that they have conveyed on screen. Essentially, the recurrent festive sequences promote an impression in audiences' minds that such extravagance was socially representative of the seventeenth-century reality for rich and poor alike.[41] This is done, however, without compromising the content of Lope's original or advocating a far-fetched interpretation of the text aimed at supporting fascist ideals.

The creation of an image of an idyllic Spanish history in these sequences was reinforced by conveying Spain's imperial past as a time of abundance, prosperity, and excess for even the lowliest members of society. For example, during the musical scene that precedes the wedding in Román's *Fuenteove-juna*, entire pigs are seen being roasted over an open flame and the villagers are seen drinking copious amounts of wine. Spectators can also appreciate that the hardworking Spanish population of the Middle Ages enjoyed free time due to their comfortable prosperity. Similar imagery is used in the tavern and plaza scenes of both adaptations of *Peribáñez*, the exuberant banquet scene in *El mejor alcalde, el rey*, and in the 1970 adaptation of *Los milagros del desprecio*. Such an idyllic past was an important illusion for filmmakers and television executives working during the dictatorship because of its possible implications for national identity and cultural unity. As Ryjik (2011) reminds us, during Francoism "it was assumed that in Lope's time there existed a certain collective identity that can be defined as Spanish and determines the behavior and cosmovision of the individuals who believe to take part in said identity" (2). García-Martín (2017) suggests that this was a unifying strategy used during Lope's time as well, arguing that the inclusion of "[singing, danc-ing, and music is] another way of calling attention to ancestral forms of ritual bonding" (138). In fostering a sense of nostalgia for such a happy time in Spain's past whose ideological orientation aligned with that of the dictatorship, these festive scenes helped to shape the public conceptualization of Franco as, in the words of Antonio Cazorla-Sánchez (2014), the "restorer of prosperity," an image that the dictator attempted to mold especially in the last two decades of his regime (185–228). For these reasons, it is increasingly evident that the authorities of the time placed minimal obstacles in TVE's and film companies' production and distribution of these types of Lope's plays, as they underscored a set of shared values that had supposedly defined Spanishness for centuries.

Perhaps this is precisely the reason why Lope's plays were adapted to tele-vision and film more than those of any other Golden Age author. Although it

is true that all plays from seventeenth-century Spain embrace Catholic doctrine and promote "proper" social conduct, Lope's were those that provided
the easiest opportunities to showcase traditions such as weddings, popular
songs and folklore, and characters from various regions of the Spanish landscape to create a sense of universal cultural cohesion among the peoples from
this part of the world. As such, producers considered them sources for films
and shows that could avoid conflicts with the regime and would require minimal effort and reasonable financial investments in order to adapt a screenplay
quickly. After all, time and money were of the essence during Spanish film
and television's infancy due to the scarcity of resources and political support.
While these aspects were not unique to him, the preference for "costumbrist"
elements over allegorical devices—fundamental to many of the works of
Calderón's oeuvre—or Counter-Revolutionary arguments—such as those
that permeate the dramas of authors like Tirso de Molina—likely made his
theater more attractive to producers who were eager to adapt theatrical pieces
for television and film audiences.

As this volume has been demonstrating thus far, film and television producers working during the Francoist regime clearly identified opportunities
to adapt Lope de Vega's works in ways that would appease the censors and
avoid conflicts with the regime's sociopolitical objectives. One should not
overlook, however, that Franco's vision for a cohesive, Catholic society
also relied on a strict adherence to a sense of morality that appears to be
reflected in the values held by the characters in many of Lope de Vega's
plays. When a Lope adaptation was produced, those in charge made sure to
accentuate these inherent morals and values, although there is no evidence
that suggests that direct manipulation of the source texts was interfere with
the original themes or motives. Whereas Pedraza Jiménez (2009) categorizes most of the plays under examination in this chapter as *comedias villanescas*, scholars from Menéndez y Pelayo (1921) to Henryk Ziomek (2014)
have preferred to label them as "Heroic-Honor Plays."[42] While it is true that
the topic of honor is an important element in the entirety of Lope's oeuvre,
plays such as *Fuenteovejuna*; *Peribáñez*; *El mejor alcalde, el rey*; *El villano en su rincón*; and *La Estrella de Sevilla* demonstrate that honor and
dignity transcend social barriers and are as important of an element in the
lowly laborer's lives as they are in the lives of the highest of nobility. The
term *honor* obviously held a different connotation during the seventeenth-
century than it did three centuries in the future, so we must ask ourselves
why this theme, so principal in all of Lope's plays under examination in
this chapter, would have been left intact in the adaptations sponsored by
the dictatorship.[43]

Taking a look at the situations in which the protagonists of these plays are
inserted helps us to approach this issue. In *Fuenteovejuna*, Frondoso is a poor

villager who earns a meager living doing manual labor for his feudal lord, just like the titular character of *Peribáñez* and Sancho in *El mejor alcalde, el rey*. Don Busto of *La Estrella de Sevilla* and Don Alonso, the *caballero de Olmedo*, differ somewhat from the others in that they pertain to the nobility and serve as knights to their kings. Despite their distinct positions on the socioeconomic spectrum, what these characters have in common is that they are all supposed to conduct themselves according to the same moral code. This point is made especially clear in Román's *Fuenteovejuna* (1947) when the Commander ridicules Esteban and scoffs as he asks him "you villagers have honor?" (00:36:30) Although the facetious, rhetorical question is never answered in the film, the implied answer is yes. No matter one's social status, one must always strive to do correct, honorable deeds according to Church doctrine and accepted social norms.[44]

Far from being seen as an irrelevant, antiquated concept to Francoists, honor was, according to the censorship and press, one of the most celebrated aspects of the adaptations. The Provincial Delegate to the censorship in Álava, for example, enthusiastically proclaimed that the adaptation put forth "those Spanish virtues of noble courtesy and honor above all . . . the themes in *Fuenteovejuna* are so Spanish, so ours, that they well deserve to be shouted to the winds during these times" ("Informes" n.p.). Pío García had already perceived this enthusiastic reception of the production a year before the film was even released, declaring "*Fuenteovejuna* . . . an eternal symbol of Spanish honor" was about to be brought to life on the big screen ("Películas en rodaje" 51). These sentiments were echoed and expanded upon after the release, when many journalists praised the film for the plot's emphasis on "the practice of a simple life [that represents] the values of Spanish and universal literature" ("Estreno de *Fuenteovejuna*" n.p.). It would appear as though this simple lifestyle was a particularly moving aspect of these plays that audiences perceived as a definer of Spanishness.

Let us not forget that another aspect that each of these protagonists has in common is that, at least at some point during the action of the play, they are the underdog of the conflict. Villagers live in a subservient role to their feudal lords, cruel and tyrannical as they may be, Don Busto is subjected to obey his king even at the expense of his own conscience, and Don Alonso is outnumbered two-to-one in the altercation in which he loses his life. Although the latter loses the fight and dies, he is still an admirable figure because he does not back down and is defeated unfairly by a gunshot during the swordfight. I sustain that it is precisely this character of the unlikely winner that Spaniards, including Franco himself, most admired during this time period for its unrelenting perseverance and ability to conquer insurmountable obstacles. Alfonso Montiel Villar, the Provincial Delegate of Jaén, for instance, noted in his censorial report that this aspect of *Fuenteovejuna* (1947) was particularly well-received by his Andalusian audience, that reacted "lively in those moments in which the Mayor firmly maintains the dignity of his duty against the Commander of Calatrava and, above all, when the masses rise up against the tyrant" ("Informes" n.p.). Villar's counterpart in Álava also referenced how this aspect of the film would likely "awaken a deep interest and sympathy not only among Spanish audiences, but also foreign ones" ("Informes" n.p.).

## THE SHADOW OF THE EMPIRE

The depiction of the noble Spaniard as the courageous underdog would have resonated throughout Francoist society as Spain found itself increasingly marginalized by the rest of the Western world. In addition to losing its position as an imperial world power a century before, Spain had largely been left off the international political stage due to an aversion to authoritarian regimes after World War II. Although I will discuss the societal and political implications of this isolation below, it is worth noting here that, in many ways, Spain's government saw itself as an alienated underdog, a sentiment that also coursed through the nation's popular culture. As such, the figure of the disadvantaged fighter in these adaptations spoke to Spaniards—especially those who worked directly under Franco's microscope such as censors and journalists—who associated these protagonists with "Spanishness" because of the country's position in the world.[45]

Nevertheless, even in light of losing its Empire, Spain would not be accused of losing its honor, even if its place in the world was strikingly different than it had been in recent memory. For some, it would appear, maintaining the patriarchal concept of honor was crucial to maintaining national dignity. Defining the term "honor" and explaining its predominance in early modern and modern Spanish culture has been the topic of much scholarly attention in recent years. Scott Taylor (2008) conceives of *honor* only in terms of *sexuality* and identifies three salient traits of honor that can be used to define and understand the concept in this manner:

> First . . . the honor of men was dependent on the behavior of the women in their lives: their daughters, sisters, and especially wives. Second, the honor of women, and therefore men, depended entirely on sexual behavior. . . . Men had to control the sexuality of their wives and women kin in order to preserve their own male honor, so adultery was the most serious threat to both male and female honor. Third, the only appropriate response to dishonorable behavior was violence. Men could protect or restore their honor only through murderous revenge. (2–3)

Although Taylor's observations here necessarily omit a great deal of crucial factors revolving around the concept of honor, such as honesty, virtue, and bravery, his identification of these traits does facilitate our analysis of the authentically Spanish values propagated by Franco's ideology of national-Catholicism.[46] Women were expected to be chaste and faithful in marriage and men were expected to defend women against any sexual transgressions and exact revenge against anyone who managed to commit such violations of the moral code.

In addition to perfectly aligning with Francoism's Catholic zeal, the strict link between sexual and gender precepts as consolidated in the early modern concept of honor were also directly correlated to the dictator's views on masculine and feminine roles in his totalitarian societal design. Under the regime, only strict heteronormative male/female relationships were acceptable, in theory. Such ideology was put into practice by passing legislation that aggressively persecuted homosexuals. As counterintuitive as it may seem, however, one sexual practice specifically condemned by Christian doctrine was still permitted. Prostitution, Conxita Mir (2013) reminds us, though not a legally protected institution, was tolerated by the regime as it was considered an "essential piece of the moral order, the safe haven of feminine virginity and the tranquility of Christian families" (167). In other words, the Francoist regime regarded prostitutes and brothels as a necessary evil because they protected the patriarchy by offering men sexual release, thus regulating the masculine sex drive. It was assumed, Mir goes on to argue, that men who could pay for sexual favors would be less inclined to rape innocent victims or stray from their families, a mentality that justified the practice as a contribution to the common good of society (168). Consequently, in strict opposition to traditional Catholic teachings on the subject, as long as it remained within the confines of a heterosexual male receiving services from a female, Spanish men could engage in sexual encounters with prostitutes without risking legal retribution or public scorn.

The societal reality of the time notwithstanding, only the highest of moral standards were to be disseminated on public platforms. As such, moments of the adaptations of Lope's plays produced during Francoism that defined or emphasized the importance and benefits of such a conservative outlook on sexuality and gender roles in the formation of Spanishness were almost always included and highlighted in the productions. At times, verbiage that could possibly be misconstrued as challenging this social construct and national identity was completely omitted. Such is the case in the 1947 adaptation of *Fuenteovejuna*. Beyond removing the controversial "sissies" (III.4, v. 1779) from Laurencia's monologue in which she confronts a room full of men who did not defend her honor sufficiently, the phrase "you're not Spaniards" (III.4, v. 1769) was also omitted.[47] It would seem as though the regime did not want a group of men whose virtue would later be exalted in the film as being regarded as anything but fundamentally Spanish, even if the exclamation reaffirms the concept of honor in its original context. In the later adaptations, however, the line was not omitted, a fact that further demonstrates the diminishing staunchness of the regime's censorship and inconsistencies in the criteria regarding what elements should be omitted.

An obvious example of how dialogues involving masculine and feminine roles were often untouched in these adaptations is the case of *Peribáñez*. Assumedly due to time constraints, a great deal of the declarations of love between the titular protagonist and Casilda are either completely removed from the adaptations or reduced significantly. Nevertheless, a lengthy dialogue in the ninth scene of the first act, in which the two lovers list a lengthy enumeration of the qualities of a good man and a good woman, offering one adjective for every letter of the alphabet (vv. 408–87), is left completely intact in both the 1967 and 1970 televised adaptations. If formatting the action of the play for a television episode required reducing dialogue, these two consecutive monologues—although astoundingly beautiful in their poetry—would have been an ideal place to at least shorten some of the lines spoken by each character, given that the interaction does little to advance the action or develop the characters in question. It is therefore significant that the exchange is left untouched in both adaptations. This is not surprising, given that the character of Casilda and her part in this dialogue was a favorite among Francoists. The priest Fr. Gabriel Orizana (1940) once posed the rhetorical question, "Where could anyone find a more gallant exposition of conjugal love, the base of the family, than in the extremely beautiful dialogue between Casilda and Peribáñez?" (111) Evidently, television screenwriters and censors saw great value in having audiences hear these seventeenth-century descriptions of "appropriate" gender roles.

The adjectives ascribed to a "good woman" (synonymous with "good wife") by Peribáñez describe a range of what is expected from her with regard to her duties to her husband and household, to God, and to her children. Essentially, she is to be a faithful, doting wife, a good Christian, and a role model for their children to admire and follow. The expectations of a good husband, on the other hand, are presented more as a list of what a man is expected not to do than what he should do: he should not be haughty, heckle his wife, be foolish, ungrateful, or difficult to get along with. Regarding what he should do includes treating her as if he were her father (meaning protect her and her honor), be gallant, honest, generous, and faithful to her. In other words, while the woman is expected to maintain the household in terms of its religious devotion, general maintenance, and child rearing, men's essential duties were fundamentally to, as Ziomek (2014) indicates, "defend the social order in the family" (45) by overseeing the woman and managing her tasks in as pleasant a manner possible.[48]

Nevertheless, one of the most successful Lope adaptations to be released during the dictatorship featured a female protagonist whose role is almost contrary to that of the "ideal" Francoist family woman. Doña María, protagonist of *La moza de cántaro*, could not be more different from Laurencia and Casilda in that she refuses to marry and takes on the heavy burden of defending her family's honor herself when her brother is murdered early in the story. Director Florián Rey, evidently aware of the problems that the censorship might have regarding María's homicidal introduction in the screenplay, took measures in his characterization of the protagonist to avoid delays in production, or worse, having the project completely banned. Rey's adaptation of María, brought to life by celebrated actress Paquita Rico, transformed Lope's valiant avenger into a ridiculous, slapstick caricature of the seventeenth-century heroine. The swordfight she engages in with Don Diego, which is absent from the text—Lope's María kills Diego by pretending to hug him, getting close enough to stab him with a dagger (I.6, v. 366)—but included in the film, probably to make the murder scene comical, shows her to be a clumsy swordfighter who only wins the duel out of a lucky strike against a distracted Diego. Unlike in the *comedia*, in which she simply covers herself with a blanket while she prepares for her sneak attack, Rico's María disguises herself as her brother by donning a complete soldier's uniform, which is comically unconvincing, as spectators can see the famous actress's face very clearly and, though she is dressed as a man, does not hide her trademark gliding, feminine gait.

Taking full advantage of the visual comedy, Rico's María remains disguised as a man well into the second act. Her less-than-convincing clandestine operation allows for even more humorous dramatic irony as other women make romantic advances on her and Don Alonso, a traveling noble who has offered to take her with him to Madrid, completely scandalizes her when he, believing she is a man, offers to share his room and bed with her. In an attempt to avoid getting into bed with him, she climbs out of the window, falls into a chicken coop where she is attacked first by the chickens, then by a pack of guard dogs, and her characterization as a source of ridicule, as opposed to calculating assassin, is completed when she screams a high-pitched shriek that contrasts very comically with her soldierly disguise.

The ridiculous aspect of the character that completely overshadows her role as murderess is sheepishly implied in a metatheatrical moment—again not present in the original—when the setting moves to Madrid in the second act. Upon seeing a *comedia* being performed in the plaza, the Count asks Ana what play it is, to which she replies, "some *comedia* by Lope or Cervantes" (00:39:02). Rolling his eyes, the Count highlights the light, jocose tone with which the adaptation was intended to be interpreted by retorting, "they write such nonsense!" (00:39:30) Later in the film, in case any part of the plot had been taken too seriously by audiences, upon hearing of what María had done in Rota, the character of Felipe IV—who is another original innovation of this adaptation—clarifies any possible confusion and avoids any possible negative societal influence by declaring that "women who take revenge into their own hands are a bad example. They're too manly" (00:55:25).

Rico's María, however, is anything but "manly" in the film; in fact, according to Don Alonso's description, she is the perfect Spanish woman. While he is still under the impression that she is a man, he begins to gloat about his travels and experiences with women far and wide. The conversation leads him to a comparison of Spanish and French women, insisting, of course, the former to be far superior. He then begins to explain that the archetypal Spanish woman is of "small waist, pretty feet, smooth hands, dark eyes," before finishing with "those are the women I like" (00:11:22). A closeup of María's face shows her blush sheepishly, realizing that she perfectly meets his idealized description. Being sure to highlight her trademark Spanish beauty, Rey's film avoids the problematic characterization of María as an avenger in the Francoist era by converting her character into a laughing stock whose vengeful homicide can be overlooked as Rico's comedic timing, charm, natural beauty, and upbeat singing numbers transform the murderess into an endearing protagonist.

Let us not forget that, in true Lope fashion, María's normally unlawful actions, like those of the townspeople in *Fuenteovejuna* and Peribáñez's murder of the Commander, are completely forgivable because they are done in an effort to serve justice upon a violator of sacred familial honor and restore the usual social order. As the lack of a political motif in the play would have made this concept difficult to translate onto the 1950s cinema screen in the case of *La moza de cántaro*, it is understandable that the director and screenwriter felt compelled to characterize the protagonist in such a way as to make the audience like her more. As such, the alteration of María's characterization cements the ideal of feminine Spanish national identity as defined by the regime and constitutes the only identifiable instance of intentional source-text manipulation on behalf of Lope's adaptors during the dictatorship.

The drastic changes were clearly necessary and reiterate our assertion that even a drama by national treasure Lope de Vega was not immune to the rigors of the regime's censorship. Rey was successful in his characterization of María and the censors showed no opposition to the film's production after reading his chaotic draft of the script.[49] Although neither censors nor journalists gave very enthusiastic opinions of the finalized version of the film, both found Paquita Rico and her protagonist to be absolutely enchanting. In his report to the censorship headquarters in Madrid dated January 8, 1954,

León Manso Menéndez, Provincial Delegate of Oviedo, even went so far as to affirm that, of all the mediocre actors, "the only exception being Paquita Rico" (n.p.). *Cine Asesor's* summary of printed reviews from Madrid from February 9, 1954—the day after the film's premiere in the Spanish capital— reveals that most journalists, despite their overall lack of interest in the rest of the adaptation, concurred with Manso Menéndez's opinion of the leading actress, reiterating it multiple times with comments like "Paquita Rico shows off her class and sympathy" (*Cine Asesor* no. 615, n.p.).[50] As demonstrated by a February 10, 1954, review of the adaptation published in *Marca*, the 1953 characterization of Doña María was so effective that some spectators were completely oblivious to her darker, potentially negative qualities. Reviewer Nieto writes that "the historical setting and the characters' acting come together to portray, by means of the situations and dialogues, the adventures of an honest woman, transformed into a waitress at an inn, whose status manages to even attract the king" (n.p.). Such an outlook on the characters, especially that of the protagonist, is contradictory on many levels; first of all, the sole reason that María is working as a waitress at an inn is precisely because she is in hiding after murdering Diego.[51] Second, she is living and working under an assumed name and identity, pretending to be Isabel, a peasant girl from Jaén. Charming as she may be, it is difficult to justify a consideration of María as *honest* in the film. The misconceptions of the protagonist's character, however, attest to the degree to which Rey utilized cinematic conventions in order to transform Doña María into a more acceptable female figure in his adaptation, in accordance with the interpretation of the play that he wanted to publicize.

While the other Lope adaptations clearly do not explicitly state family values and inherent gender roles as blatantly as *Peribáñez* does with the alphabetical poem, the context of most of the adaptations includes a similar understanding of the expectations of men with respect to those of women. The climax of *Fuenteovejuna*, for example, revolves around the men in Laurencia's life, particularly her father, doing enough to protect and defend the family honor, *El mejor alcalde, el rey* presents Sancho in a very similar dilemma with Elvira's honor, Estrella of *La Estrella de Sevilla* is also in danger of losing her honor to the king, the supposed promiscuity of Leonor and her uncle's homicidal intentions to restore the family name is central to the conflict in *Los milagros del desprecio*, and even the admired Inés of *El caballero de Olmedo* manipulates the topic of honor to convince her father that she will join a convent since she is unable to find a suitable partner. It should be noted that all of these manifestations of honor, which are central to the plots of all of the original plays, are left completely unaltered in the adaptations of the Francoist era due to their emphasis on social values that, as the regime believed, contributed to the definition of Spanishness.

The dictatorship's use of seventeenth-century morality to define Spanish gender roles seems to go far beyond a simple adherence to Catholic doctrine if we consider the societal implications of the concept of honor. It would be completely unreasonable to propose that the regime sought to create a modern parallel to works like the *comedias villanescas* or heroic-honor plays to the mid-twentieth-century reality to admonish troublesome nobles against attempting to mistreat lower-class women because it would invalidate their God-given authority and make them vulnerable to being justly murdered by either the populace or the monarch, especially considering there was no reigning monarch at the time and the position of the nobility in Spanish society had evolved to an unrecognizable figure when compared to the times depicted in Lope's plays (the titles were the same, but their societal functions, if they had any, had been greatly diminished). Instead, the topic of honor was manipulated to demonstrate that the nuclear family, presided by a vigilant, faithful husband to a chaste, loving wife was the essential element to the fabric of society.[52] In addition to providing for a utopic, homogenous society, the family life as observed during Spain's Imperial Age seemed to be a personal obsession for the dictator.

As well as the adaptations of Lope's plays, other television programs being produced by TVE in the mid-1960s to early 1970s also demonstrated the regime's preoccupation with displaying an idyllic family lifestyle. The second most highly rated program on TVE in 1964 was *La familia por dentro* (1960–1965), a 30-minute show hosted often by members of the clergy to offer advice and Biblical reminders as to how "proper" Catholic families were to conduct themselves, especially behind closed doors. The 39-episode series of telefilms titled *La familia Colón* debuted in 1966, and revolved around a nuclear family comprising a father, mother, two children, and their dog. A year later, the series *La casa de los Martínez* (1967–1971) began airing weekly segments whose format, according to Miguel Fernández Labayen (2007), was a "unique mixture of a talk show and a dramatic space that alternates between stories about the components of a family and interviews with famous [people] and musical performances" (34). Two more family-oriented series were released in 1970: *Bajo el mismo techo* and *Remite: Maribel*. The former depicted what Manuel Palacio (2012) considers "daily stories of a typical Spanish family of the time" (128), while the latter exalts the loving treatment of a family toward their rustic maid, who quickly becomes a beloved part of the family after she is hired in the pilot.

It is precisely in this dynamic television climate that a noticeable shift in the types of Lope's plays selected for adaptation on TVE can be observed. From the mid-to-late 1960s onward, "heroic-honor" dramas started to be outnumbered on television by titles such as *El perro del hortelano* (1966), *La dama boba* (1969), *La discreta enamorada* (1970), *Por la puente, Juana*

(1970), *La malcasada* (1973), and *La viuda valenciana* (1975), to name a few. It was not that TVE was making a conscious effort to align its programming with the immediate sociopolitical preoccupations of the regime by explicitly spotlighting Lope's pious, exemplary Christian female protagonists. The fact that many other types of Lope plays were being adapted during these years— namely *Fuenteovejuna* (1967), *El mundo nuevo* . . . (1968), *El villano en su rincón* (1970), *El mejor alcalde, el rey* (1970), and *El bastardo Mudarra* (1971)—eliminates this possibility. The truth is that, in spite of TVE's efforts to produce original family-friendly Hispano-centric programs, the station found itself under a cultural foreign invasion from the United States and Great Britain during these years. Series such as *Hawaii 5-0* (1968–1980), *The Mary Tyler Moore Show* (1970–1977), *Kung Fu* (1972–1975), *Little House on the Prairie* (1974–1983), and *The Waltons* (1971–1981)—among many others—had a firm grasp on Spanish television audiences and original Spanish programs, including the mythical *Estudio 1*, were desperate to compete. As such, I maintain that the shift in the types of Lope adaptations seen during this period reflect an eagerness to attract a wider audience by offering viewers more variety.[53] Again, Lope's texts were not typically problematic as far as the censorship was concerned, and they could be converted into screenplays quickly and with relative ease.

Beyond recalling Spain's illustrious history, firmly established sociopolitical order, and time-honored traditions, it is also assumed that Lope's plays also mirror an inherited Spanish national identity by putting stereotypes of early modern Spanish society in the spotlight. As Iván Cañadas (2005) explains, Lope's plays almost always depend on a cast of stereotypically Spanish stock characters, "such as the noble lovers, the obstructing father, the comic servant, or *gracioso*, and so forth" (17). As accurate as this observation is, let us not forget that Lope de Vega simply adopted this construction and placement of stock characters from a broader Western theatrical tradition derived from the *commedia dell'arte*.[54] Hence, if the stock characters' origins are Italian and they are also recurrent in contemporary English and French theatrical productions, what is it about Lope's characters that make them intrinsically Spanish and relatable to spectators in the entire country? The answer lies in the settings and situations in which these characters were all presented, which were almost exclusively in Spanish places and during significant times in Spain's past. Furthermore, his protagonists all pertained to a conceived Spanish ethnic group that all spoke a common Spanish language.

By placing his characters in both contemporary and historical Spanish settings, some critics have determined that Lope was making a profound statement on nationalism. Ryjik (2019) argues, for example, that the recurrent character of the Spanish gentleman [*caballero*] was the epitome of Spanish pride, presented as "a type of superman, an undefeatable warrior, admired by the women of other nations" (177). She goes on to argue that the importance of this figure to Spanish national identity was brought to the forefront especially when compared to the "bad vassals," who were mostly Flemish. In other words, being a Spanish subject did not necessarily equate being a Spanish person in Lope's theater. For Lope, the true Spaniard had to have been born and raised on Peninsular Spanish territory. Such a demonstration of an inherent Spanish character as witnessed in Lope's dramatic works links perfectly with what Antonio Duplá Ansuátegui refers to as Franco's insistence on a "particular Spanish personality, both individual and collective, since the beginning of time. From this point of view, Spaniards present certain innate, unalterable, and natural characteristics, [that they have had] since before recorded history" (174). In other words, Lope's portrait of the Spanish people as a homogenous group fed into Franco's cultish brand of nationalism that envisioned united, uniform society.[55]

In addition to the archetypal Spanish characters who were portrayed on Lope's stage and created an illusion of cultural unity, the playwright also demonstrates an awareness of his audience pertaining to this idealized Spanish reality. A fleeting glance at some of the titles of Lope's most successful dramas such as *Fuenteovejuna* (1612), *La viuda valenciana* (1604), *El caballero de Olmedo* (1622), and *Peribáñez y el comendador de Ocaña* (1605) reiterate a universalizing component of the public theater in Spain's Golden Age. These titles suggest in themselves that the protagonists and plots would resonate with members of Spanish society from all walks of life and a variety of Spanish regions, be they rich or poor, from large cosmopolitan areas like Valencia or small, rural villages like Fuenteovejuna. Lope considered all of these settings, characters, and plots as relatable to—and frequently examples for—every Spaniard, given their innate national similarities to spectators and readers across the peninsula. Consequently, Ryjik (2019) has conceptualized Lope's theater as a vehicle for cultural indoctrination, considering the role of public theater as a "medium of mass communication of cultural contents aimed at all layers of society in the process of development and dissemination of the national ideal" (216). The Francoist regime, she posits, saw an opportunity to make history repeat itself by adapting these theatrical works to the media that would be made most available to the Spanish population in the twentieth century: film and television. If this were true, however, there would have been more adaptations of Golden Age plays on TVE and efforts would have been made to indoctrinate Spanish youths, as the government had done earlier in the century with Cervantes's *Quijote*.[56]

In addition to spreading the national ideal throughout popular culture, uniting audiences and characters in strictly Spanish settings and situations created a view of Spain that Arco y Garay (1947) referred to as a *genius loci*, or spiritually protected haven for Spanish people. Essentially, the historian argues that Lope, via his theater, had created a sense of Hispanic superiority that derived, in part, from their attachment to such a blessed and privileged land (12). In other words, the very terrain on which they were born greatly shaped and set them above other peoples in the eyes of God.[57] Although already outdated by the time Franco rose to power in Spain, he was keen on maintaining these ideals of geographical determinism as they conveniently reinforced his perceptions of divine providence for God's faithful elect. As William Viestenz (2014) indicates, "Franco's facile displacement of the sacred onto secular discourse, promoting both Catholicism and the sacrosanct Castilian countryside as the heart of *la raza castiza*" was one of his most recurring ideological foundations for propagating national unity (21). It would seem as though, knowingly or not, Franco was promulgating Claudio Sánchez-Albornoz's idea of a *homo hispanus* that, according to Simon Barton (2009), conceived of Spaniards as pertaining to a race whose members shared a "basic Spanish temperament, shaped by the climate and terrain of the peninsula [that] had evolved even before the arrival of the Romans . . . and had evolved over the centuries" (111).[58]

The desire to create a nation bound by a common cultural, religious, and linguistic identity became an obsession of the dictator, as evidenced by the publication of his covert autobiography in 1922, titled *Raza*, which was subsequently republished in 1939 and adapted into a major motion picture in 1942 and remade in 1950.[59] The first film adaptation, as Higginbotham (1988) duly observes, was dedicated to "the youth of Spain . . . that such is the nation and thus such is the race" (19). Herein lies a crucial ideological difference between Lope and Franco that is easily overlooked. Although he uses the term "race,"[60] Franco was certainly not referring to *race* in terms of skin color or any other physical attributes.[61] Whereas early modern Spaniards frequently ridiculed the physical appearances of Jews, Muslims, indigenous Americans, and Africans, Franco most likely ascribed to the concept of *race* as outlined by one of the far right's most emphatic intellectual influences who was killed at the onset of the Civil War in 1936, Ramiro de Maeztu. In his *Defensa de la Hispanidad*, Maeztu (1934) argues that the inequality between groups of people is rooted not in their ethnic makeup, but in their respective levels of civilization. As such, he affirms, all people who pertain to the countries of the former Spanish Empire (those in Latin America and the Philippines) constitute a single "race" of Hispanics that is superior to all others because they perpetuate the language and evangelical mission that sets Hispanic culture apart from that of "inferior" peoples, such as primitive, uncontacted tribes and, especially, Protestants from Northern Europe. His argument that the "lack of geographic and ethnographic characteristics does not prevent it from being one of the most decisive features of Hispanity" (85) was most probably shared by Franco, which helps to explain why the dictator was keen on discriminating against people based on their sociopolitical status as opposed to physicality.

Regarding the film and television adaptations of Lope's plays, race—synonymous with "Hispanity"—was essentially implemented by the films breaking with the cinematic trend of the time of hiring foreign actors whose lines would later be dubbed by a native Spaniard on screen. Remarkably for the time, most of the adaptations of Lope de Vega's original dramas during Francoism boasted a strictly native Spanish cast, often with famous national actors such as Fernando Rey, Paquita Rico, Amparo Rivelles, José Sacristán, and Manuel Luna, just to name a few. Florián Rey, adaptor and director of *La moza de cántaro* (1953) and vehement opponent to dubbing in films, was the only director to pay explicit attention to race when speaking of his film production. According to the filmmaker, he enjoyed national stereotypes of people and their respective cultures and believed that perpetuating the "Spanish legend" by using exclusively Spanish elements was key to achieving success both inside and outside of Spain. "Yes, sir," he was quoted as saying in an interview published in the third issue of *Fotogramas*, "dark-haired women and Spanish music . . . we can all make bad films that bring money to our pockets; but movies with dignity are exclusive to those who are able to make them and those who know how to" ("Fuenteovejuna," *Fotogramas* n.p.). Evidently, portraying the Spanish race in films that were considered well-made brought about a sense of dignity and national pride to Spanish popular culture. It is therefore all the more ironic that Rey cast none other than North American actor Peter Damon for the leading male role of Don Juan and had his speaking parts dubbed.

Some Francoist censors seemed to agree with Rey's standpoint, highlighting the importance of the adaptations to the "race" on several occasions. After reading the proposed script of Román's *Fuenteovejuna* (1947), one censor commented that the film was a great example of "a historical theme in which the fundamental values of our race are exalted" ("Informes" n.p.). In less explicit terms, José de Juanes expressed a similar opinion in his review of the film, stating that "as Spaniards, we congratulate this new triumph" ("Colisevm" n.p.). Race was, of course, not only an integral part to defining Spanishness during Lope's and Franco's times—albeit via different criteria—but was also an essential factor used to determine who did not belong to this Spanish community. As I continue my analysis, I will examine how, if at all, Lope's conception of race was used by Franco's regime to create an idea of Otherness in Spanish popular culture.

## THE SHADOW OF THE MOORS

There are many aspects of Franco's life that make it tempting to categorize him as a racist from a twenty-first-century perspective. He had been associated, for instance, with Adolf Hitler in the early stages of his rise to power. He later went on to foster a close alliance and personal friendship with the racially motivated dictator of the Dominican Republic, Rafael Trujillo. His invocation of the Catholic Monarchs brings to mind their obsession with blood purity and the expulsion of the Jews and Muslims from their territories. Accordingly, one might expect a dictator like Franco to harbor a xenophobic attitude toward Spain's most timeless "Others"; namely, the North African Moors. Nevertheless, as I have mentioned in the previous section, Franco was not racist with regard to ethic differences. Thus, we are again faced with an ideological discrepancy between the dictator and the seventeenth-century playwright that challenges the notion that the two shared a tight ideological affinity. Whereas Lope's plays seldomly portray Jews, Muslims, *conversos*, *moriscos*, or any foreigner in a positive light, the Francoist regime's perception of "the Other" comprised mainly fellow Spaniards who did not conform to his ideal of "Hispanity." Republican and Communist Spaniards were the regime's targeted "Others," not necessarily non-nationals.

In fact, Franco was quite endeared to the North Africans and, as his dictatorship progressed, to many Muslim leaders and diplomats. Let us not forget, after all, that his rise to power began and gained momentum while he was stationed as a commanding officer in Morocco. Some of his most fervent support in the early days of his ascendance came from native Moroccans. As a matter of fact, it could even be argued that, as Payne (2018) states, "Africa made Franco" (360). Once dictator, he would not soon forget the aid provided to him by Spain's neighbors to the south; his personal bodyguards, the Moorish Guard, consisted of native North Africans who publicly accompanied Franco on horseback, dressed in traditional Muslim attire. These bodyguards remained a symbolic and nostalgic spectacle to onlookers until they were disbanded in 1958 following a conflict between Franco and the Moroccan government over the last remaining Spanish territory in the Sahara. Despite the altercation, the regime continued to treat the subject of race with utmost care throughout the entirety of the dictatorship, especially on film and television, so as to avoid any potential animosity with countries that Francoist diplomats considered helpful. Again, the adaptations of Lope's plays reflect this trend.

Although it is true that adaptations of plays like *El Nuevo Mundo descubierto por Colón* (1968) certainly included scenes that portrayed stereotypical images of the Native Americans and even a comical Muslim caricature, Lope's unflattering comments about the Moors were completely omitted from the adaptations of *Fuenteovejuna*, *Peribáñez*, *El mejor alcalde, el rey*, *La Estrella de Sevilla*, and *El caballero de Olmedo*.[62] Given that the historical context of these plays—and, by extension, their adaptations—is the Christian Reconquest of the Iberian Peninsula in an attempt to realize the Castilian ambition of forming a united society under one crown, one religion, and one language, it is somewhat counterintuitive that the Francoist regime would omit these references, especially considering the widely held opinion that Franco and his followers idealized this period. After all, a common misconception repeated by Barton (2009) is that Francoist ideology was essentially the continuation of a medieval mentality that had positioned the Moor as a hostile "other" and that the national Spanish consciousness had been wrought from centuries of fighting against Islam and its followers (111). Despite the dictator's admiration for the Middle Ages, it cannot be said that his regime ascribed to all of the schools of thought of the time period. A comparison of Lope's original texts with the dialogues of the adaptations shows a noticeable omission of any anti-Muslim rhetoric or even references to the defeat of Muslim forces during the Reconquest that serve as evidence to refute claims to the contrary.

The most salient example of an avoidance toward these types of anti-Moorish commentary is the treatment of the dialogues in *Peribáñez*, which contain the most frequent references to the ongoing war in Granada, the Commander's military prowess against the Muslim inhabitants of Andalusia, and the fear that Castilian soldiers instilled in the Islamic communities. In both the 1967 and 1970 televised adaptations, even the most fleeting references to any conflict with the Muslims are completely removed from the dialogue. For example, when spectators are introduced to the Commander and his servant Luján in Act I, even the former's comment "ever since with me you went, / Luján, to Andalusia, / I give personal testament / to your honor and bravery" (vv. 632–635),[63] is absent from both adaptations. It would appear as though, beyond avoiding any cultural insensitivity toward the Islamic community, the regime was keen on erasing any mention of an uncivil relationship between Muslims and Spaniards from popular culture.

If such a non-politically charged reference like the aforementioned was omitted, it is not surprising that more explicitly violent lines were also removed from the screenplays, such as when Peribáñez relates a conversation he heard between the Maestre de Calatrava and the king to his fellow *labradores* in which the former declared "there must be no Moor left standing / of all those who live and drink / the Betis [River], although I know well / the way in which they are received" (II.1, v. 72).[64] Another unflattering Moorish reference that is omitted from both adaptations is when Leonardo's description of "the Moor king of Granada" (III.1, v. 18) as an untrustworthy adversary of King Enrique III because of the many promises the Muslim had made to him and broken. When Blas is preparing to deploy to the south to fight in the conflict, he tells his love interest Costança, "May it please God that the Christianized Moors (*moriscos*) / make your clothing from my own skin / if I do not leave having killed / as many of them as try to flee from me" (III.5, vv. 349–352), which is also absent from both adaptations.[65] A similar exchange that takes place moments later between lovers Isabel and Belardo when she tells the soon-to-be soldier, "bring me a Moor, Belardo," to which he responds, "I have been pursuing them for days. / But, if the outcome is not in prose, / from now on I will say it in verse,"[66] (III.5, vv. 361–364) is also noticeably absent from both television episodes. In the following scene, Bras, Belardo, and Leonardo speak of the cowardly nature of the Moors and Bras recalls "seeing a Moor / . . . / I have already seen them flee" (III.6, vv. 389–391). Finally, when the king tells his Condestable to take relentless action in the conflict against the Moors, in the original text he tells his subordinate that "the mischievous Moor trembles in Granada / . . . / may his joy become a sad cry" (III.13, vv. 839–841),[67] but these lines are also absent from both television episodes. In addition to all of these lines, even the one that simply mentions the "conquest" that the Commander's weapons had achieved in Andalusia (II.4, vv. 303–306) was also cut from both adaptations.

The 1970 adaptation goes even beyond that of 1967 in its removal of any and every mention to the Reconquest or conflict with the Moors. For example, scenes 3 and 4 from Act III, in which Peribáñez says goodbye to Casilda as he prepares for his deployment to Andalusia to participate in the war, using a great deal of military language that alludes to the destruction of Moorish strongholds, are completely omitted, even sacrificing crucial aspects of the plot. For example, the dramatic irony that is created by Lope's original by having Casilda believe that Peribáñez has left Ocaña when he is really hidden in the house prepared to protect her from the Commander is an essential element of the denouement that the televised adaptation forfeits by removing these scenes. Likewise, the final scenes of Act III (18–22), in which Peribáñez also kills Luján and the King gives a patriotic speech about his advance on the Muslim south in an attempt to "leave Andalusia free, / if our army is prevented" (III.21, vv. 827–828),[68] which are present in the 1967 adaptation, are not included in the 1970 recreation.

In a very similar fashion, the adaptations of *Fuenteovejuna* all avoid the topic of Moors and/or *moriscos* or any conflictive past between Christians and Muslims in Spain. Román's 1947 film, for instance, despite its impressive battle scenes and dialogues that emphasize the friction between the Castilian and Portuguese factions of Isabel the Catholic and Juana, the "Beltraneja," makes absolutely no mention of the Reconquest of Iberian lands for the Christian kingdoms. Even Guerrero Zamora, who prided himself on respecting Lope's original text so faithfully in his 1972 adaptation, omitted lines like Flores's "because the red cross obliges / all who wear it on their chests / although they may be of the sacred order / it is understood that they are against the Moor" (I.5, vv. 465–469)[69] and, a few lines later, his reaffirmation that "they fear him even in Granada" (I.5, v. 500). Moreover, in the song that the townsfolk sing in the following scene that references the Commander's skill "conquering Christianized Moors" (I.6, v. 537) is also absent from his film. Finally, during the denouement in the final scene of Act III, the Maestre promises the monarchs that he will recompense his shortcomings in dealing with the Commander by fighting for the Christian faith in Andalusia, swearing that "and in that battle / of Granada, where you are all going, / I promise you will see / the bravery of my sword" (III.15, vv. 2326–2329).[70] These lines are completely omitted from the film. Likewise, the 1967 televised adaptation of *Fuenteovejuna* also omits all of these references, although it does maintain the Commander's threatening lines to Frondoso, in which he boasts, "That to a Capitan whose sword / makes Cordova and Granada tremble, / a worker, a young man / should put a crossbow to his chest!" (II.4, vv. 1044–1047)[71] Perhaps these verses were considered subtle enough and sufficiently important to the character development of the Commander, that they were allowed to be maintained for television audiences, although this is likely yet another piece of evidence that television censorship was less rigorous than that of film.

Although there are much fewer references to the Christian versus Muslim conflict in medieval Spain in *El mejor alcalde, el rey*, *La Estrella de Sevilla*, and *El caballero de Olmedo*, it should be duly noted that almost all of these references were also left out of their televised and cinematic adaptations. For example, in the 1970 televised adaptation of *El mejor alcalde, el rey*, an allusion to the royal court as a chess set that pits "white ones" (*blancos*) against "black ones" (*negros*) after immediately mentioning how foreigners are treated at court is completely omitted when Pelayo says, "they say that it is a sack of money / where the chess pieces are kept / to bet on their fortune / as many white ones and black ones" (II.9, vv. 1235–1238).[72] Although the original verses make an optimistic comment on the multinational integration of people at the court, it is easy to understand how adaptors in the 1970s, especially following the models of adaptations like those of *Peribáñez* and *Fuenteovejuna*, might have desired to remove the comment altogether so as to avoid audiences misconstruing the message, most of all because the archaic terms used, such as "talega" and "trebejos," could have obscured the meaning of what Pelayo was actually articulating. Furthermore, Sancho's praise of the king as supreme ruler of Castilla, whose feet he wishes to kiss because "they will soon use Granada as their pillow" and "Seville will be their carpet" (III.1, vv. 1642–1645), are also completely omitted from the adaptation. Gil's 1974 major motion picture of the work, although mostly avoiding the religious conflicts as well, does make a reference to Tello's insubordination to the king deriving from the fact that the king owes him lands taken by Muslims, asserting that "my grandfathers took many of the king's lands back from [the Moors]" (01:05:57). Granted, this comment does not carry a strong political charge and, like the adaptation of *Fuenteovejuna* before it, is so subtle that perhaps it was deemed unworthy of modification in the script.

Having established that the adaptations of Lope de Vega's works specifically omitted most references to the Moors or their social, religious, and political plight in the Middle Ages and Early Modern period on the Iberian Peninsula, one must also consider why such obvious omissions are detectable in these productions. In addition to Franco's personal connections with North Africa, Spain's international political situation of the time provides us with many clues that help to explain why such extreme measures were taken to avoid potentially offending Muslims who might happen to view one of these adaptations. Beyond the possible external diplomacy, it is likely that the regime was also hesitant to allow rhetoric that might create a negative image of Spain's Islamic allies in the collective Spanish imagination. As is the case today, Saudi Arabia was an extremely important commercial ally for Spain and the public's support for political collaboration between the two countries was certainly desirable. In addition to the internal struggles taking place in Spain before and throughout the dictatorship, the Iberian country also found itself in a precarious position with other Western nations. The failure of fascism in Italy and the catastrophic threat to world peace posed by Hitler's Germany had caused most countries in Europe and the United States to be mistrustful of authoritarian regimes that went against their democratic standard. As such, Spain became increasingly isolated in the diplomatic realm throughout the decade following Franco's rise to power. The United Nations had rejected Spain's membership on February 9, 1946, withdrawn ambassadors from Madrid (December 12, 1946), and harshly criticized the political system established following the Civil War (March 5, 1946).[73] Moreover, Spain had been completely left out of the European Recovery Plan (commonly referred to as "The Marshall Plan") that provided an exorbitant amount of funding to Western European countries following World War II. Fearing the possible disastrous implications of such an international political and economic siege from its neighbors in Europe and the United States, Franco's regime identified the immediate need to foster international relationships with other countries. Relying on the shared cultural past and mythical vision of Al-Andalus among Islamic intellectuals, the regime fixed its sights on forming an ample base of alliances that would be solid enough for the dictatorship to use to its international advantage.

Franco and his regime thus officialized a manner by which to foster the Islamic nostalgia for the utopic civilization they had built in Al-Andalus. As Algora Weber (1996) indicates,

> from here the function that the Ministry of Foreign Affairs attempted to exploit proceeds with regards to its relationships with Arabic governments. Franco's regime, acutely aware of this [utopic] conceptualization that the Arabs had of Spain, constructed a rhetoric in which this factor could be perceived. This attempted bond did not correspond to the actual possibilities of the Spanish State

in the years of international isolation, but it was used as their narrative because
it provided for an approach to Arab sensitivities. (281)

As such, the political rhetoric of the 1940s centered around courting the
Islamic countries by using pragmatic linguistic devices that would speak
to this Muslim sensitivity so as to guarantee the political support that the
isolated Spain so desperately needed. Moreover, as Mulay Hicham (2015)
recalls, Spain took the initiative in the early 1960s to combat France's cultural hegemony in North Africa by making Spanish television available in
Morocco, meaning that at least one of the Islamic countries with which he
was trying to forge an alliance had direct access to this programming (55).[74]
Spain did not, however, abandon its attempts to be seen in a favorable light
by its Islamic neighbors after it had garnered a degree of acceptance in the
Western world in the 1960s, which explains why the avoidance of negative
commentary or imagery of the Middle East persisted throughout the entirety
of the dictatorship.[75]

   In many cases, as I have demonstrated with the examples above,
preconceived notions of Islam and its professors, brought about in great
measure by the mythical Christian Reconquest that prevailed in the collective
Spanish imagination, meant that any derogatory or defamatory speech or
images against Muslims must be completely erased from popular culture
in the twentieth century. In addition to the remarks and verses taken out of
Lope's plays during the process of adaptation, it is also worth noting that,
as Román Gubern (1981) observes in his study of Franco's romanticized
autobiographical book-turned-film *Raza* (1922), omitted a passage in which
a Moor is mocked and has his ear cut off by a Spanish soldier in its reedited
edition that was released in 1939 and served as the source text for the motion
pictures debuted in 1942 and 1950. Quite frankly, it is apparent that omitting
the turbulent past between Spanish governments and Muslim cultures
was a political strategy used by the regime to prevent any cultural clashes
between Spain and the countries from whose alliance the dictatorship could
benefit. One also must not overlook the massive influence that the petroleum
industry, which could have devastated Spain's economy had it excluded the
country from purchasing the commodity at a reasonably price, also had on
international relationships during Franco's dictatorship, much as it still does
today.

## PUBLIC CONSUMPTION AND CULTURAL IMPACT

An analysis of these common features of the adaptations of Lope de Vega's
plays during the Francoist period would be incomplete without a reflection on

how audiences reacted to and evaluated these productions in terms of financial compensation for the producers and government. Although it is impossible to determine with any degree of certainty what motivated screenwriters, directors, and producers to adapt the plays that they did, the fact that public money was used to create these films and episodes informs us of the regime's tastes and preferences. Only by examining the return on their investment, however, can one try to determine whether or not these productions were of any interest to the Spanish people. If the films and television episodes were financial success stories, scholars could infer that the strategy of encoding the regime's ideology for the implied spectator was capable of causing a significant sociocultural impact. If not, then one can only assume that the ideological messages fell on deaf ears. In order to approach this question, I must examine the financial compensation of the two media slightly differently. First and foremost, film spectatorship can be quantified by identifying the amount of tickets sold for a specific title, while it is difficult to ascertain television spectatorship since audience members do not pay per episode. One can only estimate the reach of a certain program based on much less concrete data like television ratings. Second, it is indispensable to keep in mind that film audiences differ from that of their television counterparts due to factors such as the availability of cinemas and televisions throughout the Spanish landscape of the time, socioeconomic limitations of the public, and the demographics of that population. Also, filmgoers could choose between a variety of titles to view and television audiences were limited to only one channel until 1966 when TVE opened a second. Third, I must consider the amounts of financial and artistic resources that are required for filmmaking and how these vastly outweigh those needed for television. Also, the potential international reach of film was often a driving force behind production that television did not generally compete with. Let us begin with an examination of the reception of Lope's film adaptations during Francoism.

As discussed earlier in the chapter, Franco's mistrust of film and television had stunted the growth of the Spanish film industry in general, leaving a vacuum in popular culture that paved the way for, as Caparrós Lera (1983) calls it, a "foreign, euro-north American colonization" that was never overcome by Spanish film production (19). As such, legislation was enacted in the 1960s to protect Spain's damaged cinema industry. In February 1960, the National Cinematography Institute (*Instituto Nacional de Cinematografía*) was remodeled and agreements with other countries to permit international coproductions were reestablished. In 1964, the regime released what Santiago Pozo Arenas (1984) considers to be the most important piece of legislation regarding the protection of Spanish films: the "Orden del 16 de agosto de 1964" (165).[76] The ordinance is divided into nine articles that cover economic protections, distribution support, showcasing, establishing the categories of

National Interest films, short films, filming and screening licenses, and formal registration of certified production companies. Two years later, on October 12, 1966, the legislation was amended to establish a "mandatory screen quota" for film companies inscribed officially within the Film Company Registration (*Registro de Empresas Cinematográficas*). In other words, the government would send orders to the film companies requiring they produce a mandatory number of Spanish films (*películas españolas*), as defined by the 1964 ordinance, under penalty of litigation.[77]

What these governmental interventions tell us is that the Spanish public would have to be force-fed national films if they were going to view them; otherwise, the population preferred to be entertained by foreign films whose financial and artistic capabilities always managed to outshine those of Spain. Further evidence to this claim is the yearly book on cinema, *Cine para leer*, printed in Spain from 1972 until 2012. Although both the 1972 and 1974 volumes dedicate space to mention that *Fuenteovejuna* and *El mejor alcalde, el rey* had been released during those respective years, there is not a lot of critical attention given to either one or to hardly any Spanish films. Nevertheless, North American films and movie stars such as Elizabeth Taylor, Jack Nicholson, and Barbra Streisand are frequently discussed.

If one looks specifically at the factors that made Lope adaptations especially unmarketable in the national film industry, it is also easy to see how the popular culture of the time had difficulty placing the seventeenth-century playwright into the modern collective imagination. Nevertheless, adaptors seemed to be damned if they did, damned if they didn't prose the dialogues. Román's *Fuenteovejuna*, for example, was praised by censors and the press alike for its prosaic speaking parts, except in the case of the Provincial Delegate of Salamanca, who expressed disappointment in that "it was displeasing to audiences that sayings that everyone knows, because they've read the works of Lope de Vega, were taken out of context or filed down," later clarifying that "the repulsed reaction is found mainly among the large amount of viewers like students and educated audiences" ("Informes" n.p.). In other words, the censors from Salamanca believed that scholarly viewers expected a more faithful adaptation of the dialogues than Pemán had prepared. Notably, this was not a concern for any of the other delegates.

This rare exception aside, the preference of prose to verse was reiterated by comments made in the press about Guerrero Zamora's adaptation. In addition to the comment from *El alcázar* shown above, a critic's article in a November 28, 1972, edition of *Arriba* also criticized this aspect, arguing that "let's just say that the way Juan Guerrero Zamora has presented [Lope's verses] seems erroneous, mistaken, confusing, clumsy to us" ("Informes emitidos sobre el visionado de *Fuenteovejuna* (1972)" n.p.). Nevertheless, Gil's adaptation of *El mejor alcalde, el rey* also received mixed reviews about his prosing of

Lope's verse. For example, although an article in *Arriba* from May 5, 1974, lauded Gil's adherence to the "spirit" of Lope, the journalist also criticized the film, complaining that "upon losing the magic of Lope's verse, the major attraction of the original work is lost, as well. And therefore . . . the results do not manage to have the same acclaim as those garnered by [Gil's other films]" (n.p.). Essentially, despite the efforts of the producers to prove otherwise, it would seem as though the Spanish public overall conceived of these films as difficult to include in the popular culture of the day due to their difficult language, even when it was not recited in verse, and their subject matter because it was considered irrelevant to their time.

Like Román's previous adaptation, Guerrero Zamora's also did not work commercially and clearly did not spark an interest in Spanish audiences. After the adaptations of *Fuenteovejuna* had failed to generate enthusiasm for his plays, Lope de Vega would have only one more opportunity to captivate the collective Spanish imagination in cinemas during the Francoist regime. Unlike Guerrero Zamora before him, Rafael Gil was given some positive press before the release of his film in which he was afforded the opportunity to defend his decision to adapt a seventeenth-century drama and his version received great praise from the censorship. The film did collect a sufficiently larger sum of revenue at the box office during its first month in cinemas than Guerrero Zamora's *Fuenteovejuna*, bringing in a total of 3,824,227 *pesetas* (*Boletín informativo*, 1974, 246). By the end of the year, the film had earned 4,204,572 *pesetas*, nearly double that of Guerrero Zamora's adaptation. Although it was hardly a blockbuster in terms of reception and revenue, Wheeler (2008) attributes its moderate success in comparison to other Lope adaptations to the fact that it is "visually reminiscent of Roman Polanski's controversial adaptation of *Macbeth* (1971), which had recently enjoyed great success in Spain" (292). Nevertheless, it is curious to note how Lope's reception in 1974 could be due—at least in part—to a comparison with his English rival who had dominated on the Spanish film landscape beforehand.

In general, Golden Age theater had a much better reception on television than it did in cinemas. For one, although some North American telefilms based on English-language literature were broadcasted on Spanish television stations in TVE's infancy, the station found it much more feasible to adapt its culture's own literature to the new medium, given its rich supply of stories to tell that were already written in the target language and the reasonably low requirement of financial and artistic resources to do so. As such, the foreign colonization that had conquered the Spanish cinema had not infiltrated the television realm as early or quite as thoroughly. Additionally, television was increasingly more accessible to middle- and lower-class working families during the formative years and maturity of TVE following its inception in 1959. Manuel Palacio (2008) estimates that the number of television sets in

Spanish households rose from a modest 850,000 in 1963 to an astounding 3,897,000 in 1969, data that suggests that by 1966, more Spaniards had televisions than cars (58).

Moreover, the regime, who only a few years previously had warned of the dangers of the new medium, had come to tolerate and allot financial support to the growing television industry. Unlike in the case of Spanish film, which the government protected from being made completely obsolete by foreign imports, the regime supported television for its potential to foster and maintain a more cohesive cultural identity through the popular culture it had created and shaped. According to Juan Pablo Fusi (1999), by the 1960s, television, contrary to bringing about a disruptive social mobilization, had fostered a "subculture lacking political and intellectual curiosity but that is hugely popular, gaining public diffusion, and favors, through entertainment and escapism, social integration and demobilization of the country, the political objectives of the new regime" (109).

During this decade, advances in technology and greater governmental investment in the medium gave forth to the TVE's program par excellence during the 1960s: *Estudio 1*. Having already established its privileged and—as Montero Díaz and Teresa Ojer (2018) affirm—preeminent position on Spanish television, occupying the coveted *sobremesa* slot on the television timetable, the *teleteatro* genre was already a hit in the ratings during the prehistory of TVE (80).[78] Hoping to move toward a more Hispanic-centered series of adaptations, TVE proposed an idea for a show that would broadcast authentic Spanish theater, or foreign theater adapted by authentic Spanish screenwriters, in at least 85 percent of its programs. To do so, executives at TVE had decided to rework *Primera fila* into a series of higher-quality programs, complete with the new name of *Estudio 1*, dedicated to bringing Spanish theater into Spain's households.[79] Like its cinematic counterpart, televised Spanish dramas also had to compete with the influx of imported television series that were invading the industry. In 1966, a year after its debut, *Estudio 1* ranked fifth in Manuel Palacio's (2008) ranking of TVE broadcasts with an 11 percent share of spectators, while the British sitcom *The Saint* (1962–1969) and American fiction series *The Untouchables* (1959–1963) came in first and second place with 28 and 18 percent of the viewership, respectively. By 1969, the program had slipped to sixth place, but still managed a strong grip on its 7,364,000-annual spectatorship (67–70). By 1974, the preference for foreign programming had sent *Estudio 1* into such a state of decadence that production shut down.[80]

What these data reveal is that Spanish theater found a degree of success on television via *Primera fila* and *Estudio 1*. Despite the fact that there were other programs such as *Teatro de siempre* and *Cuentos y leyendas* that also adapted Spanish dramas, the former two were certainly much more widely viewed than the latter and have been paid a higher degree of scholarly attention. It is impossible to say that the success of these programs had anything to do with its adaptations of Golden Age theater—let alone Lope de Vega's plays—provided that this category only represented a very small percentage of the works they adapted. Nevertheless, the data on television spectatorship during this time does lead us to believe that the adaptations of Lope de Vega's plays likely reached a relatively large audience, thus justifying the need to carefully select which dramas would be broadcasted and how. Most of the adaptations examined in this chapter were at least highly anticipated; both adaptations of *Peribáñez*, for instance, were given an exclusive two-page spread in *TeleRadio* in the weeks preceding their premiers that were written to provoke a sense of excitement in potential spectators.[81]

Furthermore, the 1970 adaptation that aired on *Estudio 1* was given very high praise by a reviewer on the December 5, 1970, edition of *TeleRadio*, who praised the televised adaptation for every aspect ranging from its decorations, lighting, acting, directing, and contextual treatment of "one of the best and most popular classics of Spanish theater" that reached a massive audience (n.p.).[82] Likewise, both adaptations of *El caballero de Olmedo* were given special attention on the television guides of their corresponding appearances on television in the magazine. The first, announcing *Estudio 1*'s 1968 adaptation attempts to equate Lope's work to a Spanish version of a Shakespeare masterpiece, assuring readers that "it just barely falls short of equaling *Romeo and Juliet*" and emphasizing its importance by describing the adaptation as one of a play that is "one of the most important, not just for Spanish theater, but for that of the world" (n.p.).[83] The second time the drama was adapted, in 1975, *TeleRadio* simply dedicated a few paragraphs to describe the plot, evidence that perhaps the audience was not as familiar with classical Spanish drama as the former journalist optimistically hoped.[84] Notably, none of the televised adaptations of *Fuenteovejuna*, *La Estrella de Sevilla*, or *Los milagros del desprecio* were especially highlighted or given any critical attention either before or after their television release.

Adaptations of Lope de Vega's plays were somewhat frequent additions to Spain's film and television industries during the dictatorship due to the ease with which they could be adapted and the speed at which they could be produced by avoiding the ideological clashes that works from other time periods might have encountered. In other words, Lope's original content lent itself well to being revived during the dictatorship, so there was generally no need to make drastic alterations to his texts. When modifications were deemed convenient, the degree to which the adaptations were manipulated by the regime varied according to medium, time period, and sociopolitical priorities. In most cases, only minor, though occasionally significant, additions or suppressions were made to Lope's original texts as the seventeenth-century playwright's depiction of Spanish society aligned well with Francoist ideology. The changes to the text in these situations were mostly made solely to highlight more implicit messages found in Lope's original or to make the speaking parts more accessible to a modern cinema or television audience. Only in the extreme case of *Peribáñez*, however, as it was convenient for political purposes, was the source text meticulously reviewed and modified in order to be deemed suitable for public broadcast.

The preceding analysis of these adaptations and accompanying data reveal that the conversion of Lope de Vega's plays to the big screen was financially catastrophic to producers, even in the best of cases. Moreover, although televised theater fared better overall and the public seemed to be more forgiving of technical errors than in cinemas, the fact that there were no more than a handful of Lope adaptations even during the times of *Estudio 1*'s supremacy on the monopolized Spanish television program timetable shows us that, as a general trend, Lope de Vega's adapted works did not prove to be of great interests to the Spanish population during the dictatorship, no matter how much the government tried to support their use to implement its ideology into the collective Spanish imagination. Such a realization must inevitably cause us to reconsider the stereotype of the dictatorial regime that assumes that Franco actively encouraged the manipulation of Spain's past to propagate his fascist agenda. In all actuality, the fact that Franco publicly expressed nostalgia and reverence for the nation's imperial past did not materialize as a systemized process of converting Golden Age dramas into mass political propaganda apparatuses. Chapter 3 will consider whether this relationship between Lope de Vega's works and Spanish audiences took a more positive turn after the death of the dictator in 1975.

## NOTES

1. The first of Calderón's plays to be adapted to the big screen, *El alcalde de Zalamea*, was released as a silent film in 1914. During Francoism, it was remade as *El alcalde de Zalamea* in 1954 and as *La leyenda del alcalde de Zalamea* in 1973. The only other of his titles to be adapted to a major motion picture format was 1960's *El príncipe encadenado*.

2. Two notable exceptions are *Los milagros del desprecio* and *El caballero de Olmedo*.

3. Breaking somewhat from the previous tradition of categorizing Golden Age plays as proposed by Marcelino Menéndez y Pelayo in *Estudios sobre el teatro de Lope de Vega* (1949), Pedraza Jiménez (2009) groups the *comedias villanescas* together according to the following criteria: they must contain (a) bucolic descriptions,

(b) popular songs and dance in the action of the drama, (c) scenes characteristic of *costumbrismo*, (d) witty rustic characters, (e) a fable in defense of pure and true love, (f) a tragic action surrounding the concept of honor, and (g) poetic justice in which the "little guy" triumphs, after much suffering, over unjust power (8).

4. Captain General of Catalonia, Miguel Primo de Rivera began Spain's first twentieth-century dictatorship by being named president of King Alfonso XIII's Military Directory on September 14, 1923. He managed to mobilize the Spanish population by incorporating an extreme-right nationalistic ideology that, as Alejandro Quiroga (2014) explains, united the citizens against common, internal enemies such as republicans, liberals, anarchists, and Catalan and Basque regionalists (3). Apart from a disdain for these groups, Primo de Rivera also used another common denominator of the Spanish population to secure this nationalistic bond: religion. Given that Spain's religious legacy had almost always consisted of strict adhesion to the Catholic Church and Church doctrine, Primo de Rivera managed to equate "Spanishness" with Catholicism and made this the foundation for his mass nationalization of Spanish identity. At a time in which the very concept of "Spanishness" had been threatened by the recent loss of Empire, humiliating military defeats in Morocco, and rising regionalist sympathies, the emphasis on what Spaniards had in common, their faith, seemed to avoid a messy national disintegration. Along with King Alfonso XIII, Primo de Rivera was overthrown and replaced by the Second Republic in 1931.

5. Francisco Franco's Catholic faith and the influence of the church on his regime are well known. Sara J. Brenneis and Gina Herrmann's (2020) recent research into the topic provides an extensive discussion into how Catholic doctrine is directly reflected in the legislation imposed during the dictatorship.

6. These *Leyes Fundamentales* addressed issues as wide-ranging as the conditions of workers and the restauration of the monarchy. For more on the *Fundamental Laws* and their impact in the Francoist regime, see Stanley Payne (2018, 444–450) and Ylán Calderón (2017, ch. 3).

7. The regime constantly addressed this issue, as Enrique Moradiellos García (2018) recounts, given that "the legal literature of the regime never failed to underline that Franco founded his authority upon a charismatic legitimacy (not traditional, by succession, or rational, by election)" (169).

8. Franco's early military career and scant political interests, such as reforming the republican system that he believed had been corrupted by the radical Popular Front, are detailed in Payne (2012, 119).

9. More on Mussolini's idolization of ancient Roman emperors can be found in Duplá and Iriarte (1990, 186).

10. More than a mere national symbol, "the águila de San Juan" also contained profound Biblical connotations given that the eagle is one of the four "Holy Beasts" that supports God's chariot in *Ezekiel*. For an in-depth analysis of this item of Francoist iconography, see David Zurdo and Ángel Gutiérrez's (2005, 121–124) and Caldevilla Domínguez, Vallés Gonzálvez, and Lorenzo Cabezuelo (2012, 169).

11. The *Frente de Juventudes*, officially the *Delegación Nacional del Frente de Juventudes*, established in 1940, was created with the explicit purpose of educating

and indoctrinating young Spanish men to the ideals and practices of Franco's national movement, comparable, according to José Ignacio Cruz, to Hitler's Hitlerjugend (23).

12. La Barraca was a touring theater group founded and administered by a group of students, including Lorca, from the Universidad Central de Madrid. Originally a student organization intending to bring performances of classical Spanish dramas to rural area with minimal cultural outlets, the group later began infusing their performances with propaganda that supported the Second Republic. See Robin Greeley (2006).

13. Outside of Spain, as Samson and Thacker (2008) indicate, this "radical" understanding of the play also explains its popularity in countries like Russia. The play has enjoyed various renditions in Russia since its first Tsarist production in 1876, which gave way to continuing success in the twentieth century and culminated in the removal of the monarchical figures in 1919, a tradition that prevails in the staging of *Fuenteovejuna* in that country even today (120–123). Veronica Ryjik (2019) has also recently published an entire monograph on how Lope de Vega's dramas have been used in Soviet and post-Soviet Russia.

14. Here it is important to recall the observations of Dennis Cutchins (2017): "What is being adapted in any particular case cannot be the text alone, nor the essence of the text, but rather a particular understanding of the text" (79).

15. *Rojo y negro*, long believed to have been lost to the fire at the Madrid Films Laboratory in 1945 which destroyed a significant amount of Spanish productions, resurfaced in 1996 when an unofficial copy was found at the Cepisca production and distributing offices on Madrid's Gran Vía. Although, as Duncan Wheeler (2012) asserts, no archival evidence has yet to be found to prove why the film was prohibited after only a few showings in cinemas (138), Augusto Torres (2004) posits that the film's depiction of street violence and destruction of national monuments cast a negative light on the Falange and, by extension, Franco himself (29–30). Román Gubern (1981) recalls that the film was only removed from cinemas after the dictator saw a private viewing and vehemently disapproved of its graphic representations of the events of the Spanish Civil War (68).

16. The movie *Raza* would be remade yet again in 1950 to be more responsive to the new international climate (specifically the fall of Nazi Germany) and Spain's new role in it as it wished to pursue collaboration with powerful European countries and the United States.

17. José Pemán, in addition to being highly regarded by the regime, was also used as a promotional tool to tease the upcoming adaptation in an article penned by Rafael de Urbano that was published in *Primer plano* on May 26, 1946, more than a year before the film was released in cinemas. In the article, Urbano highlights the picturesque family life of the screenwriter, as well as his "fuertes sentimientos de cristiano" (9). The article exalts the phenomenon that the adaptation is certain to become in Spanish popular culture by arguing that "verdaderamente, hay que pensar que el verbo de España está en José María Pemán con fuerza atropelladora" (9).

18. The biblical passage referenced by the abbot is Matthew 23:12, which states that "whosoever shall exalt himself shall be abased; and he that shall humble himself shall be exalted" (*Authorized King James Version*, Matthew 23:12).

19. The moral resemblance between this scene and *El burlador de Sevilla's* theme as exemplified by Don Juan's repetition of "¡qué largo me lo fiáis!" is, although beyond the parameters of this study, certainly a topic for further consideration.

20. Although promising the restoration of the monarchy, Franco was sure to maintain absolute control over the process of choosing his royal successor, specifying in the thirteenth article that "El Jefe de Estado, oyendo al Consejo del Reino, podrá proponer a las Cortes queden excluidas de la sucesión aquellas personas reales carentes de la capacidad necesaria para gobernar, o que, por su desvío notorio de los principios fundamentales del Estado o por sus actos merezcan perder los derechos de sucesión establecidos en esta Ley" (3273).

21. The Golden Age plays broadcasted on *Primera fila* were *La dama duente* (1963), *La Estrella de Sevilla* (1964), *Casa con dos puertas es mala de cerrar* (1964), *Peribáñez y el Comendador de Ocaña* (1964), and *El astrólogo fingido* (1965).

22. *Teatro de siempre* (1966–1979) was a series created after *Primera fila* that, instead of staging performances in a studio, recorded them on-site, often at authentic "corrales de comedias." *Estudio 1*, on the other hand, was essentially a re-formatted "spin-off" of *Primera fila* that adapted plays and other literary works in such a way that they resembled short films more than live performances. Most of the adaptations aired on these two shows are still available to view in RTVE's audiovisual archives.

23. Paul Preston (2012) gives specific examples of the antagonistic manner in which Franco treated the future king of Spain (115–120). See also Philippe Nourry's *Juan Carlos: Un rey para los republicanos* (142–150).

24. Antonio Cazorla-Sánchez (2014) goes into great detail about Franco's preoccupation with his own death and how his regime's sociopolitical design would survive after his passing (185-95). Moradiellos García also sheds light on this issue in his *Francisco Franco: Crónica de un caudillo casi olvidado* (208–220), as well as in *Franco: Anatomy of a Dictator* (146–150).

25. In addition to leaving the speaking parts in Lope's original verse, the only notable alteration of the text is the substitution of "maritornes" in Laurencia's heroic monologue for the derogatory "maricones" used in the original. Wheeler erroneously states that the term "maricones" was replaced with "maritornes" in Román's adaptation (2008, 287), but the film avoids the term completely by omitting the sentence altogether. Wheeler's mistake is most likely due to a confusion between the 1947 film and this episode. In any case, Pepe Coira (2005) reports that Román did manage to go against the demands of Spanish censorship and re-shot the scene with the controversial term intact for the versions of the adaptation that were to be released overseas and were, therefore, not subject to Francoist censorship (123).

26. *Fotogramas* no. 1145. It should also be noted that the cover of the issue announced the article as "FUENTEOVEJUNA: La película escándalo de TVE."

27. Guerrero Zamora did speak, albeit briefly, to journalist Mery Carvajal for her November 20, 1972, article in *Pueblo* titled "No asisto al estreno de *Fuenteovejuna*" (15). In addition to reiterating his faithfulness to Lope's original, Guerrero Zamora continues to defend his adaptation due to the changing social climate of the times. Although he doesn't specify exactly what he's referring to, it can be inferred that the waning dictatorship is one of the driving forces of the social changes taking place.

28. In addition to the interviews with Pemán and Román discussed earlier in the chapter, a full-page promotional poster of the 1947 adaptation was included in the film magazine *Primer plano* on April 6, 1947 (4). Newspapers and magazines such

as *Ya*, *Arriba*, and *Fotogramas* also published smaller-sized ads in the weeks prior to the premiere and all three published ads on November 20, 1947, to promote the premiere at Cines Coliseum that took place that same day. In 1972, nothing at all was said about *Fuenteovejuna*'s debut in the weeks leading up to it (November 17, 1972), nor was it reviewed afterward. There was even an issue of *Fotogramas* released that day and it did not even advertise it. It is also curious to note how the two films were both released at the end of November of the respective years.

29. Regarding the positive reviews, an article in *TeleRadio* from February 1973 stated that "Me parece que [*Fuenteovejuna*] sigue vigente. Es más: creo que en estos momentos será mejor recibida y comprendida por el gran público. Y estoy refieriéndome a la temática" (25). The negative reviews, on the other hand, dealt almost exclusively with how poorly they considered the cinematic aspects of Guerrero Zamora's adaptation. Pascual Cebollada, for instance, in his critique of the film in a November 25, 1972, article in *Ya* objected to the cinematic aspects of the production, mentioning "un tratamiento cinematográfico equivocado, con una planificación desigual y caprichosa y con elementos extracinematográficos como punto de apoyo de toda la realización" (n.p.). A week later, a similar scathing report was published in *ABC*: "Guerrero Zamora quiso hacer cine. Lo que se le había encargado era, naturalmente, televisión que pudiera ser proyectada en pantalla grande. Su error no podía ser más grave" (n.p.). No review, however, was more devastatingly negative than the one published on March 22, 1972, in *El alcázar*, which berated the film for its lack of vision and direction with regard to proper film production in which the—anonymous—reviewer stated, "He de confesar mi estupefacción ante esta película. ¿Qué es? ¿Qué quiso ser? ¿Dónde está el cine aquí? ¿Qué idea del cine tiene su director? . . . En primer lugar, el error de cambiar el sistema de proyección. . . . El cine es vida. El verso, no. . . . De toda esta confusión (cine, teatro, telecine, teleteatro, televisión), Guerrero Zamora ha engendrado *Fuenteovejuna*. La película donde todo efectismo tiene su asiento, toda ilógica su lugar, y toda ruptura es posible . . . ha resultado monstruosa" (n.p.).

30. Original: COMENDADOR: ¡Vino sin taza, ventero! / Despertad y abrid la cama. / Vosotros, por que la fama / corone a este majadero.

MUJER: Ayuda, por Dios, ayuda, / dejadme, soltadme, perros.

HOMBRE: Si no es sonando cencerros, / dudo que nadie te acuda. / Mira cómo se me emboba.

MUJER: Auxilio a mujer casada.

HOMBRE: Sirve la parte fiada, / no soy yo quien te la roba.

COMENDADOR: Y al fin, por que no se diga. / que abuse de lo prestado, / quien viéndolo se desdiga / diga el pueblo su degrado / esta mujer no me obliga / a complacerle el ardor / y si para los ardores / curas son comendadores / descuidare sus fervores / siendo yo comendador.]

31. This idea is corroborated by the fact that horror films, particularly those of Alfred Hitchcock, had enjoyed great success in Spain since the 1950s. See Dona Kercher (2015, 34–40) for an overview of how the American filmmaker's productions were handled by Francoist censorship and how they possibly influenced Spanish cinema in the 1960s and beyond.

32. Original: ISABEL: Y es bien ganar por la mano /las pretensiones de Juana / a la corona que gana, / que no se entretiene en vano. / Si Juana la Beltraneja / pudiera con su marido / anidar en nuestro nido, / fuera avispa más que abeja. / No es el trono de Castilla / para quien le quiera mal / y Alfonso de Portugal / le malquiere como villa / unida al reino vecino / y no estado soberano. / Mas el reino castellano / no es agua para tal vino.

33. The 1972 report from the *Boletín informativo del control de taquilla* graphically demonstrate how the public perceived the film, which corroborates the negative press. Guerrero Zamora was cited claiming that the film cost 17 million *pesetas* to make in *Fotogramas* no. 1145 (6–7), yet it only generated 2,695,109 *pesetas* in revenue from its first month in theaters (*Boletin informativo*, 1972, 293).

34. Here I am referring to the period known in Spanish as *La Transición*, which will be discussed more in depth in chapter 3.

35. In Spanish, the period of openness is referred to as *aperturismo*, whereas the uncovering period is called the *destape*.

36. The only negative comment about the film found in the censorship documents was the censor's regret that he could not rate the film as suitable for audiences under 18 years of age, defending his assessment by saying, "aunque hubiese sido mi deseo darla para 14 y menores, [es imposible] dado que está hecho de manera bastante tosca y cruel" (Box no. 36/04445, Archivo General). As such, the film was deemed suitable only for eighteen years and above.

37. Established in 1962, most likely to strengthen Spain's case for entering the European Common Market, the category of "interés especial" was designated to films that offered "realistic narratives dealing with contemporary settings and current problems, [and were] often critical of Spanish society" (Higginbotham, 1988, 61). Many film scholars consider this classification a catalyst in the creation of the "nuevo cine español."

38. It should also be noted that scholars are divided as to whether or not *Peribáñez* was also derived from a popular song that included the lyrics: "Más quiero yo a Peribáñez, / con su capa la pardilla, / que a vos, Comendador, / con la vuesa guarnecida." As Steven Wagschal reminds us, the lyrics have often been attributed to Lope himself (viii).

39. Original: *bailan y danzan, folía y voces*

40. Given the intervention of the censorship in the final cut of the film, it is impossible to know whether or not it was the screenwriter and director's decision to leave this scene so short. Given the film is just over two hours in duration, this sequence takes up a very small percentage of the total run time.

41. Mark Burnett and Adrian Streete (2011) have applied this concept to the Showtime miniseries *The Tudors* (2007–2010), in which they deduce that the feast and banquet scenes contribute to creating a homogenizing implication of the elite society in Tudor England that draws direct parallels to modern celebrity culture and, of course, the popularity of the British Royal Family within Western cultures in the twenty-first century (196–197).

42. See Menéndez y Pelayo (1909, 208–216), Entreambasaguas's *Los estudios de Menéndez y Pelayo sobre el teatro de Lope de Vega* (1969, 145–148), and Ziomek (2014, 51–58).

43. Covarrubias defined *honor* in his *Tesoro de la lengua castellana o española* (1611), as having to do specifically with reputation and dignity, defining the term broadly as a synonym of *honra*, "reverencia, cortesía que se hace a la virtud, a la potestad; algunas vezes se haze al dinero." In other words, honesty, courtesy, and avoiding public scandal were the basic foundations of the seventeenth-century definition of the term.

44. The motif of the lowly being subjected to the same standards of honor as the powerful was recurrent in the theater of Spanish Golden Age, as is made evident by its prevalence in plays such as Calderón's *La vida es sueño* (1635), *El gran teatro del mundo* (1655), and *El médico de su honra* (1637).

45. Kercher (2015) also goes into how Spain's self-fashioning in national films of the time portrayed Spain and its people as courageous underdogs who, despite their disadvantages, were superior in strength and morality to their enemies and therefore always came out of their conflicts victoriously (35).

46. The term used in Spanish to refer to these National-Catholic ideals is *nacionalcatolicismo*.

47. The Spanish word for "sissies" in this case is *maricones*, which is also an extremely derogative term for homosexuals.

48. José María Pemán, the screenwriter of the 1947 adaptation of *Fuenteovejuna* and militant Francoist, was very fond of this binary conceptualization of masculine and feminine roles, as he clearly establishes in his *De doce cualidades de la mujer* (1947) by linking the masculine/feminine dichotomy to the Catholic creation story, arguing "cuando Dios quiso sancionar el pecado original, impuso a la mujer un doble castigo: el dolor en su maternidad y la sujeción al varón, que la dominaría" (840).

49. The copy of the script that was submitted for review was a disorganized rough draft that, as many censors noted, lacked page numbers and sequence indicators. It is likely for this reason that the final production had technical errors that had to be fixed and resubmitted to the censorship *en revisión*.

50. Similar comments were published on the same day in *Arriba, ABC, Ya, 7 Fechas*, and *Dígame* (*Cine Asesor* no. 615, n.p.). Keeping in mind that all of the censors and, most likely, journalists of the time were men, it is probable that their favorable reviews of the actress have less to do with her interpretation of Doña María and more to do with the actresses' flirtatious and witty demeanor in the film, in addition to her physical beauty. As Susan Martín-Márquez (2008) reminds us, placing beautiful women to perform impressive musical numbers in otherwise lackluster films was a common marketing technique in the 1950s, especially in Spain. Along with Lola Flores, Carmen Sevilla, and Sara Montiel, Martín-Márquez specifically lists Paquita Rico as one such actress who was used for this misogynistic purpose (185). This is especially true of Andalusian women, like native Sevillian Rico, due to the exotic and folkloric prestige that Southern Spanish women enjoyed in Franco-era cinema Ruiz Múñoz and Sánchez Alarcón (15–17).

51. The term for "waitress" used in the original was *moza de mesón*.

52. The importance of the traditional family to the regime is made clear by the fact that non-normative sexual relationships were not only illegal but actively persecuted during the dictatorship. This aspect of Francoist social control has been

vigorously studied in recent publications like Vicente Domínguez's *Tabú: La sombra de lo prohibido, innombrable y contaminante* (2006), Javier Pérez Ugarte's *Una discriminación universal: la homosexualidad bajo el franquismo y la transición* (2008), Lucas Jurado Marín's *Identidad: Represión hacia los homosexuales en el franquismo* (2014), and Víctor Mora Gaspar's *Al margen de la naturaleza: La persecución de la homosexualidad durante el franquismo: leyes, terapias y condenas* (2016).

53. Of course, there were also financial benefits to acquiring foreign shows as opposed to producing original Spanish ones. As Montero Díaz and Ojer (2018) remind us, "la adquisición de estos programas resultó muchísimo más barata que su realización" (102).

54. We see, for instance, all three of the aforementioned character types in contemporary English dramas like Shakespeare's *Romeo and Juliet* (1591–1595). For more on the *Commedia dell'arte*'s international reach throughout Europe, see Christopher Balme (2018, 65–130).

55. William Viestenz (2014) identifies a "cult-like" mentality of the regime, stating, "like a religious cult, civic duty in Francoist Spain demanded unflagging commitment from its members, and a stress on national unity led to an obsession with purification" (5) and comparing the dictatorial goal of creating a pure, Catholic race to a construct of a *raza castiza*, insists that "Spanish national identity [. . .] came to resemble an exceptional sacred cult" (6).

56. Following the loss of the last overseas colony of the former Spanish Empire in 1898, the curricula of Spanish elementary schools was changed to include *Don Quijote* so that the nation's children could participate in what was considered the greatest source of Spain's national pride. See the prologue to Jesús García Sánchez's *Visiones del* Quijote *desde la crisis española de fin de siglo* (2005) for a discussion of this scholastic modification.

57. Although such a cosmovision of geographical determinism originated in Spain, it was hardly a novel idea to either Lope or Franco, having developed by Saint Isidore of Seville in his *Etymologies* (600–625). Benedict Anderson (1991) acknowledges that the issue of being indigenous to the Spanish landscape has been a critical component to the construct of a sense of Spanishness for centuries. He highlights the distinctions made in the eighteenth and nineteenth centuries between creoles born in the Americas versus "Spain-born Spaniards" as a means of justifying the former's treatment as inferior in the metropolis, which followed the concept that "born in the Americas, [the creole] could not be a true Spaniard" (58). Although he doesn't explicitly name the concept, Anderson is undoubtedly referring to what Antonio Feros (2017) has denoted "scientific racism," a belief arising out of the seventeenth century that maintained that biological alteration was the result of environmental factors like exposure to native flora, fauna, and climate. As Feros goes on to explain, it was believed that any European that experienced an overexposure to these natural elements could be negatively affected by them, and thus it was commonly held that "Spaniards born on the American continent were brutish imbeciles, resembling Indians" (225). This theory served as the basis for justifying the discrimination against creoles and Native Americans and lasted well into the nineteenth century.

58. Barton came to this conclusion by reading Sánchez-Albornoz's *España*, vol. 1, pp. 20–22. President of the Second Republic, Sánchez-Albornoz was, naturally, a controversial figure during the dictatorship and spent the four decades of the regime's duration in exile. He is best known for his views on Spanish nationalism that sparked an intellectual feud with fellow exiled compatriot, Américo Castro. See Kevin Ingram (344–353) for more on the feud and ideological clash between the two scholars.

59. The autobiography was advertised and sold as a work by Jaime de Andrade, Franco's pseudonym as a war piece for political propaganda.

60. In Spanish, *raza*.

61. In fact, as early as 1914, October 12 was celebrated as the *Fiesta de la raza* by the Ayuntamiento de Madrid to extol the shared traditions of the greater pan-Hispanic community. The name was changed when King Alfonso XIII officially declared the commemoration a national holiday in 1918.

62. As Esther Fernández (2018) indicates, Lope's *Nuevo Mundo* was broadcasted to commemorate the discovery of America and does not posit any political motivations behind its production. Instead, she argues that the broadcast's influence in future Lope adaptations was merely stylistic, noting how "el reparto multitudinario de más de una veintena de actores, los decorados múltiples o el creativo diseño de los créditos atestiguaban una incipiente grandiosidad que se volvería más común en las realizaciones dramáticas de los setenta" (15).

63. Original: "desde que fuiste conmigo, / Luxan, al Andalucía, / y fui en la guerra testigo / de tu honra y valentía."

64. Original: "no ha de quedar moro en pie / de cuantos beben y viven / el Betis, aunque bien sé / del modo que los reciben." The term "Betis" here refers to the Guadalquivir River in southern Spain. The Roman name for this body of water, Baetis, stylized as Betis" in Spanish, is used here as a likely way to avoid using the Arabic name.

65. Original: "Plega a Dios que los moriscos / [vuestras prendas] hagan de mi pellejo / si no dejare matados / cuantos me fueren huyendo!"

66. Original: "días ha que ando tras ellos. / Mas, si no viniere en prosa, / desde aquí le ofrezco en verso."

67. Original: "tiemble en Granada el atrevido moro/ . . . / convierta su alegría en triste lloro."

68. Original: "libre pienso dejar la Andalucía, / si el ejército nuestro se previene"

69. Original: "porque la Cruz roja obliga / cuantos al pecho la tienen, / aunque sean de orden sacro, / mas contra moros se entiende"

70. Original: "y que en aquesta jornada / de Granada, adonde vais, / os prometo que veáis / el valor que hay en mi espada."

71. Original: "¡Que a un capitán cuya espada / tiemblan Córdoba y Granada, / un labrador, un mozuelo / ponga una ballesta al pecho!"

72. Original: "dicen que es una talega / donde junta los trebejos / para jugar la fortuna / tantos blancos como negros."

73. The international retaliation against Franco's regime was signed into law via the Resolution R.39/I of the UN General Assembly in December 1946. For many

scholars like Algora Weber (1996), this legislation marks the official beginning of Spanish isolation on the world stage (23).

74. Studies on the cultural impact of Spanish television, radio, and press in North Africa are available in Vicente Coscollá (2005, 25–26), Javier Tusell (1999, 534– 546), the Fundación Pública Andaluza: El legado andalusí's *Andalucía y Marruecos* (36), and Paloma Gómez Crespo (2004, 50–59).

75. Virginia Higginbotham (1988) highlights the importance of the year 1962 in the Franco Regime's intentions to be politically and culturally favored by other European nations, as his government was eager to join the European Common Market and made its first attempts to enter this economic agreement that year. She recognizes that "in a concerted effort to demonstrate that Spain, at least culturally, was no longer the retrograde, fascist backwater of Europe, a new era of *aperturismo* was integrated" (60). During this period of *aperturismo*, the censorship was much less rigorous than in previous years, and increasingly more foreign films were allowed into the country without such a high degree of the regime's manipulation of the content. Although these steps to appear more democratic in the eyes of its European peers was seen favorably by the other countries on the rest of the continent, it would be over two decades later and following the installation of a democratic constitutional monarchy before Spain was officially admitted into the European Common market in 1986.

76. The legislation in question is referred to in the BOE as Decreto 2283/1964, published on August 18, 1964. For information regarding similar legislative protectionary measures of Spanish film between 1960 and 1964, see Santiago Pozo Arenas (1984, 165–167).

77. Pozo Arenas (1984) offers data that reveal that, even with these ordinances in place, Spanish films never acquired more than a 30 percent share of the film market in Spain during the decade of 1960–1970. Spain's average of 115–120 annual films was eclipsed by cinema giants from the United States, Italy, and France in its own market (186).

78. Montero Díaz and Ojer (2018) refer to the *prehistoria* of TVE as ranging from the first experimental programs broadcasted by the station in 1952 to the first publication of the television-based magazine *TeleDiario*—renamed *TeleRadio* a year later—on December 31, 1957.

79. A journalist writing for *TeleRadio* no. 405 advertised *Estudio 1* as a program that would "ir paulatinamente introduciendo textos que, o bien hayan sido espresamente escritos para TVE, o que al menos hayan sido adaptados por escritores españoles de reconocida solvencia profesional y que se ajusten a nuestros criterios normativos" (28). The same journalists also explains the change of name from *Primera fila* to *Estudio 1*, assuring that it was "un título amplio que, sin comprometerse en cuanto a su contenido, alude a algo esencialmente televisivo y acentúa la obligada vinculación teatral que tenía *Primera fila*" (28).

80. Patricia Diego, Elvira Canós and Eduardo Rodríguez Merchán (2018) do remind us that a short-lived revival of the program, given the name *Teatro*, did appear in 1975 and was sometimes advertised as *Estudio 1* because, like "es de Lope" in the seventeenth century, the phrase *Estudio 1* became associated with quality televised

theater and "sirvió para designar a todos los dramáticos estelares que adaptaban obras teatrales preexistentes" (85).

81. *TeleRadio* no. 337 (n.p.) and no. 646 (n.p.), respectively.
82. *TeleRadio* no. 647.
83. *TeleRadio* no. 566.
84. *TeleRadio* no. 929.

*Chapter 3*

# Lope's Leading Ladies

## *Adaptations for the Democratic Era (1976–2020)*

Francisco Franco died on November 20, 1975. From our twenty-first-century vantage point, it would be easy to conceptualize this date as the beginning of a period of Spanish history known as *La Transición*, during which Spain immediately shed its dictatorial regime and took steps toward integrating a democratic system of government.[1] In all actuality, the dictatorship did not end that abruptly at all.[2] After all, as Javier Tusell (1999) observes, Spaniards were extremely skeptical about and hesitant to embrace any structural, political changes, given that said transition "occurred when it was not at all clear that the consolidation of democracy that was later demonstrated in practice would happen" (6). Recent national controversies, such as the exhumation of the former dictator's mortal remains on October 24, 2019, have reopened the discussion on how to classify the regime's end and the dawn of a new democratic era to such an extent that the very idea of a concluded transition has been called into question. Supporters of the Catalonian Independence Movement, for instance, have argued on social media outlets that any semblance of a complete transition to democracy is impossible as long as the monarchy, Franco's approved successor to his regime, is still in power.[3] Very recently, the dispute over Francisco Franco's mortal remains, which culminated in the exhumation of his body and reburial in 2019 further demonstrates the lingering sociopolitical conflicts that his legacy still sparks in modern Spain.[4] In other words, despite the passing of several decades and the fact that the Spanish political situation has arguably stabilized since 1975, the dark cloud that the Francoist regime casts over the country has yet to dissipate completely. Proof of the dictatorship's lingering effects into the current century can be seen by the passing of the "Historical Memory Law" (2007) under the Spanish Socialist Workers' Party (PSOE) president José Luis Rodríguez Zapatero and the controversies that this law has sparked over the last decade among opposing political parties.[5]

The uncertainty surrounding which direction the Spanish government would take regarding its sociopolitical future in the mid-1970s created shock-waves of confusion and tensions throughout the country. On the one hand, the dictator was indeed dead, which opened an abundance of revolutionary possibilities for some, but on the other hand, little would change in society in the two years immediately following his death. Thousands of anti-Francoist prisoners were still held captive in Spanish jails, those exiled by the regime for their political persuasions remained outside of the country, and Franco's prized tool of social control, the State's censorship of mass media outlets (including film, television, and the press), was not officially dissolved until December 1, 1977. Quite simply, despite the temptation to categorize Franco's death in 1975 as a definitive demarcation of past and present in Spanish society, it is essential to consider the lingering sociopolitical instabilities of the time—and their prolonged consequences—in any analysis of post-Francoist popular culture.

During this period, opinions varied widely regarding fundamental issues such as freedom of speech, censorship of the press and mass media, international cooperation, and even the very concept of Spanish national identity.[6] Voices from all sides of the sociopolitical spectrum were eager to reach as many Spaniards as possible with their opinions, observations, and arguments for and against certain political structures. By 1977, 93 percent of Spanish households owned televisions that they reportedly watched daily for updates on sociopolitical issues, as opposed to the 33 percent who claimed to still read newspapers and other printed publications for their informative content, and 83 percent of the surveyed rural population admitted to receiving the news exclusively through television broadcasts, preferring not to consume newspapers at all (Martín Jiménez, 2018, 320). Consequently, TVE became a driving force behind the early stages of the democratic *Transición*. One must not, however, overlook the fact that TVE continued to be a governmental entity. The political conundrum of these years is perfectly illustrated by the astounding turnover rate of TVE's administration. From 1975 to 1982, the role of general director of TVE was held by no less than six men, switching administrations and political inclinations nearly annually. The following table provides a list of these directors, their official titles (which also frequently changed), their time in office, and their political affiliations, which, not surprisingly, reflect the alternating political parties that rose to power in the Spanish government during these years:

| Director's Name | Official Title | Time in Office | Political Party |
|---|---|---|---|
| Gabriel Peña Aranda | Director General de Radiodifusión y Televisión | November 27, 1975– July 23, 1976 | Francoist |
| Rafael Ansón Oliart | Director General de Radio y Televisión | July 23, 1976– November 9,1977 | UCD |
| Fernando Arias-Salgado Montalvo | Director General del Organismo Autónomo RTVE | November 19, 1977– January 25, 1981 | UCD |
| Fernando Castedo Álvarez | Director General del Ente Público RTVE | January 26, 1981– October 24, 1981 | PSOE |
| Carlos Robles Piquer | Director General del Ente Público RTVE | October 25, 1981– March 15, 1982 | AP/PP |
| Eugenio Nasarre Goicoechea | Director General del Ente Público RTVE | March 15, 1982– December 1, 1982 | UCD |

Translated from Enrique Bustamante (2013, 316) and elaborated upon to include political party and end of term of each director.

These data reveal that, with the exception of Fernando Arias-Salgado Montalvo, none of these general directors maintained their positions for much longer than one calendar year, if even. Arias-Salgado Montalvo's administration is, nonetheless, extremely significant for our study, given that it would be during his time in office that television censorship would officially be lifted and, one year later, on December 29, 1978, the Spanish Constitution, which specifically defined the kingdom as "a social and democratic State of law and order" (Preamble, Article 1), was approved by the courts and officially established Spain as a constitutional monarchy. Furthermore, it is interesting to highlight that his administration ended less than a month before the attempted *coup d'état* of February 23, 1981 by Francoist sympathizers, thus emphasizing the tumultuous sociopolitical climate in which TVE had to navigate. It is also worth noting that his time in office corresponds to the time in which the Central Democratic Union (UCD), led by Prime Minister Adolfo Suárez, firmly held the reins of the reformed Spanish government. Moreover, it is also telling that the PSOE was in charge of TVE for almost the entirety of the year prior to their landslide victory in the 1982 general elections, even though the more conservative *Alianza Popular* (later *Partido Popular*) would manage the television airwaves during the year of this decisive election.

Beyond the political arena, the list of general directors also informs us that change was the only constant for TVE during the months and years immediately following Franco's death. Whereas the sociopolitical climate would have to wait for significant change, TVE's leadership changed within a mere three business days of the dictator's passing when Gabriel Peña Aranda took

over from Jesús Sancho Rof. Understandably, this was an exceptionally difficult moment in which to manage Spain's most effective means of mass
communication, which had been propelled into a state of crisis due to harsh
criticism by the press, devastating budget cuts, and hostile internal discord
(Martín Jiménez, 2018, 322). It is, therefore, not surprising that in just eight
months, Peña Aranda would be replaced by Ansón Oliart, a successful busi-
nessman who many hailed as "an expert in the fields of creation and public
relations" (323). Enrique del Corral, a fierce critic of TVE in the mid-1970s,
published an article in the July 25, 1976, edition of *ABC* in which he laid out
the challenges facing Ansón Oliart in his new role:

> Mr. Ansón is arriving at an especially significant moment derived from the lack
> of a budget to attend to the growing needs of the medium, on one hand, and the
> inevitable deterioration of the material, on the other. Both of these problems,
> added to the unavoidability of the technical and tactical demands of television as
> a new social mass-communication medium, turn this into an especially difficult
> and even conflicting intramural house because of the discontent of the person-
> nel, and extramural because of the audiences' disinterest, with whom it is urgent
> to regain credit. (94)

Such descriptions of TVE's dismal possibilities for future success made public the knowledge that the single Spanish television station was under attack
from both internal and external forces. As such, a failure to act on warnings
like Del Corral's would have been detrimental to the company. Accordingly,
TVE decided to take the risk of revamping its programming to offer its viewership productions that were more responsive to the sociopolitical climate in
which it lived.

The traditional midday news broadcasts, for instance, were transformed
into debate platforms upon which political scientists, politicians, and journalists could present their positions to the majority of the Spanish population.
Such a drastic innovation was immediately received positively by spectators;
a survey published at the end of the 1976 calendar year by the *Spanish Journal of Public Opinion* demonstrated that, out of 100 participants, nearly half
(48 percent) agreed that the new format of the *telediarios* was an improve-
ment upon the former structure (420–428). Such a verdict from the viewers
caused TVE to redesign its programming and invest more resources into
producing debate-oriented talk shows and expanding upon those that already
existed. By 1978, informative programs such as *Los reporteros, ¿Quién es?*;
*¿Qué es?*; *Hora 15*; *La prensa a debate*; *España, hoy*; *Opinión pública*; *Más
- menos*; *Cara a cara*; *Siete días*; *Hablamos*; *Gente hoy*; *Gaceta cultural*; and
*Primera página*, among many others, dominated the Spanish airwaves. The
political persuasion of the general directors shaped the ideological overtones
that were transmitted by these programs. In an attempt to separate society

from its recent dictatorial past, the general directors fomented programs that dealt with more democratic issues such as amnesty, freedom of expression, gender equality, Spanish cultural diversity from an array of perspectives, and intellectual advancement. In other words, "in this context, the *telediarios* became one of the principle mechanisms for democratization and support for the process of transition" from the late 1970s onward (Arias et al., 2018, 335–336). More importantly, by 1978, TVE had become a promotional vehicle for the Spanish Constitution.

With such an influx of informative, politically oriented programming, it is only natural that shows produced for their entertainment value—with the massive exception of live sports—declined from 1975 to 1980. Instead of investing in original productions, TVE began purchasing the syndication rights to foreign entertainment programs. By 1980, series such as *Heidi* (Japan), *Dallas* (the United States), *Poldark* (UK), *Eight is Enough* (the United States), *The Mary Tyler Moore Show* (the United States), and *Rich Man, Poor Man* (the United States) had scored the highest positions in the Spanish ratings, beating out original Spanish shows such as *Curro Jiménez*, *Cañas y barro*, and *Fortunata y Jacinta*, (Montero and Ojer, 2018, 110). As the latter titles indicate, when TVE did attempt to make an original program, it still tended to rely on adaptations of national literary works.[7] Surprisingly enough, those of Spanish origin, few as they may have been in comparison to the surplus of imported programs, were preferred to those of foreign authors; although, as José Carlos Rueda Laffond and María del Mar Chicharro Merayo observe, "there was a clear preeminence of contemporary Spanish novelists," as opposed to more historical literary adaptations (2006, 376). As a result, televised adaptations of classical theatrical dramas fell to the wayside to accommodate the dynamic and evolving tastes of TVE's viewership.

Many scholars, such as Robert Bayliss (2015), Walther Bernecker and Sören Brinkmann (2004), Veronika Ryjik (2011), and Duncan Wheeler (2012)—have argued that Spanish society was so eager to abandon Francoism—and any cultural artifacts associated with it—that it attempted to completely obliterate the Golden Age's presence.[8] They argue that specifically more conservative figures of the era like Lope de Vega have regularly faced efforts of being erased from mainstream popular culture in the years immediately following Franco's death. On one hand, such claims are certainly substantiated by looking simply at television programming records and the titles of films released during this time; on the other hand, it is also important to consider that there were only four adaptations of Golden Age plays broadcasted at all from 1975 to 1980.[9] Of these four, only two were new productions; *Don Gil de las calzas verdes* (1978) was a re-broadcast of *Estudio 1*'s 1971 adaptation and *El mejor alcalde, el rey* (1977) was a re-release of the 1970 episode, also from *Estudio 1*. Quite simply, the argument cannot be made that Lope de Vega was singled out for his association with Francoist ideology. Based on the aforementioned data, it would be possible to substantiate the opinion that any Golden Age play, not just those attributed to Lope, would have been avoided due to the popular assumption—factual or not—that Francoists exalted the Early Modern period as the epitome of Spanish nationalism.

Agustín Díaz Yanes, the director of *Alatriste* (2006), even goes so far so as to directly blame modern Spaniards' disinterest in their country's literary past to the fact that the Francoist regime tainted the historical memory of the Early Modern era altogether. According to the cinematographer, the lack of interest in Spain's history by the Spanish people "is due to the dictatorship: it created such a division in the country that it's still too soon for people to be reconciled with their past" (Romero Santos, 2014, 80–81).[10] The source text's author, Arturo Pérez-Reverte, had already expressed a similar belief to *El País* reporter Miguel Mora in an exclusive interview in which he revealed that one of his biggest motivations for preparing a scholastic edition of his novel *Las aventuras del capitán Alatriste* (1996) was to prevent the younger generations from perpetuating attitudes about the past that stemmed from "imperial prejudices from Francoism [and] the forgetfulness and ignorance caused by the LOGSE" (Mora, 2001, 38).[11] As we can see, even some of Spanish popular culture's most successful and renowned influencers have contributed to perpetuating the belief that Francoism had generated a post-dictatorial aversion to Spain's imperial history.

It seems much more likely, however, in the years immediately following the death of Franco, that Golden Age theater had temporarily fallen out of the collective Spanish interest due to the more pressing societal issues and evolving tastes and composition of TVE's spectatorship. After all, as Kristin Bezio and Kimberly Yost (2018) assert, "popular culture provides a distillation of the concerns facing a civilization at particular sociohistorical moment[s]," which are extremely dynamic and frequently change, thus altering what is "popular" at a certain time to a particular people (2). In the sociohistorical context of 1975–1980 in Spain, it seems much more likely that, instead of a collective drive to ignore all early modern memorabilia, the Spanish audience's attention had simply shifted; rather, as opposed to what the aforementioned critics have argued, it is much more plausible that instead of an active attempt to counteract any possible contamination of Lope de Vega as a Francoist cultural symbol, TVE was simply responding to its consumers' more immediate concerns. The result of this change was a preference for different types of entertainment than in decades past. Considering the lucrative imperative of appeasing audiences, it was not feasible for TVE to invest in Golden Age adaptations during these years.

Moreover, popular culture cannot—and should not—be analyzed solely on television and cinema trends. The dissolution of the censorship ushered in a newfound interest in the theater in the late 1970s, which had suffered greatly during the dictatorship.[12] Reflecting on his motivation for creating the *Compañía Española de Teatro Clásico* in 1979, the director of the national theater company, Juan Antonio Castro, lamented in an interview with *El País* that "if writing in Spain is frustrating, making theater—especially classical theater—is even worse" (n.p.), a problem he hoped to correct with his new company. Considering that their first production was none other than an adaptation of Lope de Vega's *El perro del hortelano* (1979), it hardly seems accurate to argue that the Phoenix had lost all relevance in the popular culture of this time. Furthermore, as I will demonstrate below, an interest in Golden Age literature—especially that of Lope de Vega—would re-enter the collective Spanish imagination in the early 1980s, short lived as the phenomenon may have been. Within the first three years of the decade, an astounding seven adaptations (more than two per year) of Lope's works were adapted to television:

1. "La dama boba" (*Estudio 1*, 1980)
2. "La discreta enamorada" (*Estudio 1*, 1980)
3. "El despertar a quien duerme" (*Estudio 1*, 1981)
4. "Porfiar hasta morir" (*Estudio 1*, 1981)
5. "La moza de cántaro" (*Estudio 1*, 1981)
6. "El perro del hortelano" (*Estudio 1*, 1981)
7. "La viuda valenciana" (*Las pícaras*, 1983)

This list of adaptations provides some curious insights. We see, for example, a brief "Lope boom" in 1980–1981, precisely as the UCD's administration over TVE was coming to an end. It seems logical that, as the sociopolitical climate began to stabilize after the confusion and uncertainty of the late 1970s, TVE was again prepared to produce programs that had been popular with their audiences before. Nonetheless, the production of such adaptations would come to a more permanent halt at the beginning of 1982, the year in which political debates leading up to the general elections that would place the Spanish government into the hands of the PSOE, dominated the public television arena (Palacio, 2012, 94). A noticeable outlier in this list, 1983's *La viuda valenciana*, took the most radical steps in changing the manner in which Lope's theater has ever been adapted to the screens. Curiously, it would also be the final Lope adaptation to be released on Spanish screens until *Función de Noche* revived *La discreta enamorada* in 1996.

Meanwhile, in the theater, Adolfo Marsillach took Castro's initiative even further in 1983 when he became the director of the company and changed its name to the *Compañía Nacional de Teatro Clásico.* The director in an interview with *El País*'s Rosana Torres (1987) said, "The goals of this company were to be to take up again the tradition of classical theater montage that has been interrupted in Spain and has existed in other countries" (n.p.). As the article leads us to understand, the reintroduction of a classical theater tradition in Spain aimed to contribute to the country's aspirations of culturally integrating itself into modern European culture, given that "the French have *a way* of performing Molière and the English have a method of approaching William Shakespeare's texts," whereas Spain had no established tradition of consistently maintaining its own classical literature in modern popular culture (Torres, 1987, n.p.). There was, it would seem, a societal motivation to elevate Spain's rich literary tradition to a point to which it would no longer be overshadowed by that of its European rivals. Spain was using its newly revived theatrical tradition to defend, from a cultural standpoint, its rightful place in the broader European society. It can hardly be considered a coincidence that such an initiative was being put into practice at a time in which a collective national desire was centered around joining the European Union, in which it would secure membership shortly thereafter, in 1986.

That same year, the National Classical Theater Company began its first season with adaptations of two Golden Age plays: Calderón's *El médico de su honra* (1986) and Lope de Vega's *Los locos de Valencia* (1986).[13] In stark contrast to claims that Lope de Vega had lost any relevance or appreciation in post-Francoist popular culture, the fact that the company has, to date, adapted 35 of Lope's dramas since its debut season demonstrates that—at least in their original medium—they seem to have found a stable place in Spanish performance culture, much more so after than during the dictatorship.[14] While it may be difficult to comprehend how literature from the Early Modern period—and especially that of Lope de Vega, whose works allegedly fit so easily into Francoist ideology—could possibly be considered relevant in a society that wished to erase its imperial and dictatorial histories from the collective national consciousness, a consideration of the academic culture of the time could help us understand this apparent contradiction. Javier Moreno Luzón and Xosé Núñez Seixas (2017) highlight the importance of Professor Manuel Tuñón de Lara's innovative approach to Spanish historiography that introduced a conceptualization of Spain's past to its young scholars in ways that had not been accepted previously. For the first time, Moreno Luzón and Núñez Seixas argue, Spanish university students of the *Transición* were becoming familiarized with terms like "hegemony," "power bloc," and "social formations" that became the basis for the field of social history (27). The resulting unprecedented interest in Spain's imperial, hegemonic past in academic culture transcended the educational realm and inserted itself into popular culture in the early 1980s.

Notwithstanding the short-lived televised "Lope boom" of 1980–1983, as the 1980s advanced into the 1990s, Lope's plays would be confined to their original medium: the theater. During this time, film and television had taken a drastic turn toward revolutionizing Spanish popular culture in ways that had not been possible in previous decades. The *destape* era of the latter years of the dictatorship had essentially evolved into a hypersexual and polysexual free-for-all.[15] Overly sexualized women, homosexuals, transvestites, prosti- tutes, and transgender characters had gained an increased level of acceptance in Spanish society and were allowed a prominent place on Spanish screens, especially in film.[16] Filmmakers such as Pilar Miró and Pedro Almodóvar took advantage of this creative freedom and helped propel Spanish cinema into postmodernity with their innovative characters and provocative plots.[17] Lope de Vega's plays, of course, would not be a natural addition to this new cinematic and television orientation; however, it is notable that, instead of disappearing altogether, adaptations of his dramas have maintained a steady—albeit infrequent—presence in these media. More importantly, when they have appeared, they seem to demonstrate the dynamic cultural climate of their time in very specific ways. The following is a list of all of the adapta- tions of Lope's works that have been released, to date, since 1983:

### Motion Pictures

1. *El perro del hortelano*, Dir. Pilar Miró, 1996
2. *La dama boba*, Dir. Manuel Iborra, 2006

### Television

1. "La discreta enamorada" (*Función de noche*, 1996)
2. "Los melindres de Belisa" (*Función de noche*, 1997)
3. "La viuda valenciana" (*Estudio 1*, 2010)

It is interesting to note that, although TVE's monopoly of the Spanish air- waves came to an end with the inauguration of *Antena 3* in 1992, all of the televised adaptations of Lope's plays have continued to be products of the government-controlled TVE. Moreover, the motion picture adaptation of *El perro del hortelano* (1996) was also funded, in part, by TVE. Perhaps not surprisingly, one should also keep in mind that all of the post 1980s adapta- tions were created and produced at times when the PSOE was in control of the Spanish government. Although this could be entirely coincidental (the PSOE has, after all, managed to maintain control of the government more than any of its rivals since the onset of the constitutional monarchy in 1978), it is still worth keeping in mind that public funding was used to at least subsidize the costs of producing Lope adaptations by a political party whose social standpoint has supposedly been the advancement of progressive ideology and corresponding legislation.

One of the PSOE's biggest attempts at influencing popular culture was its incentive to promote adaptations of great literary works of Spain's national past on TVE. Following in the footsteps of a policy put in place by the UCD in 1979, the socialist government allocated 1,300,000,000 *pesetas* to TVE in 1987 in order for the television station to create and distribute, in cooperation with film production companies, a new canon of Spanish productions for the small screen that gave special priority to adaptations of great literary texts (Palacio, 2012, 202). The government did not, however, specify what kinds of adaptations were most preferable, or which works were considered "great." The PSOE's investment did not materialize into adaptations of Golden Age texts, but rather of nineteenth- and early twentieth-century novels that accentuated the vulnerable state of Spanish society prior to the Civil War that would serve as a cautionary tale for contemporary audiences. Francisca López (2009) interprets this trend as a "way to guarantee a future in which [that bellicose conflict] would not be able to happen again" because the instability of the times had conjured ghosts of the war that had catalyzed a newfound obsession with the violence of the previous century in the collective imagination (95). I consider this further evidence that the democratic governments that followed the dictatorship took an active role in influencing sociopolitical discourse by attempting to intercept perceived threats to the new, fragile political environment.

To reiterate what the data of the times continue to demonstrate, it is important to avoid the pitfalls of categorizing post-Francoist Spanish sociopolitical and popular cultures as a single, homogenous unit. As is typical in all modern democracies, political factions and societal trends change frequently and rapidly, which is often seen reflected in their cultural products. Nevertheless, the thematic correlation of all of the adapted plays that have been produced since the mid-1970s is also significant. Each Lope play adapted after 1975, apart from taking place in urban, noble settings, centers the action around love and its complications, all revolving around a female protagonist. Thus, in keeping with the democratic spirit of giving women more visibility in popular culture, every Lope de Vega adaptation has focused the spotlight on strong, powerful women, who many directors and screenwriters have interpreted as opposing the patriarchal constructs of the past. Of course, some of these types of plays had been adapted during the 1960s and 1970s, following the cultural current of the time, a phenomenon that Esther Fernández (2012) identifies as a result of Spanish women's more active role in society (12–13).

Naturally, the adaptations produced after the dictatorship were considered as an opportunity to represent Lope's women in a new, proto-feminist light, which was facilitated by the more radical sociopolitical changes that occurred after Franco's death. The very concept of feminine national identity had changed alongside the political climate of the country and some television producers and filmmakers saw the modern Spanish woman reflected in her early modern counterpart as presented in the works of Lope de Vega. Based on the adaptation styles and reception of these productions, I argue that post-Francoist screenwriters and directors have drawn a parallel between the pioneering seventeenth-century protagonists and the late twentieth-to early twenty-first-century feminist movements in Spain that they wished to highlight with their interpretation of Lope's plays.[18] Essentially, like their Francoist counterparts before them, they have attempted to create and develop a widespread interpretive community that fosters an interpretation of the Phoenix's plays that better aligns with the societal shifts and ideological currents that were prominent during their respective times. This objective is exemplified by many of the advertisements and promotional materials used to generate public interest in these films and television episodes. For example, the promotional materials for *La dama boba* (1980) depict Lope's original story as an early manifestation of feminist thought, affirming that the play advocates the "woman's right to decide in love, to choose on her own behalf, to disrupt paternal authority, the *machismo* of the times, conquering males with wily weapons" ("Estudio 1" 2010, 20).

The adaptors of the 2006 motion picture version of the play shared this interpretation of Lope's original, telling journalists at *El País* in a March 13, 2006 article that the women protagonists of *La dama boba* were examples of proto-feminists because "they evade the male chauvinistic society of the times in two very different ways; the first through books, the second one, by playing dumb" (n.p.).[19] Likewise, a promotional article in *TeleRadio* for the 1983 adaptation of *La viuda valenciana* commented upon the play's relevance to modern women, arguing that modern female viewers would appreciate the themes therein because the "hunt for a man is no longer the objective to which women set their sights," given that the protagonist Leonarda is unwilling to remarry ("La viuda," 1983, 26). A feminist interpretation of a Lope drama was never stated more precisely, however, than when Pilar Miró confessed to Gregorio Morán of *El País* in 1997 that the aspect of *El perro del hortelano* that most attracted her to converting it into a screenplay was its "almost feminist essence" that surges from the protagonist Diana's taking control of her own love story (47). Beyond an attempt to merely modernize the motif of Lope's dramas for a late twentieth-century audience, these statements suggest that the adaptors in the democratic era desired to dismantle any possible association between Spain's Golden Age literature and the fascist regime's propaganda from earlier in the century. Essentially, the blossoming democratic society would not necessarily have to renounce its illustrious literary patrimony as part of its rejection of the ideals propagated during the dictatorship. The key to doing so was to be found in the interpretation of the central arguments.

Although not all of the post-Francoist adaptations of Lope's plays were marketed as relics of early modern feminism, an analysis of the films and television episodes will be necessary to detect whether or not a feminist impulse truly guided their adaptors during production. Considering the implications that a feminist interpretation of Lope's texts could have on the overall public opinion of the author—and, by extension, the entire Golden Age—in modern society, I will examine this aspect of the adaptations first. In order to study these cultural artifacts and contemplate a possible evolution of Lope's female characters on the Spanish screen, I will limit the majority of my attention to those plays that were produced both *during* and *after* Francoism, namely *La moza de cántaro* (1954, 1981), *El perro del hortelano* (1966, 1981, 1996), *La dama boba* (1969, 1980, 2006), *La discreta enamorada* (1970, 1980, 1996), and *La viuda valenciana* (1975, 1983, 2010). I will analyze, especially, the differences that exist between the Francoists' portrayals of these protagonists and their post-dictatorial counterparts.

## POST-FRANCOIST CHARACTERIZATIONS OF LOPE'S FEMALE PROTAGONISTS

The 1974 adaptation of *El mejor alcalde, el rey* had already begun to introduce novel broadcasting techniques in its portrayal of nudity, an example of the newfound artistic freedom enjoyed during the *destape* era, when Felicia's unclothed backside and breasts are shown while she bathes in the river. Nudity and more sexually explicit material had been increasingly becoming—albeit slowly—a part of Spanish visual culture in the final years of Francoism. Scholars like Isolina Ballesteros (2001) attribute this period of artistic risk-taking to the influx of foreign tourism that had been moving onto Spanish shores in the 1960s and, more than anything else, the heightened eroticism in European and North American cinema in the early 1970s (175). Franco found himself powerless against the increasingly progressive societal trends that were invading his moral fortress of *nacionalcatolicismo* from abroad and yielded to popular demand as a political strategy to protect and preserve his regime.[20]

In addition to allowing characters and situations once considered taboo by the dictatorship to take center stage on Spanish screens, one of the most prominent ways that Spanish popular culture distanced itself from its conservative past was by abandoning the portrayal of characters that had been idealized by the regime. Such discriminatory attitudes toward the type of Spanish person depicted on mass media outlets is certainly made evident by the choice of Lope's plays that were adapted after the end of the dictatorship. As opposed to the Casildas and Laurencias of days past, whom Francoists held dear for their roles as faithful, loving wives, considering them—in the words of Fernando Valls (1983)—an "excellent example of the Spanish woman" (151), the decades since the dictatorship have witnessed the portrayal of a completely different type of Golden Age Spanish woman in cinemas and on television screens. Essentially, as Montero and Ojer (2018) state, a "new world demands new women" (101). In direct opposition to the *machismo* that had defined and characterized the Francoist male ideal in decades prior, ideas of feminine inferiority and women's place in society had—at least in the major metropolitan areas and, in turn, popular culture—changed for the better. More egalitarian and tolerant perspectives had become cultural goals for Spanish society. More than a mere altruistic ambition to create a more open-minded, civil community, modifying the depictions of women on Spanish screens was considered to be a measure by which Spain could better involve itself culturally on an international scale. The dictatorship had hindered the types of Women's Liberation movements that had prevailed in Europe and North America during the 1960s and 1970s and the post-dictatorial society was anxious to make up for lost time.[21] As Cristina Martínez-Carazo (2012) affirms, Spanish history was one aspect of the country's culture that filmmakers and television producers were most eager to reconstruct in order to modify the nation's image both inside and outside of its territory (149). Consequently, some alterations to Lope's original plays have been necessary in order for them to resonate better with modern audiences, especially with respect to the portrayal of women in his dramas. Post-Francoist screenwriters certainly had their work cut out for them, given that the types of women represented in Golden Age literature were very far removed from the women of the 1980s. Lope's female characters were no exception to this general rule.

Some critics like Melveena McKendrick (1974) have maintained that Lope de Vega was an influential promoter of feminist tendencies on the Golden Age Spanish stage (73). Be that as it may, the fact that his female protagonists had to be modified so that these adaptations would respond to the more inclusive, anti-misogynistic post-Francoist rhetoric that has permeated popular culture discourse throughout the past 40 years suggests the contrary. In her authoritative volume on *Woman and Society in the Spanish Drama of the Golden Age: A Study of the* Mujer Varonil, McKendrick (1974) substantiates Lope's feminist inclination by arguing that many of his female protagonists pertained to a type of rebellious, proto-feminist category of "manly woman," which she subcategorizes into distinct types of leading female roles. McKendrick's study, however, completely overlooks the fact that, at least in Lope's plays, the "defiant" manly woman always succumbs to the societal expectations of her time and resumes her place in the "natural" social order (as it was considered then) by the end of the plot. Moreover, it is often precisely through his women's virtue that the established order can be restored and maintained.[22]

Leonarda, the young widow from *La viuda valenciana*, for example, certainly qualifies as an "elusive woman"[23] in Lope's original in the sense that she refuses to marry any of her numerous gentlemen callers, despite society's—and her uncle's—fervent objections, which are always voiced by male characters. Leonarda is, nonetheless, also presented as somewhat of a scholar in the first act, as she is seen reading mystic poems by Fray Luis and proclaiming her love of literature. It is precisely Leonarda's elusiveness that the press most comments upon after the release of the 1983 adaptation on the series *Las pícaras*. As a reviewer in *La Nueva España* described it, the play's appeal in the 1980s was the result of the depiction of a "widow besieged by beaus, who are dying for her tokens and her dowry, [but are] rejected by the beautiful woman who is inclined to mysticism" (42). Similar sentiments were echoed by a journalist from *TeleRadio* when he suggested a parallel between the modern Spanish woman and her seventeenth-century predecessor, given that the protagonist is initially opposed to finding a new husband in Lope's original (M. A., 1983, 26). The press seems to be commenting upon the adaptation based on their interpretations of the original work, not the episode that actually aired. It is tempting to question if, after decades of watching renditions of the plays that hardly adapted the source texts, the reviewers bothered to watch the episode at all.

In any case, their commentary stems from a fundamental misunderstanding of the play. The original Leonarda's literary interests are not the result of a fascination with mysticism or any desire to pursue a formal education; she admits to reading only for pleasure in the source text.[24] The fact that she possesses her own library and has leisure time to indulge in her hobby helps to characterize her as an affluent, independent widow who does not need either the company of a man or any financial assistance. On the contrary, being married would greatly deplete her sizable economic resources, as she explicitly tells her uncle Lucencio by narrating an imaginary lovers' quarrel in I.2:

> He'll come home late, I'll be jealous, he'll squander my money, we'll fight over who is right. I'll save and he'll squander, he'll make me liable for his debts, the officers of the law will come and there'll be kicking and screaming. Every night and every day we'll have trouble in this house because of him.—"Show me the dowry!"—"Leave the money alone, it's mine!"—"Abide by what is written here!" (vv. 277–289)[25]

In the 1983 adaptation, however, Leonarda is anything but *esquiva*; she is portrayed as a young woman obsessed with achieving admiration from men. The adapted character shows no interest in reading any kind of literature, but rather is seen frequently playing with girls her own age.

Ironically, despite the press's zeal to promote the episode as a culturally relevant revival of a classic work, the observations in the press regarding Alfredo Mañas and Francisco Regueiro's 1983 adaptation never seem to address the version of the play that was broadcasted on *Las pícaras* at all. First of all, Mañas and Regueiro's Leonarda, played by Cristina Marsillach, is not a widow until nearly a third of the way through the episode, when her husband dies from an apparent heart attack upon discovering that she has taken a lover (00:12:30).[26] Far from Lope's devoutly religious widow that was depicted as late as in the 1975 televised adaptation, Mañas and Regueiro characterized the protagonist as a hypersexual adulteress who, contrary to the report in *TeleRadio*, certainly employs several "burlesque feats" to accommodate the man she believed to be her "secret beau" during his nightly visits.[27] Her servants, for instance, including an African prisoner, disguise men in order to smuggle them into her chambers. Her promiscuity is highlighted when, immediately after her husband's funeral, her servant Julianilla (an adapted form of Lope's Julia from the original) reveals herself to be a boy. Leonarda, seen nude in a tub of milk, invites Julianilla to undress, touch her exposed breasts, and join her in the bath before initiating a series of sexual encounters with him (00:16:13–00:20:15). Far from being the untouchable elusive scholar from the seventeenth-century original who had faithfully been brought to life on *Estudio 1* less than a decade earlier, Marsillach's Leonarda is an uncontrollable, boy-crazy teenager whose only similarity with Lope's protagonist is her young age.[28] In fact, it is interesting that her youth is highlighted so intensely by her costuming—which is, during most of the production, strikingly visually reminiscent to the ladies in Velázquez's *Las meninas* (1656)—and surroundings (children jumping rope and singing playground songs) at various points throughout the episode.[29]

The visual and situational emphases on Leonarda's youth in the 1983 adaptation deserve a close examination. When compared to the version that had been aired in 1975 and the one broadcasted in 2010 (as discussed below) this was the only rendition of *La viuda valenciana* to base its depiction on Lope's characterization cues by placing a young actress in the title role.[30] It could, of course, be argued that the casting directors were simply following the marketing concept that "sex sells" by hiring an attractive adolescent for the episode. Nevertheless, though it is not specifically remarked upon by the press or critics of the time, Leonarda's age identity contributes a great deal to deriving a new interpretation from the old play.

The young age of Marsillach's Leonarda could be considered a critique of early modern social conventions. Though commonplace in seventeenth-century Europe, modern spectators are likely to find the visualization of a child widow to be utterly absurd, if not disturbing. In doing so, the episode questions the practices of a time that had recently been propagated as the zenith of Spain's illustrious imperial history. According to Shannon Brown-lee (2018), such reconsideration emerges naturally from the absurd spectacle because "absurdity illuminates the arbitrariness of social convention" (164). Hence, the drastic change in characterization of Leonarda in the 1983 adaptation sheds a negative light on the social conventions of the allegedly idyllic Early Modern age by showing how girls could be forced into marriage—and thus subjected to adult realities and tragedies like widowhood—while they were still children and, therefore, did not have the opportunity to mature and develop properly throughout a nurturing childhood. Nevertheless, contemporary critics did not detect any such criticism of Golden Age societal norms. In fact, an April 1983 review of the episode in *TeleRadio* hinted that the radical changes to the protagonist had nothing to do with making any kind of cultural statement, but rather was an artistic device designed to categorize Leonarda as a complex character. According to the reviewer, Leonarda possesses a peculiar psychological curiosity and a "manly eroticism contemplated with joyous indulgence, which makes the character of Leonarda an almost singular feminine personality in seventeenth-century theater" (27). Unique as the character may be to the time period of her conception, the episode of *Las pícaras* does not demonstrate any of the psychological traits as her counterpart in the source text.

In 2010, TVE launched a reboot of its mythical *Estudio 1* in hopes that it would become a regular addition to the station's weekly programming. The program debuted with a third televised adaptation of *La viuda valenciana*, starring Aitana Sánchez-Gijón in the leading role of Leonarda. The decision to cast Sánchez-Gijón, who was in her early forties when the episode was filmed and released, already broke with the characterization of Lope's Leonarda, a "beautiful young widow," which, as stated above, was only respected in the 1983 adaptation.[31] The age difference aside, which was likely a decision made to aesthetically align the character with a modern conceptualization of a widow, the fundamental aspects of the character remain intact in comparison to Lope's original. Spectators were introduced to an avid reader, though not a scholar, who passes her abundant free time reading poetry by Fray Luis and becomes hostile to the idea of marriage when it is presented to her, using the same versified dialogues as her seventeenth-century counterpart. Sánchez-Gijón's Leonarda is still, however, highly sexualized; for example, she is introduced as reading nude in a bathtub (00:00:36). Additionally, in her second encounter with Camilo (II.17, vv. 1797–1992), the sequence is highly eroticized by placing the young gentleman nude in the same bathtub filled with rose petals while Leonarda, wearing only a thin robe that she soon sheds, bathes him and sensually kisses and massages him (00:40:00–00:42:10).[32]

In an interview for the "Making of" featurette released alongside the adaptation on DVD, Sánchez-Gijón asserts that the episode's eroticism is an essential element to Leonarda's characterization, saying that, although the widow has accepted and come to terms with a life of romantic solitude, her defining characteristic is that "she does not resign herself to having a man close, but rather to love and enjoy" (00:11:10). She goes on to explain that such traits were essential to Lope's characters, given that—as she understands—his overall theatrical objectives were to cleverly disguise his social criticisms. Sánchez-Gijón argues that Lope understood that one needed to "maintain appearances so as to cause no scandal and be left alone, but one has to know how to play without getting one's clothes dirty; so to say, allow your body its pleasures, but maintain appearances" (00:12:02). Essentially, the producers and actors of this adaptation wanted Leonarda's sexuality to be explicit, much more so than it was presented in 1975, but significantly more moderate than in 1983.[33] I find the evolution of Leonarda's sexuality from 1975–2010 to be an illustrative, visual representation of the progression of female sexuality in Western society in which Spanish popular culture was eager to participate from the end of the dictatorship to the first decade of the twenty-first century. Patricia Politzer (2010) has noted that during the twentieth century, feminine sexuality was increasingly legitimized and showing this to the public—as Marsillach's Leonarda does in the 1983 episode—became a duty in order for women's ability to enjoy and satisfy their sexual desires to be an accepted societal actuality (111). In other words, by 2010, Leonarda's sexuality was still considered an important aspect of her characterization, but social acceptance of this element of her persona eliminated the need to place the scandalous spectacle of it at the forefront.

In similar fashion to *La viuda valenciana*, *La dama boba's* co-protagonist Nise is also *esquiva* at first, because her limited dowry and high intelligence make her an unsuitable match for any of her contemporary pretenders. Nise, like the widow Leonarda, is also portrayed as literarily inclined, though her studious quality is much more emphasized than in the case of the latter. In both instances, however, the women do not demonstrate ambitions to continue their education to an inappropriate—or, as McKendrick would assert—"manly" degree, and both of their academic inclinations are replaced by their infatuation with a man. Whether she is a scholar or *esquiva* was indifferent to the journalist who wrote a promotional description of the work to advertise the 1980 adaptation in the newspaper *ABC*, who saw Nise's inconsistent and malleable personality not as a negative trait, as it was seen in Lope's day, but as a tribute to Lope de Vega's emphasis on women's rights to make their own decisions regarding courtship (20).[34] As this comment suggests, the strong female character of Nise has been conceptualized as an opposing force to the patriarchal societal model, which could possibly explain, in part, her noticeably reduced presence in the adaptation from a decade prior.

As indicated by an editorial in *ABC* from March 1969, "[the character] Nise—the intellectual sister—is more suggested than performed" (67) in the 1969 adaptation of *La dama boba*. Although this comment is quite an exaggeration, it is true that her part is significantly reduced from the source text and the role is certainly eclipsed by her sister Finea. Several scenes and dialogues that develop her strong, independent character are completely omitted. For example, an excerpt of the dialogue from an early scene in the first act is altered so as to omit the part of the conversation between Octavio and Miseno in which they discuss Nise's intellect and domineering personality (I.6, vv. 269–272). In the second act, her eloquent conversation about love with Duardo, Celia, and Feniso, in which she demonstrates a thorough understanding of intricate concepts like neoplatonic love attraction and its force over human beings, is also completely removed (I.2, vv. 1063–1194). Though it would be tempting to attribute these omissions to an intentional effort to "dumb the character down," it seems much more likely that these parts were removed in order to edit the piece for time or to avoid dense, neoclassical intertextuality that might confuse or bore audiences.

Despite the fact that the character of the studious, elusive sister is not developed much in the 1967 adaptation, the review published in *ABC* highlights that director Alberto González Vergel compensated for this omission by focusing the character development on co-protagonist Finea, who he figured could bring an element of transcendence to the episode. He justified his decision to reporters at *ABC* by reaffirming that the production "had an actress in its ranks able to give Finea all of what she has inside, because Finea is perhaps the only consistent character in the whole play" (1969, 67). In doing so, Lope's contrast of the two feminine extremes—total ignorance and obnoxious intelligence—are lost and the motif of the play becomes distorted. Intelligent women, it would seem, could be ignored or moved to the back burner in the 1960s without the fear of damaging the episode's reception. Ignorance was not necessarily an obstacle to overcome in order to find a suitable man and be happy, but cleverness did not make for an attractive leading woman. After the dictatorship had ended, however, an assertive, intelligent woman was the only kind of feminine protagonist that directors and screenwriters were interested in giving a voice to.

The 1980s interpretation of the play would be the one to prevail into the new millennium, as evidenced by Iborra's 2006 adaptation of the drama. In his adaptation, Iborra contrasts the two sisters by providing them with virtually equal screen time. The omissions to his screenplay do not favor one sister over the other and Nise is allowed to flaunt her intelligence and eloquence throughout the entire production. Considering the film adaptation's high degree of adherence to the source text—which in no way deviates from seventeenth-century patriarchal norms, given that, in the play's resolution, both women end up marrying young, attractive, rich men that correspond to their elevated social status—we must ask ourselves: Do the protagonists really evade the misogynistic currents of their society in the film?

Despite the fact that some visual additions such as swordfights and dance sequences are inserted into the film for increased visual impact and the reorganization of some scenes is employed to enhance dramatic effect, the action is essentially identical to the original.[35] With the exception of some overly passionate kissing at times, neither Finea nor Nise behave in the film in any way that would have challenged the *machismo* of the seventeenth century. If anything, the characteristic traits of both protagonists are embellished in the film to a possibly insulting degree; Silvia Abascal's Finea is so forcibly ignorant that the character exudes an almost cartoonish quality, while Macarena Gomez's disapproving glances and unpleasant demeanor take Nise's disinterest in men to an almost hostile extreme. The added non-verbal cues take a high degree of artistic license to re-characterize the protagonists.

In terms of the characterization of the play's deuteragonists, there are two modifications to Lope's text that could have inserted some type of progressively feminist overtone in the film, but the significance of both is quite unremarkable. Ironically, the first deals with a masculine character: Nise's partner Liseo. Although he is a typical, affluent gentleman in Lope's play, Iborra's 2006 adaptation presents him as a weak, spoiled, arguably effeminate *indiano*, who is continually shown overdressed and wearing heavy, carnivalesque makeup.[36] He is humiliated and emasculated on more than one occasion by Laurencio, who is depicted as a "bad boy" scoundrel type, who defeats him in swordfights and is shown as superior on many levels throughout the film. It could be construed that, by pairing the domineeringly intelligent Nise with a more effeminate partner, Iborra's choice of characterization illustrates the dissonance that many modern adaptors of historical literature or period pieces have experienced when attempting to converge premodern masculinity and postmodern feminist ideals. By assuming that strong women and effeminate men are a perfect match, the patriarchal dichotomy of a "dominant and dominated dynamic," as gender scholars Susan Duggin and Jason Pudsey (2006) name it, is maintained, even if the traditional gender roles are swapped (115).[37] Thus, popular culture products like *La dama boba* (2006) that attempt mirror the present with the past in order to highlight the work's contemporaneity commit the fallacy of maintaining cis-heterosexual paradigms, even if the characters' sexes are reversed. Considering one of the film's primary objectives—according to adaptors and the press—was to convey entirely the opposite message and illuminate the importance of female characters whose bravery shined in such a dark, backward time that modern society has left far behind, it is only fitting that the film has generally been considered a failure, both commercially and artistically.

Regarding characterization, the second attempt at a progressive and/or feminist intervention that could be detected in *La dama boba* (2006) deals with the replacement of the protagonists' father Octavio with their mother, Octavia. With the exception of the name change, little more is altered from the original text. In fact, other than the suppression of the scene in which Octavio explains the unequal dowries of his two daughters (I.2, vv. 25–61)— which is replaced by an intertitle at the beginning of the film—and the occasional adjustment to the ends of adjectives for gender agreement, almost all of Octavia's dialogues and actions are identical to Octavio's in the original. Accordingly, the responsibility of protecting her family's honor, primarily through the excessive vigilance of her daughters' conduct, falls entirely on her. Such a reversal of genders was likely meant to make a statement in favor of women's ability to equal a man in complying with familial duties: not only does the switch from Octavio to Octavia blatantly attempt to suggest that the assigned gender roles from the seventeenth century and adhered to by Francoists were, by 2006, an antiquated and obsolete social construct, but Octavia's skillful swordsmanship in the penultimate scene graphically imply that her gender in no way impedes her from fulfilling her parental obligations. In any case, the reversal of gender roles is hardly sufficient to make a profound feminist or progressive statement, given that, despite being executed by the hand of a woman, the family dynamic being defended does not cease to be overtly patriarchal.

Octavia's assumption of the traditionally male responsibility of protecting the family honor would categorize her, according to McKendrick's criteria, as an "avenger" type of "manly woman." Naturally, as McKendrick also recognizes, the avenger was the most scarcely depicted type of female protagonist in Golden Age literature because of her atypical willingness to confront men in physical altercations (261), so it is logical that Lope would have opted not to place the parental burden in *La dama boba* on a mother. Such a radically irregular feminine character would naturally have also been unpopular during the dictatorship.

Diana, the Countess of Belfor from *El perro del hortelano* (ca. 1613) represents another possibly unlikeable female lead during Francoism, but this did not prevent the play from being brought to screens many times, both during and after the dictatorship. The play's popularity in the twentieth century is attested to by the fact that it was adapted three times, once as a major motion picture and twice on television. There is a crucial difference, however, between being well-known and well-liked and, as the reaction from the contemporary press reveals, the 1966 and 1981 adaptations of *El perro del hortelano* were far from the latter.[38]

Enrique García Santo-Tomás (2000a) has already indicated that *El perro del hortelano* is an incredibly difficult text to adapt, calling attention to the way that it presents a

> series of spaces of indetermination, "voids" that make a favorable reception of it difficult. Within this very stage of his career, Lope's placement within the literary canon also perfectly demonstrates the synchronic model in which a series of speeches (trends, administrative aspects, edicts disguised as philanthropy, etc.) flows and cannot be left aside. His artistic legacy, and this is what matters at the end of the day, acquires new interpretive nuances upon presenting it in this new context; it becomes transgressive in its design, it challenges the mechanisms of tolerance among its audiences, it dares people to accept a controversial and scandalous situation. (244)

What García Santo-Tomás duly recognizes in this statement is that *El perro del hortelano* is a prime example of how good literature offers its readers a plurality of interpretations. According to John Guillory (2013), this malleability is precisely what makes canonical literature an invaluable product of cultural capital, arguing that "literary works must be seen as the vector of ideological notions which do not inhere in the works themselves but in the context of their institutional presentation, or more simply, in the way in which they are taught" (ix). In the case of film and television adaptability, I find it necessary to expand the verb "taught" to "presented" in order to demonstrate that Lope's play could be utilized in the formation of an interpretive community outside of a pedagogical context in popular culture. In other words, the plays studied in this chapter, including *El perro del hortelano*, naturally lend themselves well to being ideological vehicles for any sociopolitical current depending on the ways in which they are presented. As such, the characterization of the protagonist Diana—who, despite her *esquiva* quality, is a highly atypical feminine protagonist in Lope's theater—is a critical factor in presenting the work in a certain fashion, perhaps even more so in this play than in many others.

In this context, the televised adaptations' unflattering critical reception both during and after Franco's regime is still, however, somewhat surprising; Lope's protagonist Diana, around whom the entirety of the plot revolves, displays characteristics that would, in theory, be appealing to the cultural and ideological currents of both pre- and post-Francoist popular culture. For Francoists, Diana's obsession with chastity and honor, as expressed by declarations like "but I hold honor / as a greater treasure / than the respects of whom I am [which] I adore / and even thinking about it I consider lowliness"

(I.8, vv. 325–338),[39] would have perfectly encapsulated their vision of proper feminine social conduct. The post-Francoists, on the other hand, would have admired the woman's defiance to social norms and her open, physical aggression toward Teodoro which culminates in her slapping him twice in the face (II.27, vv. 2221–2222). The 1966 adaptation is not conserved in TVE's archives, which makes it impossible to comment upon Diana's characterization in that version from a first-hand viewing. It is remarkable, however, that the screenwriters and production crew of the 1981 adaptation took certain measures to characterize Diana in a manner concurrent with the more open-minded attitudes toward strong leading females after the conservative attitudes of the dictatorship had begun to disappear. Yet again, we see that the source text was manipulated far more by the democratic adaptors than their Francoist predecessors.

The 1981 Diana's infatuation with Teodoro, for instance, is not made nearly as clear as in Lope's original. The monologue in which she realizes that she is in love with and consumed by jealous rage for him is completely omitted from the adaptation (I.7, vv. 325-38). Although it is possible that these lines were removed for time constraints, as seems to be the logical reason behind some other omissions, the fact that the entire tenth scene of the second act, in which Diana's jealousy toward Marcela finally boils over, is also absent from the episode (II.10, vv. 1580–1591) substantiates that the alterations were strategic characterization techniques on behalf of the screenwriters. Other moments in the play that might contribute to a characterization of Diana as anything other than strong and composed are also left out of the adaptation. Her soliloquy in Act III, for instance, is also cut so as to avoid the audience perceiving the vulnerability that she expresses by saying:

> Eyes, since you have fixated on such an unequal thing, you should pay the price for such mistaken sights, since I am not at fault. But I don't want my eyes to cry, since crying also soothes the eyes, I'd rather they felt their pain. If you look wrong, cry right. They probably have already thought of an excuse: the sun looks upon the mud and it does not stick to him. Then it's appropriate that they do not cry. Eyes, stop crying, feel your pain. If you look wrong, cry right. (III.8, vv. 2656–2671)[40]

These lines, as poetically pleasing and emotionally charged as they may be, were not conducive to constructing an image of the strong female persona that the adaptors aimed to characterize Diana as. The suppression of the lines in which Diana impugns women's ability to evaluate situations, "aside from being a woman / subject to every error" (I.13, vv. 808-09),[41] is further evidence that substantiates my claim that the adaptors of the 1981 television episode wished to mold Lope's Diana into a more contemporary feminine figure.[42]

How, then, could Diana be characterized and presented in such a way so as to be embraced by modern Spanish audiences? Unlike the televised versions before it, the 1996 film adaptation of *El perro del hortelano* was a critically acclaimed commercial blockbuster.[43] Directed by the post-Francoist feminist film pioneer Pilar Miró, one of her top priorities in preparing the production was to properly characterize what she considered to be the play's virtually feminist essence (Muñoz, 1996, 47). Doing so, she admitted, required very little artistic intervention on her behalf during the process of adapting the text to a motion picture screenplay, as she already conceived of Lope's original Diana to be, besides a simple countess, a lady who "fights for what she wants, for the man she wants, lying to him and behaving in a thousand ways to, and it's no small feat, to manage to enamor and then marry a commoner" (47). Diego Galán, in a March 2004 article printed in *El País*, recalled an interview he conducted with Miró in which she elaborated on her perception of the protagonist in her adaptation, explaining that she saw Diana as a woman who was "owner and lady of her own will [and] uses her ingeniousness and her position to get what she wants, how she wants it. [She is] corrosive, malicious, intelligent, and fun" (n.p.). Although her observations of these characteristics are absolutely correct, her perception of these traits as "almost feminist" elements of the play is highly debatable.[44] Nevertheless, Miró's thorough study of the play, integral knowledge of its plot, and profound understanding of the protagonist is made evident in her skillful execution of Lope's original verse, supplemented masterfully with twentieth-century cinematic conventions.

Many of Lope's original verses are cut from Miró's film, though sometimes they are compensated for by focusing on a certain character's facial expression or widening the camera angle to enhance the viewer's perspective, rendering some utterances obsolete. Such is the case with Diana's soliloquy offered above (III.8, vv. 2656–2671). Like the 1981 adaptation before it, the protagonist's *romances* are completely left out. Instead, a close-up of Diana allows spectators to view the character as she noticeably struggles to defiantly hold back her tears. As opposed to the 1981 version that removes the sequence entirely so as to not compromise the characterization of the strong leading lady, Miró's adaptation provides audiences with a visual depiction of the difficulties the character has maintaining her composure, thus emphasizing her emotional strength. The brief moment greatly enriches Diana's characterization as a strong willed, yet still very human character.

Along the same lines, although executed slightly differently, is Miró's inclusion of Diana's soliloquized sonnet in Act I (vv. 325–338), which I have established could have been omitted from the 1981 version to characterize Diana as a more serious, less infatuated countess. The sonnet is left in its entirety in Miró's version, but is recited as an off-screen narration, heard while Diana goes to greet Teodoro in the courtyard (00:09:20). From an artistic standpoint, the inclusion of this reflective moment simultaneously engages audiences and humanizes the protagonist, as spectators are given the sensation of hearing her thoughts. Additionally, the voice-over removes the need for Diana to be alone on the set while the soliloquy is being pronounced, as is indicated by Lope's stage direction. Additionally, it is also interesting to note that Diana's fits of jealous rage against Marcela (I.7, vv. 325-38; II.10, vv. 1580–1591) and her utterance of "aside from being a woman / subject to every error" (I.13, vv. 808–809) are also left completely intact in this adaptation (00:21:30). Clearly, as evidenced by the film's enthusiastic critical reception in both academic and popular cultures and its financial profitability, Miró's version has set a standard for Lope adaptations that has yet to be matched, much less surpassed. More interestingly, as Wheeler (2012) asserts, is the impact Miró's film has had on its source text, which has now "been over-identified with the director at the expense of the playwright" (297).[45] Consequently, after the release of the film, many seasoned literary and theatrical critics now include *El perro del hortelano* within the category of feminist Spanish literature.[46] *El perro del hortelano* (1996), therefore, has proven itself to be an authentic tour de force of Spanish cinematography, even with Lope's characterization of Diana largely unaltered.

What Miró also accomplishes by including these moments is, like in the case of the post-*Transición* adaptations of *La viuda valenciana*, marking a milestone in the evolution of Spanish popular culture in which there is no longer a drive to overcompensate for the dictatorial repression as it had done in the 1980s. By the mid-1990s, the drastic measures taken to ensure the depiction of an era-appropriate female protagonist were no longer as necessary as they had been a decade prior. This is quite possibly the result of the enduring stability of Spain's political climate that suggested that the democratic system of government would prevail long term. As such, it is logical that the early 1980s adaptations of works such as *La moza de cántaro* (1981), *El perro del hortelano* (1981), and *La viuda valenciana* (1983) were careful to avoid a tone reminiscent to that of conservative Francoist ideology by explicitly introducing female protagonists that were representative of the progressive social attitudes that predominated the immediate post-Franco period. Once these types of embellishments ceased to create such a shocking spectacle for audiences, fewer efforts were put into changing the characters so drastically. In the following section, I will examine what strategies, beyond the characterization of the protagonists, were used in their post-1975 adaptations to set these films and television episodes apart from the previous film and television manifestations of the same titles.

## ARTISTIC REACTIONS TO PREVIOUS ADAPTATIONS

José Álvarez Junco (2016) asserts that the "grand narrative" of Spain's imperial past that attempted to utilize a historical paradigm "with pretensions to hegemony" began to die a slow death that began in November 1975 along-side Francisco Franco and did not end until the signing of the Constitution in 1978 (31). Consequently, he goes on to argue, official national symbols associated with his nationalist narrative—namely the Catholic Monarchs' yoke and arrows crest, the red and yellow Spanish flag, and the national anthem—became, to varying degrees, stigmatized cultural artifacts that were closely linked with the dictatorship in the collective Spanish imagination.[47] Luis Moreno-Caballud (2018) would later refer to this process as a "cultural democratization" which contributed to establishing Spanish cultural products as pertaining to "cultures of anyone" in order to foster "collective intelligence" during the democratic age (4). As this volume has previously established, many scholars have argued that, along with the crest, flag, and anthem, Lope de Vega was another national symbol claimed by the dictator-ship to support his nationalist ideology. Such arguments represent a common fallacy that cultural scholars must avoid. Elevating Lope's presence during the dictatorship to that of a national symbol used to legitimize the regime is to give more importance to the Golden Age author during this period than is accurate. What is true, however, is that the post-Francoist entertainment industry certainly took strides to culturally democratize mass media outlets, since they had been so restricted during the previous decades. The effect that this cultural democratization of national symbolism had on film and televi-sion was often manifested in a hypercorrection of the artistic suppression experienced during the dictatorship. As such, gratuitous nudity, sexually explicit sequences, and profane language became commonplace on Spanish screens during the late 1970s and 1980s to the extent that they gave the term *españolada* an entirely new meaning.[48] Naturally, even manifestations of Golden Age literary works were susceptible to these trends.

No piece of Golden Age Spanish literature would naturally fit into this new television and film culture due to the radical sociopolitical differences brought forth over time. Moreover, the association between the historical period and Franco's regime that had been cemented during the 40 years of the dictatorship's duration had, as discussed above, made television and film producers wary of creating programs that represented the early modern time period. Television viewers who still harbored a taste for traditional adapta-tions of classical Spanish theater would be catered to with programs like the revamped *Estudio 1* and its spinoff *El teatro* that continued to transmit filmed stage performances of Golden Age plays onto the small screen well into the 1980s. Meanwhile, more progressive directors and screenwriters saw an opportunity to attempt to make Golden Age literature a part of the modern popular culture movement, at least on television. Thus, the idea to dedicate an entire miniseries to female picaroons—a literary figure that had been com-pletely absent in the 13-episode series *El pícaro* (1974–1975)—resurfaced in

1982, after having been rejected by TVE years earlier. With the participation of 6 film directors and over 40 actors, *Las pícaras* debuted on April 8, 1983.[49]

Again, one must consider the sociopolitical context of this time in recent Spanish history. The PSOE had just won the general elections in December 1982 and a leading PSOE figure, Fernando Castedo Álvarez, managed the television station in the months leading up to his political party's victory. As Julio Montero and Teresa Ojer (2018) assure us, TVE was very aware of its critical position in propelling the *Transición* throughout Spanish society and was determined to engage the increasingly liberal masses by implementing gradually progressive programming (100). Live variety shows and game shows had been intermittently introduced into TVE's program schedule since the early 1970s, but their popularity, along with many other original TVE shows, had plateaued by the end of the decade. By 1979, most of these types of programs had been canceled due to low ratings (Montero and Ojer, 2018, 115). Taking heed from international television shows and the "boom" of weekly tabloid magazines that generated hype by publishing scandalous stories about national and international celebrities, TVE realized the importance of "shock value" to keeping its audiences tuned in to its programs. The television of the post-1982 socialist era, Charo Lacalle (2018) observed, is defined by a heightened degree of eroticism and new, more risqué series were frequent additions to TVE's lineup, in stark contrast to the "prudery of Francoism" (620).

In response to the new entertainment trends in early 1980s Spain, Francisco Regueiro's contribution to *Las pícaras* went far beyond simply adjusting dialogues or suppressing certain scenes of *La viuda valenciana* to differentiate his adaptation of Lope's text from its Francoist predecessor. Instead, advertised as a "free adaptation," the progressive director created and distributed a total perversion of the Golden Age play. Forfeiting any semblance of a coherent plot, Regueiro's version of the drama hardly *adapts* Lope's play at all, but rather includes some elements of the original—such as character names and the overall concept of a woman breaking sexual moral codes—in a completely different series of events.[50] Regueiro's objective in making the episode, therefore, seems to have been simply to join together a collection of loosely—if at all—related sequences to saturate the episode with provocative, shocking visual material designed to test the limits of postmodern acceptance and tolerance in visual culture.

Leonarda's maid Julianilla, for instance, is a boy in disguise who, in addition to engaging in sex acts with the protagonist, also develops a sexual relationship with a male African prisoner (whose role in the episode is never made clear). Furthermore, the men brought into Leonarda's chambers to sleep with her are outfitted with a phallic-shaped headdress that covers their faces. One of these men is, unbeknownst to him, led to the chambers of a female African servant to gratify her instead of the beautiful young widow. Additional signs of the director and producers' eagerness to implement elements into the episode that would have been absolutely off limits a decade earlier are moments like a cardinal being portrayed by a very young, albeit extremely eloquent, child, who lies leisurely on a sofa while nuns and priests attend to him, and the repetitive singing of a reverse counting nursery rhyme in colloquial Valencian (00:05:50; 00:07:25; 00:54:15).

The song in question, "Little apples," is a children's song that counts backward from five as apples fall from a tree. Although the song appears three times in the episode, including being sung over the closing credits, it does not bear any significance to the play or its televised adaptation, nor is it present in the textual witnesses of Lope's original. As such, its two functions in the episode appear to be (1.) as stated above, to emphasize Leonarda's youth, and (2.) to create the illusion of an authentic Valencian setting.[51] As one of Franco's ideals for national unity revolved around Spaniards speaking only one Spanish language, the minority language would most likely not have been afforded such a prominent position had the episode aired during his regime.

The aforementioned elements were, I believe, counter-reactionary measures against Franco's censorship used to demonstrate that Spanish television had entered into a more modern aesthetic and thematic era, which was executed at the expense of Lope's original. As opposed to the censorship's criteria in the early days of Francoism, literary value was no consideration for the 1983 audience, as is demonstrated by the warm reception provided by the press of the time. A April 28, 1983, review of the episode printed in *El País*, for example, praised the play's innovative approach to the adaptation, which the reviewer likened to the aesthetic of Luis Buñuel's films, suggesting that the episode marked a before and after in TVE, adding that "one had to rub his eyes in disbelief: 'is it possible that this is TVE?' Owing as much to the, occasionally exceptional, quality of the images as well as to its sexual and oneiric charge, the holy chastity of our small screens was torn asunder" (66). The reviewer even went on to congratulate Regueiro for being able to successfully "destroy and glorify a text by Lope de Vega, but also . . . destroy some taboos that had remained on TVE" (66). In direct opposition to what other scholars have argued about Lope adaptations being used for ideological purposes during the dictatorship, this adaptation—and the press's response to it—demonstrates that the clearest example of moralistic manipulation of one of his dramas occurred after the Franco regime was no longer in control of TVE.

A 1983 issue of Spanish tabloid *Interviú* that was published the same week as the release of the episode dedicated an entire three-page spread to Regueiro's *La viuda valenciana* but did not even address the content of the adaptation, much less its literary roots (70–73). Instead, the article "Cristina

Marsillach's first nude scene" lived up to its title by including two full-page stills of the actress appearing topless in the episode, along with three smaller images of the nude sequences. The accompanying text only complements the "naturalism" and bravery with which the actress performed the nude scenes (72). Clearly, Regueiro had his thumb on the pulse of what was important to his audience: content had become secondary to spectacle.

Despite stripping the work of any seventeenth-century conventions and distorting the plot beyond recognition, Regueiro's production is to be applauded for its attempt at merging past with present to promote an interest in and appreciation for Lope de Vega's work. As Glenn Jellenik (2017) has argued, transmedia adaptations should necessarily be responses to dynamic cultural conditions, given that, in essence, they are "different approaches to processing a changing world" (38). Timothy Corrigan (2017) develops this idea further, maintaining that "filmmaking offers the same expressive and creative freedom as writing" (29). Let us also not overlook the fact that, like many of Lope's plays, a great deal of scholars have considered *La viuda valenciana* a transmedia adaptation of a *novella* by Matteo Bandello.[52] In fact, in terms of Robert Stam's (2012) criteria for assessing adaptations from a perspective of "comparative stylistics," which encourages us to question "to what extent are the source [text] and the film adaptation innovative . . . and if they are innovative, are they innovative in the same way" (86), Regueiro's production is indisputably a solid contribution to Lope's filmography. According to Teresa Ferrer Valls's interpretation of the original play, despite her return to orthodox behavior in the denouement, Leonarda's conduct was innovative during her time in that it went contrary to the quotidian reality and prescribed behavior assigned to her by the day's moralists (46). Likewise, Regueiro's emphasis on Leonarda's promiscuity in his adaptation, as we have seen expressed in the aforementioned article in *El País*, was similarly innovative.

By taking precisely the opposite approach to the adaptation process as Regueiro's episode, the adaptors of *La moza del cántaro* (1981) also managed to create an equally different type of production to distance their adaptation from its 1954 predecessor; again, this was done to align the production aesthetically with the ideological undercurrents of its time.[53] Although not quite to the same degree as the 1983 adaptation of *La viuda valenciana*, Rey's *La moza de cántaro* was, despite not being advertised as such, another "free adaptation" that greatly modified Lope's text. Beyond completely recharacterizing the protagonist, Doña María, Rey also incorporated various folkloric songs by moving the central setting of the play to a typical *mesón* that many townspeople frequented to be entertained while they ate and drank. Effectively, Rey transformed Lope's drama into a 1950s *españolada* that exalted an idyllic, cheerful Spanish past that could not be further from the tone of the original.

Such a cinematographic approach was an exemplary manifestation of the director's filmmaking philosophy that he defined in a 1929 interview by affirming that "I firmly believe that without a film industry there is no nation. Currently, the filmmaker is the most effective medium of national expression. Therefore, every state has been preoccupied with encouraging and favoring it, giving it is own characteristics" (Marquina, 1929, n.p.). In other words, Rey saw film not as a "mirror" of a country's reality, but rather as a living image of what the nation should strive to be, in addition to spotlighting its values and ideologies for international audiences to admire. Surprisingly, even though it was released during a time in which the topic of national identity and patriotism permeated popular culture and were encouraged by the government of the time, the film neither impressed audiences nor censors.[54]

Whereas Florián Rey's version modifies Lope's text to a nearly unrecognizable degree, the 1981 adaptation is among the strictest in terms of its reproduction of the original text. In an unusual technique for *Estudio 1*, which had taken great strides in its inception to avoid resembling a series of recorded theater performances, its *La moza de cántaro* (1981) embraces and exaggerates the theatricality of the drama with its props and decorations. The windows and doors painted into the background, for example, are obviously not functional, a fact that is made increasingly evident by the characters entering and exiting scenes from the sides of the soundstage. Moreover, title cards displaying "Lope de Vega's *La moza de cántaro* Act I/II/III" appear during the intermissions that coincide perfectly with the division of the action in the original. As opposed to the 1954 adaptation, in which added folk songs and dancing are a frequent occurrence in accordance to the original, the only singing in this version occurs during the wedding that takes place in the drama's final scene. Even in this situation, a group of four gentlemen simply walk across the visual field, lightly strumming on a guitar and singing Lope's verses "in the village of Madrid / Leonor and Martín wed / bulls run and reeds are played with" (III.23, vv. 2559–2561; 01:37:40).[55] Clearly, the episode's producers in no way desired for their interpretation of the play to even remotely remind audiences of the drama's treatment during Francoism.

Although attempting to offer audiences as authentic of an experience as possible by respecting Lope's text to the letter was hardly an innovation of the early 1980s adaptations, it does seem to have been the preferred production strategy from the end of the dictatorship until 1983. Although *Porfiar hasta morir* (1981), *El despertar a quien duerme* (1981), and *El perro del hortelano* (1981) all cut more of Lope's verses than *La moza de cántaro* (1981), they resemble the latter by highlighting the original theatricality of the dramas using minimalist cinematography and maintaining virtually the entirety of the seventeenth-century text. Most of the textual omissions seem to be made as courtesy to modern audiences, as most of the suppressed verses

contain either archaic language or obscure classical references and metaphors. Nevertheless, in the case of *El perro del hortelano* (1981), it does seem
that screenwriters, directors, and actors were careful to try to avoid the harsh
criticism that the 1966 adaptation faced in the press for its poor recitation of
Lope's poetry. A reviewer in *ABC* described the speaking parts as "kind of a
race and in a hurry to get the lines out," and ridiculing the actors for putting
on "period frippery [so as to] give themselves an unsuspected importance . . .
to put on a play, not to perform it" (94). Taking these criticisms into consideration, *Estudio 1* made sure to assign the leading roles to televised theater
veterans Concha Cuetos and Manuel Gallardo, who had both been starring
in Golden Age television adaptations since the 1960s. Despite the fact that
the only press the adaptation received was negative due to poor planning
on TVE's behalf, the impeccable recitation of Lope's original verses shows
that the dialogues were certainly a priority in this production and somewhat
redeem Lope's play from the possible negative reputation it might have garnered from the 1966 version.

When Miró set out to create her own adaptation of *El perro del hortelano*
(1996), she aimed to correct the errors of the past that had made the previous
televised adaptations so unpopular with audiences and the press. In an interview with *El País*, the director and screenwriter admitted that her first priority, unlike the early 1980s adaptation, was to distance her production from
its predecessors "by making an adaptation that is not at all like a theatrical
performance [which] had not been done until now" (Muñoz, 1996, 47). Her
goal was for audiences to, at least to some degree, disregard the theatrical
roots of the work while watching her interpretation. To achieve this objective,
Miró did away with soundstages and fabricated settings, preferring to film
on location in an actual palace in Sintra, Portugal that is visually reminiscent
of an Italian Renaissance palace, which respects Lope's original setting in a
palace in Naples.[56] This decision allowed for the use of elaborate, colorful,
even grandiose interior and exterior shots that highlighted the plot's noble
setting and created a beautiful aesthetic for spectators to enjoy. Furthermore,
by moving the action into a setting that visually transported spectators to a
different time and place so effectively, the director believed that she was
paying homage to the Golden Age playwright and using his literary strategy
to connect past and present. As she told journalist Rosana Torres (1997),
by setting plays in different times and places, his social critiques "seem
less scandalous [because] he is talking about what is going on around him,"
which allowed him to clandestinely comment upon his own societal realities
(n.p.). By being constantly pictorially reminded of the time period in which
the play was written, *El País*'s Diego Galán (2004) argues, Miró was able to
efficiently transmit a powerful message with her production, that "feelings
don't belong to any century" (n.p.).

Although Miró and Galán's explanations of the importance of the authentic setting are quaint and somewhat true, we cannot accept them as the most effective justifications for this artistic decision. Every other Lope adaptation ever produced in Spain also provided a great deal of visual cues to remind viewers of the centuries that separated them from the action of the film or episode, so it could be argued that they all attempt to demonstrate that human emotions don't pertain to just one time period. After all, as Laura Vidler (2014) has properly observed, one of the principal objectives of reviving works from previous time periods has always been to highlight "a gaze of the unrepeatable by way of the eternally reproducible" that demonstrates the continuous thread of human experience (124). It seems, therefore, as though Miró's objective, far from camouflaging any potentially scandalous social criticism, was simply to break with the techniques used by the previous adaptations of the play of using unimpressive studio sets, so as to offer spectators an awe-inspiring spectacle to accompany the action. This is especially evident by Miró's recurrent use of exterior shots to take full advantage of film's virtually unlimited visual resources that are not available to theater producers.[57] For example, the first dialogue between the lovers takes place as the characters stroll through an exterior courtyard (I.9, vv. 511–600).

Likewise, the scene that concludes the first act in Lope's play (I.19, vv. 1023–1186), during which the two star-crossed lovers share a long conversation about the social barriers to their love, also takes place in an exterior setting as Teodoro rows the two of them in a boat in the palace moat (00:28:44–00:35:12). The ability for spectators to appreciate the immensity of the palace from both inside and outside emphasizes Diana's elevated social status and authority while also eclipsing the poorly constructed sets used for *Estudio 1*'s previous adaptations of the drama. Furthermore, the artistic decision to "air out" the play in this manner creates an elevated form of realism, which Sánchez Noriega (2005) has identified as the principle benefit of this filmic technique, given modern film audiences' insistence upon increasingly realistic visual experiences (17). This authentic quality of the spectacle is likely another reason why Miró's film has widely been considered the only successful modern film adaptation of a Golden Age drama.

Even though her risky endeavor to use such an elaborate staging repelled many potential investors, it was praised by film critics when the film debuted. In his article in a 1996 edition of the magazine *Nosferatu*, film and literary critic Miguel García Posada (1997) declared that "Pilar Miró has made a wonderful spectacle . . . full of color [and] what seemed impossible came true" (n.p.). The critic further elaborated on the possible influence this film could have on Golden Age literature's presence in the postmodern world, indicating that

Miró has accomplished a product with exquisite results and it makes us forget the awful pieces that have been made whilst attempting to adapt the classics. We leave the cinema reconciled with our filmmakers. We leave behind the good-intentioned yet poorly-executed experiences from before . . . new expectations are now ahead of us, a horizon is opened the we believed closed forever. (n.p.)

Contrary to such predictions, the film did not spark newfound interest in Spain's classical theater adaptations on the big screen. At any rate, such praise from García Posada, a Hispanic philologist specializing in poetry, is especially impressive, given that Miró made the decision to keep the seventeenth-century verse in the film, a choice for which audiences had ruthlessly condemned Guerrero Zamora's *Fuenteovejuna* (1972).

Although Miró's unconventional staging of the drama proved that *El perro del hortelano* was not only suitable for low budget, disinterested television adaptations, her insistence on maintaining Lope's verse provoked apprehension in possible investors, who feared this decision would jeopardize its financial performance in cinemas. These naysayers made Miró acutely aware of this risk, as she recounted to Diego Muñoz (1996), they "they called me crazy for wanting to bring a classic to the screen, especially in verse" (47). Again breaking with the 1981 adaptors' approach, the casting directors of Miró's film did not place veteran Golden Age theater actors in the lead roles. Neither Emma Suárez (Diana) nor Carmelo Gómez (Teodoro) had ever acted in films or television shows in which the speaking parts were recited in verse.[58] While discussing the challenges of working on the film with host Cayetana Guillén Cuervo during a pre- and post-screening colloquium on the adaptation, Suárez discussed that this was one of the most difficult obstacles to overcome in her portrayal of the protagonist, stating, "we worked a ton on the verse, we worked with Alicia Hermida" (00:03:26). Hermida, veteran TVE actress and acting coach, was able to instruct the actors in reciting the verse properly, but with their own natural interpretations so as to prevent their diction from sounding too traditionally theatrical.[59]

The result of this kind of verbal delivery was that Miró's film demonstrated that the seventeenth-century speech patterns did not hinder the twentieth-century audience's understanding or enjoyment of the production. The film's Director of Photography, Javier Aguirresarobe, commended the actors' success in handling the verse, which he supported in the colloquium by repeating comments he had overheard at the premiere: "Ten minutes into it people said that they started to understand the verse as if they were speaking normally" (00:29:37).[60] Aguirresarobe even went so far as to attribute the success of the film to its use of verse. Whether or not he is correct in assuming so, it is certain that due to the actors' ability to make the verse intelligible to modern viewers, Miró's adaptation managed to find a place for an authentic Lope play in modern Spanish cinema culture, a feat that has, to date, yet to be matched, despite its noteworthy success.

Following in Miró's footsteps and also taking a Lope adaptation in a completely different direction than its 1980s counterpart, Manuel Iborra debuted his version of *La dama boba* (2006) 10 years after *El perro del hortelano* made cinema history. In an interview with *Fotogramas*, the director expressed what motivated him to take on the project, saying "it is shocking to me that, after the experience Pilar Miró had with *El perro del hortelano*, nothing similar has been done. I have always really liked the theater and Lope de Vega and it was a marvelous new adventure to bring one of his works to cinemas" (Pando, 2016, 128). This quote, in my opinion, reveals Iborra's motive for creating the adaptation; he sought the financial compensation and national acclaim that Miró had secured a decade earlier. While it is possible that he truly desired to contribute to Spain's collection of big-screen Lope adaptations, it is clear that he had the potential awards in mind from the onset of production. There are many aspects of the film that corroborate this claim.

The film contains many stylistic elements that suggest that he modeled his approach to the adaptation after that of Miró. As in *El perro del hortelano* (1996), *La dama boba* (2006) also maintains Lope's verse. Additionally, Iborra, like Miró before him, did not rely on the participation of actors who boasted a lot of experience with versed theater. Instead, probably in an attempt to make a truly comical *comedia*, almost all of the actors hired for the production had mainly performed in the humor genre.[61] The production even copied Miró's decision to hire Alicia Hermida as an acting coach to guide the actors in their delivery of the verse, which Iborra believed—as he revealed in an interview with the newspaper *El País*—"it does not have to be archaic, it can be lively, vibrant, and exciting" (2006, n.p.). Hoping that his actors' recitation of the verses would create a similar effect with spectators as that of *El perro del hortelano* (1996), José Coronado was quoted by the same newspaper as preparing audiences for a "verse that was neither enthusiastic nor solemn and that made it to viewers [with hopes that] after five minutes they would forget the verse and laugh along with it" (n.p.). The attempt to create a popular culture phenomenon like Miró had done a decade prior could not have been made more obvious by the filmmakers and cast.

Nevertheless, critics vehemently disagreed with the director and Coronado; the press's reaction to Iborra's film was strikingly different to that of Miró's production. Whereas the 1996 adaptation was congratulated for its precision in executing the rhymed lines, José Luis Martínez Montalbán made it very clear that he was not impressed with the manner in which the verses were recited in Iborra's film. In the January–June 2006 edition of *Cine para leer*, the film reviewer wrote that

Iborra's insistence on transferring a *comedia* by Lope to a screenplay is revealed as a total failure and it's result is a bland film, with no ambition, that is born dead. Besides, the arguable pretension to maintain the verse shocks spectators who are not accustomed to hearing it and the scarce preparation of the actors to say it, leaving us with a highly disappointing finished product. (n.p.)

In a complete reversal of fates, Lope's *La dama boba* had gone from being highly praised in its 1960s and 1980s adaptations to being extremely unpopular in the twenty-first century. The only positive reinforcement the film received at all was for its beautiful sceneries and implied feminism perceived by some to be the function of the protagonists, as exemplified above. Unfortunately for modern Golden Age enthusiasts, any place in Spanish popular culture that had been forged by Miró in the 1990s had disappeared before—or, perhaps, because of—the release of Iborra's adaptation.

## THE CONTEMPORANEITY OF LOPE'S DRAMAS

Following suit with the post-dictatorial push to emphasize the concept that being Spanish was not necessarily antithetical to being modern, almost all of the efforts made on behalf of the producers of the adaptations studied in this chapter centered on convincing audiences that the works were inherently relatable to contemporary audiences. To do so, the democratic adaptors employed adaptation techniques that were far bolder than those actions taken to adapt the works during the dictatorship. I have mentioned that films like *El mejor alcalde, el rey* (1974) had already begun to incorporate aesthetic elements that foreshadowed the cinematographic style of the *Transición* and beyond, but it did not anticipate the more drastic alterations that would be made in the following decade. Likewise, regarding Lope adaptations on television, steps had been taken by TVE to spark an interest in the plays broadcasted by accompanying the episodes with brief introductions that highlighted the play's historical context and literary importance as early as the 1960s. The episode of *Los milagros del desprecio* (*Teatro de siempre*, 1967), for instance, begins with an off-screen narration that highlights the work's importance as one of Lope's most characteristic *comedias*, adding that "Lope de Vega was in his best moment when he wrote *Los milagros del desprecio*" (00:00:00–00:01:11).[62] *Estudio 1* would later adopt this technique with its emissions of Lope's dramas in the years that would follow. *La dama boba* (1969), for example, begins with a lengthy introduction by veteran actor and host Ángel Losada, in which he exalts Lope's genius and inexhaustible sources of inspiration before transitioning to an introduction of the drama with

Tonight, *Estudio 1*, with Spring having recently sprung, is pleased to offer you *La dama boba*: a piece with joyous entanglement and that is fun, that Lope de Vega wrote for the theater around the year 1613. We will see in it the contrast between two feminine personalities: Finea and Nise, the silly girl and the smart girl, so that by the end we will not be able to determine which one is truly silly and which one is truly smart. The play ends with a wedding, yes, as these love-story *comedias* usually do, but beforehand many things will happen. There are two ladies and two beaus and there is, especially, the marvelous and in-depth study of a character who, over the course of the three acts, evolves, baffles, and surprises, until the play concludes with a brilliant and happy final solution. (00:01:54)

Perhaps it is not surprising that the producers of the show found it necessary to justify their programming choices and promote the episodes in this fashion, considering *Estudio 1*, voted as the most popular Spanish show by 43 percent of participants in 1964, had fallen in the ratings to sixth place by 1969 (Montero Díaz and Ojer, 2018, 105–109).[63]

Instead of rewriting Lope's texts, pre-democratic adaptors utilized the mechanism of introducing the episodes with a brief narration describing their entertaining qualities for modern audiences. These mechanisms had evolved into increasingly creative ways for TVE to advocate for the contemporaneity of Lope's dramas. *La viuda valenciana* (1973) offers us an extremely novel example for how producers were desperate to convince viewers of Golden Age relatability in the twentieth century. The episode begins with electric guitar music before a metadramatic moment in which the actors and directors perform an out-of-character skit that highlights how Lope's play is equally as relevant and entertaining as any modern production. During the skit, the actors are seen rehearsing for filming a different adaptation when the director interrupts them to announce that the episode in question has been canceled. Disappointed, they begin to discuss alternatives when the following exchange occurs:

ACTOR 3: After all, what we're trying to do is make a fun, very spicy, very interesting, and very entertaining play and all that, aren't we?
DIRECTOR: And with a great cinematic feel.
ACTOR 3: Well, then, you'll be fine with it having a television feel, huh?
DIRECTOR: Yeah, I wouldn't mind that.
ACTOR 3: Well, I just read a play that gathers all of those features and we wouldn't have any problem with the author.
DIRECTOR: Hey, hey, hey . . . and who is this author?
*Crowd gets silent. ACTOR 3 exclaims proudly, almost shouting*:
ACTOR 3: Lope de Vega!
*Crowd gets restless, annoyed, obviously does not like the idea. Close-ups show eye rolling, etc.*

*Actor 3:* Yes, a classic, a classic . . . a classic that is much more interesting and more fun than the majority of current authors.
*Director:* Well, we'll just have to . . .
*Actress 2:* (Interrupting.) And what's it called?
*Actor 3:* (Shouting again.) *La viuda valenciana!*

   *Actress 2 pauses, looking perplexed, contemplating the suggestion. Camera zooms in on her. Next shot is of her dressed in early modern garb behind a title card that reads "La viuda valenciana by Lope de Vega."*

Such an insistence on the modern appeal of a seventeenth-century play is all the more significant because the rest of the episode's script adheres strictly to Lope's original text. As Esther Fernández correctly affirms, the inclusion of such a presentation attempts to serve two purposes: (1) to demonstrate that Golden Age plays do not necessarily have to take place in an authentic theatrical setting to be enjoyable and (2) it endeavors to demystify the hesitancy that the average television viewer might have toward the classics ("Lope de Vega" 19).[64] I must add, however, that the sequence also attempts to make the film look fashionably attractive and modern to young viewers. The continuing decline of Lope adaptations on TVE that would be seen over the following decade would, however, call into question the effectiveness of this modernizing technique.

   Either as a result of the inefficiency of these types of introductions to inspire audiences' interest in classical theater adaptations or a simple response to the dynamic audiovisual trends of the times, the next version of *La viuda valenciana* (1983) to be aired on TVE, as we have seen above, chose to *show* and not *tell* audiences how a Lope play could be made to fit into modern popular culture. The only certainty in this regard is that TVE was eager to address criticisms it had faced in the press over the past several years about its choice of broadcasts. Columnists Enrique del Corral and José Baget Herms, for example, had recently expressed frustration with TVE, the former arguing that the station should be more keen on providing experimental programs as opposed to playing it safe with formulas that had been successful in the past, and the latter agreeing with him, insisting that the mission of TVE should be to provide "dynamic programming, modern and adapted to the new realities" of the country (Herms, 1975, 134). The ever-increasing influx of foreign programs meant that Spanish television would have to reconsider everything from its content to stylistic choices if it was going to compete with these televised imports.

   Thus, *Las pícaras* (1983), as opposed to offering traditional renditions of Golden Age works, took any and all artistic liberties to distort the originals in order to make them appealing to audiences who were ready for something new. According to the reviews in the press, audiences greatly appreciated their efforts. The commentary in the April 18, 1983, edition of *El País* lauded TVE for breaking Spanish television orthodoxy with the episode of *La viuda valenciana* and finally broadcasting a "groundbreaking play for our television; a film that is no doubt going to create equal measures of love and hate and that, even if only for this reason, is worth being regarded as a point of no return in the history of Prado del Rey" (66).[65] Unlike critics from a decade prior, this journalist was exceptionally pleased with the disregard for Lope's version of the story, highlighting his elation upon seeing the innovative adaptation, which he indicates was achieved by "Mañas and Reguiero grabbing one of these licentious stories of Lope de Vega by the end-seam in Reguiero's script, getting increasingly disheveled in the production, and managed to add an erotic dimension to the licentiously charged original, with a super-real strength [that] is surprising" (66). Critic J. M. B. (1983) also favored the radical treatment of Lope's play, arguing that it created a space for a genuinely Spanish sociotype to be represented in modern Spanish popular culture, writing "[picaresque characters] today busy themselves with little more substance than getting out of a marriage or, for example, finding a fail-proof way of hiding a handful of *pesetas* from the authorities" (26).[66] What these reviews reveal to us is that the plays no longer fit as easily into the evolving popular culture as they had in previous sociopolitical circumstances. According to these critics, the possibility of bringing classical works into post-Francoist modernity was only successfully attainable by making drastic changes to them. If Lope's plays were going to survive in the post-Francoist collective imagination, they would have to be molded to fit Spain's new reality.

Clearly, despite being applauded by the press, this approach also proved impotent against the public indifference toward the Phoenix's masterpieces on television, as it would be over a decade before a Lope adaptation was displayed on Spanish screens again. Virtually three decades would have to pass, however, before *La viuda valenciana* would again be adapted for television. As the "making of" featurette reveals by showing excerpts from the two previous adaptations of the play, the creators were extremely aware of how TVE had handled the work in the past. In what seems to be an attempt to correct their perceived errors of the play's treatment in the other versions, Carlos Sedes's 2010 adaptation combines the techniques used in 1973 and 1983 and leaves the explicit commentary of its contemporaneity to the episode's cast and the press.[67] Leading actress Aitana Sánchez-Gijón (Leonarda) was among the cast's most prominent promoters of the modernity of the play, highlighting in an interview with RTVE that "the modernity of the chosen play really stands out; we're talking about a women who, at that time, was a widow who discovers that she doesn't want to renounce her dreams, nor her freedom, nor her sexuality" ("TVE recupera," 2010, n.p.). The actress uses this perceived modernity to encourage audiences to give the episode a chance in the featurette, asserting that "I would love for audiences to feel inspired to watch *La viuda valenciana* because I believe that they are going to find a very funny, modern text; they are going to take a jump back in time, but, of course, with a starting point, a story, some characters that transpire and breathe anxieties for freedom and satisfaction of their desires within an intriguing carnival setting" (00:01:58). In an interview with *El País*, Lola Molina, TVE's Director of Programming and Content, assured that *La viuda valenciana* "is one of the most modern pieces by Lope because 400 years ago the protagonist fought to conquer her personal freedom" (Gallo, 2010, n.p.). Despite their efforts to prove to audiences that the work could still be culturally relevant, audiences were not easy to persuade. The anticipated reboot of *Estudio 1* was not successful.[68]

TVE's marketing technique of promoting Lope plays as modern was not an original idea; it had been used for both of the post-Francoist major motion picture adaptations. Nearly 15 years earlier, Pilar Miró made sure to mention *El perro del hortelano*'s contemporary relevance in almost every promotional interview she did for the film. For instance, she remarked to Diego Galán (2004) that she was

> absolutely convinced of its efficiency and currency. . . . My victory is having demonstrated that a classic is not something rotten. The success that the film is having, both here in Spain and abroad, the seven Goya awards, and especially the reception of the audiences, are one of the greatest professional satisfactions I have had in my life. (n.p.)

According to the actress who portrayed the film's protagonist, Emma Suárez, the director encouraged the cast to act as naturally as possible in their performances in order to make the characters more culturally relatable to audiences, even at the risk of introducing anachronistic elements to the production. Reflecting on how she was concerned about acting flirty on camera by batting her eyes, she told hostess Cayetana Guillén Cuervo in a behind-the-scenes colloquium about the film, "I did it without realizing what I was doing and Pilar liked it . . . I told her, 'no way . . . that's not right for the period, how am I going to make such a progressive gesture?' and Pilar said to me, 'no, no, do it'" ("Coloquio" 00:32:20). In hindsight, Suárez realized the importance of the modern gestures and other such hints at Diana's modernity, a quality she assured the hostess was part of the central argument of the film. "The film is very current. . . . One of the features of the characters is precisely that, that she's such a vanguard, you know? She's ahead of her times," she reiterated (00:13:55).

The contemporary relatability of the play seemed to resonate well with both the press and academic critics. Journalists like García Posada (1997) considered the film the beginning of a new tradition of bringing Spain's most renowned works to the big screen, writing that "what Miró has done is something else: it's the joining together of the classics with authentically modern cinema. . . . Our classics work for the cinema, I believe they do. And if it works for a small, minor, very minor play like *El perro del hortelano* is, imagine the hit that the big texts could be. I have here a bet that is for our cinema" (n.p.). Outside of the popular culture realm, scholarly specialist in Spanish cinema José María Caparrós Lera (1992) also identified how Miró emphasized the cinematic elements of Lope's text in order to make it a true comedy for the twentieth-century audience. According to the film historian, "as Lope de Vega would have done, *El perro del hortelano* includes jokes and funny anecdotes; so fans of our times can accept the play the same way as an illiterate viewer from the Golden Age would have, without getting into its critical background, one just might be impassioned by the story and the humorous details of the action" (65). Even early modern theater scholars—often the harshest critics of modern film and television adaptations of classical works—praised Miró's adaptation for its ability to involve spectators in a reconsideration of the past in terms of the present and vice versa. According to García Santo-Tomás (2000a),

> The contact that is achieved with Golden Age theater through Pilar Miró's re-reading of it places the end-of-century audience in a situation that not only forces them to contemplate a series of codes from the past itself, but also obliges them to reformulate the conditions that determine our cultural present. The encounter of the past with the needs of the present results in the past ceasing to be the past. (59)

If one considers the uses of Lope's plays during the dictatorship alongside García Santo-Tomás's evaluation of the power of a re-reading of historical works, it becomes evident that—although likely not politically motivated—Miró's adaptation manages to appropriate a symbol once supposedly associated with Franco to new, modern cultural needs. Far from the dictatorial rhetoric of national unity and uniformity, Miró's version uses Lope de Vega's work to advocate self-realization and personal liberty.

In spite of its critical acclaim and the optimism about its potential to spawn a new age of Golden Age adaptations in modern Spanish popular culture, Miró's *El perro del hortelano* remains a cinematic anomaly to this day. The slim possibility of lightening striking twice, however, did not deter Iborra from essentially copying Miró's marketing strategy when promoting his adaptation of *La dama boba* (2006) as an old text with cultural relevance for the new millennium. In an interview with *Fotogramas*, the director discussed how one of his principal objectives in making *La dama boba* was to dismantle stereotypes about classical Spanish literature, suspiciously using Miró's exact phrasing from the previous decade to argue that "there are those who may believe that Lope or Calderón are something rotten and antiquated, but it is not so" (Pando, 2016, 128). In doing so, as he clarified to a journalist writing for a March 23, 2006, issue of *El País*, he hoped to continue Miró's project of instilling a newfound national appreciation for Golden Age drama adaptations that would culminate in a new cinematic subgenre. "If the film would work as an inspiration to have one or two classic texts made per year," he told the reporter, "it would be marvelous, because in Spain we have some stupendous texts" (n.p.). While film critics mostly ignored the movie, academics like Verena Berger (2009) did not share Iborra's optimism and specifically referenced the film's inability to involve modern spectators into the action enough for them to care about the plot (67–68).

In other words, it would appear as though Iborra failed to "constitute a familiar world produced in an unfamiliar form," which, as Wolfgang Iser (1993) reiterates, is an artist's primary responsibility (7). Simply put, cinematic devices must be used when adapting Golden Age texts to present a familiar world in dynamic ways that will pleasantly surprise audiences if they are going to make successful films. Whereas Miró's film presented a familiar unrequited love story, Iborra's *La dama boba* did not comply with this obligation as viewers did not see a familiar world reflected in this unfamiliar setting. This is likely due, in part, to the idea of true love "curing" stupidity, which is not a common literary *topos* that modern audiences can relate to, especially considering the cartoon-esque nature of the characters in the film that remove any sense of realism and relatability from the story.

I daresay that the major flaws in Iborra's film have to do with timing, aesthetics, and its inability to distance itself far enough from previous adaptation styles. In the 14 years that had passed between Miró's and Iborra's adaptations, cultural preoccupations had shifted significantly. The gender politics of the previous decade had somewhat faded in Spain's collective imagination and political debates, and there was now more public concern with other societal issues, such as the "recovery of historical memory." This topic was such a hotly debated cultural phenomenon in the mid-2000s that the Spanish government signed the *Ley de Memoria Histórica* into effect on December 26, 2007, the year following the release of Iborra's adaptation (BOE-A-2007-22296). As such, a film that promoted itself as exalting two women confronting the patriotic norms of their time was a bit tone-deaf to the current cultural fixations. In any case, it is also in questionable taste to release a film whose supposed goal is to praise independent, defiant women when the emphasis on the protagonists' features as a stubborn shrew or insufferable imbecile—as Wheeler (2012) correctly assesses—"borders on the offensive" (187). Be that as it may, Spanish cinematic feminism had transformed into a much more realistic and precise discourse that relied on more profound characters and social problems than noblewomen in a quandary about which wealthy suitor to marry, as evidenced by the fact that Almodóvar's *Volver* (2006) was the second highest grossing film of that year.[69]

Moreover, considering that *Alatriste* (2006) was the highest grossing film of 2006, it is also impossible to argue that the film's early modern setting was at all problematic. It therefore seems that the disconnect with audiences is found, in part, in the director's artistic and promotional decisions that provoked an immediate comparison to its predecessors, chiefly *El perro del hortelano*. By mimicking Miró's aesthetic too closely and not achieving the same visual quality as she did, Iborra automatically created an inferior production. Additionally, Iborra's version did not contribute any innovations as far as the adaptation style is concerned, which would undoubtedly have disappointed audiences familiar with Piró's work. Modern moviegoers, it would seem, are only willing to give adaptations of old works a chance when they can see them in a new, creative way, as they had with Miró's film in 1996. Unsurprisingly, as I will demonstrate below, the inability to generate excitement in audiences translated to very poor performance at the box office.

## CRITICAL RECEPTION AND CULTURAL IMPACT

It can be very difficult to gauge television spectatorship in Spain during and immediately after the end of Francoism. Studies on mass media in general reveal a great deal about popular culture and the public's interest in Lope adaptations. As episode guides demonstrate, despite the absence of any new Lope adaptations from 1975 to 1980, a small "boom" of Lope adaptations occurred in 1981. According to Félix Arias et al. (2018), such a fluctuation on television screens is characteristic of the first few years after the end of dictatorships as mass media outlets tend to focus their resources on producing material that is immediately responsive to the changing sociopolitical tides (350–351). The unstable political situation in which Spain found itself during this time was reflected in public television's uncertain direction with regard to its programming.

In a curious turn of events, Lope de Vega is indeed much more alive in Spanish popular and academic cultures now than he was during the Francoist dictatorship, despite what other scholars have argued. Although his televised adaptations—along with nearly all remakes of theater on Spanish screens— have almost completely vanished from regular programming schedules, his plays have led to a vast amount of public and scholarly attention in the decades following the end of the regime, mainly due to their presence in the theater.

Regarding Lope film adaptations, Pilar Miró's *El perro del hortelano*, for example, was a nominee for 12 Goya awards and winner of 7, and temporarily generated excitement for the author's plays. It was the seventh highest-earning film of 1996 and earned an astounding 165,269.789€ from 287,094 spectators during its cinematic run. When compared to Manuel Iborra, who faced a disappointing financial reality when his adaptation of *La dama boba* (2006) debuted, we can understand that the key to reviving Lope's place in the collective Spanish imagination is directly related to choosing works that respond to coetaneous realities and societal preoccupations and adapting them appropriately.[70] Lope was always able to keep his audience's attention by writing about issues that mattered to them in ways that kept them entertained and excited to see more.

Times have changed, and Lope's conservative perspective on issues such as national identity, gender roles, and politics have naturally been rendered obsolete by the passing of time; nevertheless, recent history shows us that an appropriate amount of creative license can make a Lope de Vega play a well-received popular culture artifact by viewers from a wide variety of sociopolitical and sociohistorical circumstances. What this phenomenon leads us to understand is that the playwright's name is vaguely familiar to modern television and film consumers, even though they rarely know why this name rings a bell. Outside of those films and television episodes that revolve around the author's scandalous escapades or insert original risqué material in free adaptations, as in the case of *La viuda valenciana* (1983), there is almost no public interest in creating, supporting, or consuming direct adaptations of his seventeenth-century texts. Although I am certainly not the first to recognize this nonchalant attitude, I disagree with those who have attempted to attribute it to an association between Lope and the Francoist regime. Instead, I have found that twentieth- and twenty-first-century adaptors have mostly failed to manipulate the original texts to an extent that makes their seventeenth-century themes relatable to today's societal preoccupations. The problem, therefore, lies in their inability to encode their productions properly with meaningful discourse for a modern audience. More evidence to this claim is to be found in the twenty-first-century's interest in Lope de Vega himself, as will be discussed in chapter 4.

## NOTES

1. One must keep in mind that the Spanish population had, in many ways, resigned itself to the possibility that the dictatorship would never end, even upon the death of the regime's leader. Attempts had been made to install a de facto political successor in Luis Carrero Blanco. Although Carrero Blanco did not survive until the end of Franco's life, his actual successor, Don Juan Carlos de Borbón, was expected to maintain the dictatorial *status quo*. The idea that Francoist ideology would continue to permeate Spanish politics and culture contributed, in great part, to public skepticism and uncertainty that will be explored in the following section.

2. Whereas some scholars like Omar Guillermo Encarnación (2008) have claimed that the Spanish population immediately began to democratize its sociopolitical environment after the dictator took his last breath (2), the truth is that the process of consolidating a renovated, more modern system of democratic government would be far from instant or transpicuous. Bénédict André-Bazzana (2006) exemplifies the years immediately following Franco's death to argue that Spain has manipulated its own history of an "ideal transition" to democracy in order to advance its international "self-fashioning" as a progressive, intellectual state. As he calls it, Spain has engaged in propagating a "transition myth" (15–24).

3. The issue has been brought to light several times in the press over the past couple of years. See the Letters to the editor from a August 28, 2018, edition of *El País* titled "La autocrítica sobre 'la Transición' es una asignatura pendiente," as well as Martín Caparrós (2018, n.p.), and Juan Cofiño (2018, n.p.).

4. The preoccupation of Franco's legacy and the importance of the symbolism of his remains being removed from the Valley of the Fallen is still being widely contemplated and discussed in the Spanish press. See, for example, Manuel Vicent's November 7, 2021, opinion article printed in *El País* titled "Franco todavía" and David Trueba's reflection on the exhumation on November 30, 2021, titled "Aquí es distinto," just to name a couple of examples.

5. The Partido Popular (PP), for example, has actively defied this law by not applying it—when it holds high political offices—on national, local, and regional levels. Former president of the Autonomous Community of Madrid, Esperanza Aguirre, was quoted in 2017 as saying "somos muchos los que rechazamos la 'Ley de Memoria Histórica.' Es un siniestro intento de reabrir heridas que habían cicatrizado por la voluntad de concordia" (Treceño n.p.). See also Ricard Venyes's *El estado y la memoria: Gobiernos y ciudadanos frente a los traumas de la historia* (2009).

6. It is imperative to remember that the sociocultural uniformity that Franco so desperately desired to foster in Spain had begun to unravel even in the final years of his life. His hand-selected Prime Minister and would-be successor to his sociocultural ambitions for the country, Luis Carrero Blanco, had been assassinated by the radical Basque separatist group ETA in 1973. The implementation of the Antiterrorist Law of August 1975, which specifically targeted "separatistas" alongside "comunistas," demonstrates that the central government continued to feel threatened by such organizations even after the assassination of Carrero Blanco (*BOE* 205, August 27, 1975, 18117–18120).

7. *Cañas y barro* was an adaptation of the homonymous novel by Blasco Ibáñez and *Fortunata y Jacinta* was also a televised adaptation of the novel of the same name by Benito Pérez Galdós.

8. Wheeler (2012) posits, for example, that the lack of adaptations of Lope's plays on Spanish screens—or Golden Age dramas in general—after Francoism "was most probably a consequence of the fact that, in this transitional period, Golden Age drama was often thought of as a reactionary art form that had enjoyed special treatment under Franco" (293). Ryjik (2011) concurred with this deduction, reaffirming that "durante los años de la *Transición*, la reacción a la noción de la España 'una, grande y libre,' difundida por la propaganda del régimen, llevó a un replanteamiento

y subsiguiente cuestionamiento del concepto de la nación española," which, in turn, made Lope an obsolete figure in the collective Spanish imagination (7). Bernecker and Brinkman (2004) also attribute this indifference to the *comedia* to the fact that the traditionalist and Catholic vision of Spain, the pillars of Lope's works that the dictatorship found so appropriate for public diffusion, lost all authority and pretensions of validity after Franco's death (6–7). Bayliss (2015) reaffirms these assumptions by considering the radical changes to the concept of "españolidad" during the years immediately following Franco's death as a catalyst for "un despojo de los iconos y símbolos (como Lope de Vega) propagados durante la dictadura" (717).

9. Tirso's *El burlador de Sevilla* (*Teatro Estudio* 1976), Lope's *El mejor alcalde, el rey* (*Teatro Estudio* 1977), Calderón's *Don Gil de las calzas verdes* (*Estudio 1* 1978) and *La dama duende* (*Estudio 1* 1979).

10. It should be noted that the film adaptation of Arturo Pérez-Reverte's *Las aventuras del capitán Alatriste*, unlike the source text, does not feature Lope de Vega as a character, though a brief moment of a performance of *El perro del hortelano* takes place in the background of one scene.

11. LOGSE is an abbreviation for the "Ley Orgánica General del Sistema Educativo de España," a Francoist incentive from 1970 that sought to further cement the religious nature of Spanish public-school curricula in official legislation.

12. For a fascinating commentary on the suppression of theatrical production and protest strategies embedded into Francoist theater, see Marina Ruiz Cano and Anne Laure Feuillastre's introduction to *El teatro de protesta: Estrategias y estéticas contestatarias en España* (13-20).

13. Although the productions were initially the target of hostile attacks on the concept of reviving such an antiquated artform and the first season received mixed reviews after its debut, the Compañía Nacional had become a popular and well-liked institution by the end of the 1980s.

14. To date, Lope de Vega is the author whose works have been most adapted by the Compañía Nacional. Calderón comes close with 22 adaptations, although significantly less of his titles have been performed because many are repeated season after season. The Compañía's complete production history is available on their official website: http://teatroclasico.mcu.es/categoria/programacion/por-autor/.

15. The *destape* era was a moment that began during the final years of the dictatorship in which more risqué visual and verbal content was beginning to make its way onto Spanish screens and in the press. Far from being a revolutionary movement rebelling against the previous repression during the more rigorous censorship of early Francoism, it was sanctioned by the regime as a way of integrating Spanish popular culture into the European mainstream. See Rodríguez-Díaz and Maestre (2015, 98–103).

16. *Homosexuality* enjoyed a particularly prominent presence in the popular culture of the *Transición*, likely as a reactionary topic to combat the dictatorship's opinions of homosexual people—and, naturally, homosexual acts—as dangerously detrimental to Spanish society. From 1954 to 1970, the *Ley de Vagos y Maleantes* established the right of the government to maintain rigorous vigilance and control over homosexual individuals, who were likened to pimps and other sexual deviants in

this ordinance. In 1970, the law was modified and renamed as the *Ley de Peligrosidad y Rehabilitación*, which, in theory, decriminalized homosexuality, but maintained penalties for homosexual acts among men (female homosexuality was completely ignored), on the basis that it constituted a "social threat."

17. As Isolina Ballesteros (2001) reminds us, women tended to be depicted as eager to leave the domestic space and be incorporated into the public sphere. He interprets such a portrayal as a denouncement of their role as victims of the dictatorship, and began to redefine their position in post-Francoist society in films as early as *Asignatura pendiente* (1976), *Los placeres ocultos* (1976), and *Cambio de sexo* (1976). Nevertheless, she argues, it was Miró who firmly established a real effort to bring feminine desire and sexuality to the forefront with her 1980 film *Gary Cooper que estás en los cielos* (178). Two years later, Almodóvar continued this tradition and broadened it to include homosexuality in his *El laberinto de los deseos* (1982).

18. The issue of feminism and feminist movements in Spain is quite complex. Some scholars, like Grażyna Grudzińska (2009), posit that there have only been three waves of Spanish feminist movements: the first, its initial organization (1975–1979), the schism between radical and socialist feminists (1979–1982), and its disintegration and failure (1982–1985) that saw an end to Spanish feminism (150–152). Others, however, like Barbara Zecchi and Jaqueline Cruz (2004), argue that a timeline is irrelevant, preferring to focus on tendencies that have spanned throughout Spanish feminism since the end of the dictatorship, ranging from disorganized activist groups, women's associations that are affiliated with political parties, and actual feminist political parties (169). Considering the fact that the Partido Feminista de España—organized in 1975 and officially incorporated as a political party in 1981—is still active in annual conferences and its leader, Lidia Falcón, continues to produce brief theatrical productions of a feminist nature, I am inclined to agree with Cruz and Zecchi in that, at least to some degree, there is a feminist current that has continued to thrive in Spanish popular culture since the 1980s.

19. The same interpretation of the plot of *La dama boba* was expressed virtually verbatim by López López (2017, 87).

20. See Ballesteros (2001, 175–178) and Caparrós Lera (1983, 353) for more on this patriarchal-oriented eroticism in the Spanish cinema of late Francoism. According to the latter, the masculine sexual prowess highlighted by these films, combined with scenes of bullfighting and other traditional Spanish customs, created a series of *españoladas* that would characterize the Spanish cinema of the *Transición* and beyond (353). As Catalan screenwriter Domenich Font (1976) observed a year after Franco's death, it was in the State's best interest to create the illusion of increased sexual freedom in popular culture during these years in order to maintain and perpetuate the dictatorship's moral principles and camouflage the "pobredumbre social y política del actual sistema de poder" (321). Whether or not this latter period of *destape* was an effective sociopolitical distraction for the regime is extremely arguable, mainly because the sexual material on display was, in accordance with Francoist ideology, strictly patriarchal and confirmative to conservative masculine fantasies geared toward defining and exhibiting the concept of the *macho ibérico*.

21. Such stunted cultural growth is still made evident to this day, as reflected in contemporary scholarship on Women's issues around the world in the mid-to-late twentieth century. Kristina Schultz's study titled *The Women's Liberation Movement: Impacts and Outcomes* (2017), for instance, is just one example. Whereas Women's Liberation movements in countries like the United States, France, Italy, Germany, Sweden, Great Britain, and Russia have entire chapters devoted to them, Spain is only mentioned twice in the entire volume, both times in passing.

22. The six types of *mujer varonil* as identified by McKendrick (1974) are: (1) the *bandolera*, who takes an offence against her own honor out against all men, (2) the *mujer esquiva*, who possesses a natural disdain for men and marriage and refuses to be wed to anyone, (3) the amazon, the leader, the warrior, who, often dressed as a man, goes into combat, (4) the scholar, the career woman, who desires nothing more than an education equal to that of a man, (5) the *bella cazadora*, who is a skilled hunter and is often free to roam the countryside like a man, and (6) the avenger, who takes revenge against men into her own hands for offences against her or her family's honor. Despite her oversight of how these character contributed to maintaining the established social order, her terminology has equipped Golden Age literary scholars with an artillery of critical language that still aides us in categorizing feminine characters from early modern Spanish literature. As such, we will be referring to and utilizing certain elements from her taxonomy in our analysis.

23. McKendrick's term, in Spanish, is *mujer esquiva*.

24. Leonarda's words in the source text are "como he dado en no casarme, / leo por entretenerme, / no por bachillera hacerme" (I.1, vv. 29–31). It is also telling that these verses are present in all of the televised adaptations of the play, with the exception of the 1983 episode of *Las pícaras*.

25. Original: Vendrá tarde; yo estaré / celosa; dará mi hacienda; / comenzará la contienda / desto de si fue o no fue. / Yo esconderé y él dará; / buscará deudas por mí; / entrará justicia aquí, /

voces y aun coces habrá. / No habrá noche, no habrá día, / que la casa no alborote . . . /

"—Daca la carta de dote. /—Soltad la hacienda, que es mía /—Entrad en esta escritura."

26. It is interesting to note that Cristina Marsillach is the daughter of Adolfo Marsillach, the first director of the Compañía Española de Teatro Clásico (1979–1983).

27. The "secret beau" in question is repeatedly referred to as the *oscuro galán* in the episode.

28. All editions of the text, including the 1620 *princeps* published in *Parte catorce de las comedias de Lope de Vega Carpio*, refer to Leonarda as a *viuda moza* in the dramatis personae. Although the term *moza* is not registered in Covarrubias's *Thesoro* (1611), it is undoubtably used as an adjective to mean young, precisely as it is defined in *Autoridades*.

29. It should be noted that Manuel España Arjona (2018) does not consider the episode to be an adaptation of Lope's play of the same name at all, but rather considers it a disguised retelling of Miguel de Cervantes's *novela ejemplar, El celoso extremeño*.

30. Lope specifically included the verbiage "Leonarda, viuda moza" in his dramatis personae.

31. Likewise, actress María del Puy, who portrayed Leonarda in the 1975 adaptation, was 34 at the time the episode aired, and no efforts were made to accentuate the character's young age.

32. Sánchez-Gijón's Leonarda is seen disrobing again (00:19:25) and is eventually caught in bed by her uncle and servants with Camilo at the end of the adaptation (01:10:40).

33. By casting Fernando Guillén Cuervo as the male lead in the 1975 adaptation, the directors and producers cleverly insinuated the sexual nature of Camilo and Leonarda's relationship to Spanish television audiences of the time. Guillén Cuervo was famous for portraying womanizing men on Spanish television during the dictatorship. In addition to bringing the infamous seducer don Juan Tenorio to life twice in the 1960s, he also portrayed the galivanting Lope de Vega in "El mejor mozo de España" (1970).

34. The 1980 adaptation of *La dama boba* is unavailable for viewing today. According to RTVE digital archivist Yolanda Martínez Villamar, although the episode is listed in the archives, a copy of the episode is not conserved.

35. For example, Laurencio's soliloquy about the power of love and how it has controlled men and women since the beginning of time and lamented in literature since Antiquity (II.1, vv. 1083–1122), is removed from the second act and is used to conclude the film, dividing the lines spoken by Laurencio in the original among Nise, Liseo, Pedro, and Finea (01:30:30–01:32:00).

36. In seventeenth-century Spanish literature, an *indiano* is a character who has travelled to the American territories (*las indias*) and made a fortune there before returning to the Iberian metropolis to retire to a life of luxury.

37. Janice North et al. (2018) concur in their analyses of modern Anglo-Saxon period pieces, arguing that such characterizations are entirely counterproductive to advancing gender equality causes (12).

38. The review in *ABC* of the 1966 adaptation mostly criticized the actors' poor handling of the verse, while an article in a May 1981 edition of the same newspaper shows disapproval of TVE broadcasting the episode at a time when a theatrical adaptation of the play was enjoying its run in Madrid; arguing that the televised adaptation naturally paled in comparison to the theatrical reproduction (117).

39. Original: "mas yo tengo honor / por más tesoro; / que los respetos de quien soy adoro / y aun el pensarlo tengo por bajeza."

40. Original: Ojos, pues os habéis puesto / en cosa tan desigual, / pagad el mirar tan mal, / que no soy la culpa desto; / más no lloren, que también / tiempla el mal llorar los ojos, / pero sientan sus enojos; / quien mira mal, llore bien, / aunque tendrán ya pensada / la disculpa para todo, / que el sol los pone en el lodo, / y no se le pega nada. / Lüego es bien que no den / en llorar. Cesad, mis ojos, / pero sientan sus enojos; / quien mira mal, llore bien.

41. Original: "fuera de que soy mujer / a cualquier error sujeta."

42. By omitting the lines in which she shows her emotional responses to situations, the screenwriters eliminated the stereotype of the "emotional woman" that has been

vigorously challenged by even the first feminist proponents like Mary Wollstonecraft in her *A Vindication of the Rights of Woman* (1792), as it portrays women as inferior to, or incomplete without, the reasonable, emotionally stable man (279). Feminist scholars continue to confront this perception of women as "overly emotional," and as such, weaker than the "unemotional" or "reasonable" men even today. See especially Rosemarie Tong (2018, 14), Deborah Lupton (1998, 106–127), and Rachel Falmagne and Haas (2002, 2).

43. As we will see in the section on reception, this film was nominated for a dozen Goya awards and had unprecedented success at the box office for an adaptation of a Golden Age drama.

44. It is worth keeping in mind that, although certainly not encouraged or practical, it was not unheard of for seventeenth-century nobles to have romantic feelings toward a subordinate; it was only socially unacceptable for the two to act upon those feelings by initiating courtship. Diana's dilemma stems from her strict adherence to the established social order. Her marriage to Teodoro is only made possible after he inherits a noble title via the will of a man that he had deceived into believing was his father. In other words, no social norms are technically broken in the play, nor does it advocate foregoing these customs in the name of love. Furthermore, neither Lope's nor Miró's Dianas fight for what they want; rather, out of jealous spite, in both versions she tries to prevent the young secretary from being happy with another woman. For these reasons, I find it challenging to defend a feminist interpretation of either the play or its film adaptation.

45. This phenomenon provides adaptation scholars with a superb example of what Cutchins (2017) has denominated "interdetermination," or, simply put, the mutual influence that two versions of the same text exert upon one other for people who have experienced both, which allows a newer adaptation to affect the meaning of the original (75).

46. Janet Pérez and Maureen Ihrie, for example, include an entire segment on Lope de Vega in their *Feminist Encyclopedia of Spanish Literature* (2002), in which they highlight their perceived feminist undertones in the original play (2: 649–643).

47. For a historiographical description of the decline of these symbols in the popular Spanish imaginary, see "The Flag and the Anthem: The Disputed Official Symbols of Spain" by Javier Moreno-Luzón and Xosé M. Núñez Seixas (2017, 33–36).

48. See Luis Borau (2003, 84).

49. The six-episode miniseries adapted one Golden Age literary work per episode, including Cervantes's *La tía fingida* (April 8, 1983), Alonso de Castillo Solórzano's *La guarduña de Sevilla* (April 15, 1983), Lope's *La viuda valenciana* (April 22, 1983), López de Úbeda's *La pícara justina* (April 29, 1983), Francisco Delicado's *La lozana andaluza* (May 6, 1983), and Barbadillo's *La hija de Celestina* (May 13, 1983). Information regarding the conception of the miniseries and, its origins, and the influence of contemporary film on its production is provided in the "Zoom" column of the April 7, 1983, edition of *Marca* (2).

50. I use the phrase "series of events" here so as not to say "plot," given that the episode does not have one that I have been able to definitively identify.

51. The lyrics, in Valencian, are as follows: "Cinc [quatre, tres, dos] pometes té el pomer, de cinc [quatre, tres, dos] una, de cinc [quatre, tres, dos] una, cinc [quatre, tres, dos] pometes té el pomer, de cinc [quatre, tres, dos] una tira el vent. Si mireu el vent d'on ve, veureu el pomer com dansa; Si mireu el vent d'on ve, veurem com dansa el pomer."

52. See Fucilla (1959), Gasparetti (1939), Kohler (1939), Scungio (1981), Rull (1968), and de Armas (1980, 3–5) for more on Bandello's influence in Lope's theater.

53. Notice here that the title of the television program distorts the title from the source text. The contraction "del" is not found in the title of the source text or any other adaptations. It is likely an error made by the television production team or an attempt at modernizing the title for television audiences.

54. Despite the fact that none of the censorship reports on file recommend the script for an *interés nacional* rating, the film did, somehow, score the distinction after the final production was released.

55. Original: "en la villa de Madrid / Leonor y Martín se casan: / corren toros y juegan cañas."

56. Although the artistic decision to use more authentic settings is, as most critics agree, a principal contributing factor to the film's success, it came at such a large financial cost that production had to be halted for several months while Miró sought additional funding for the project. See Wheeler (2008, 293–297).

57. This is a prime example of a successful application of Sánchez Noriega's definition of "airear la obra" that we saw attempted by Perpiñá and Torrente Ballester in chapter 1.

58. Curiously, Gómez did have a small, uncredited appearance in the television miniseries *Don Quijote de la Mancha* (1991–1992) and Suárez would go on to play a duchess in *El caballero don Quijote* (2002).

59. Alicia Hermida was a frequent participant in TVE's earliest *teleteatro* productions in the 1960s, even making sporadic appearances on *Primera fila*. Prior to working on *El perro del hortelano*, she had already gained experience with Lope de Vega's works by playing Clara in *La dama boba* (1969), Beatriz in *Los milagros del desprecio* (1967), and Fenisa in *La discreta enamorada* (1970), in addition to 18 other episodes of *Estudio 1* and 28 episodes of *Teatro de siempre*.

60. García Posada (1997) also commented on the transparency of the verse that made the film easy to follow, attributing it to the fact that "la mayoría de los actores consiguen evitar el tonillo, aunque sin duda por este camino se puede todavía mejorar mucho. El verso del teatro clásico es verso dramático, lo que parece una obviedad, pero no lo es en el sentido de que pausas y énfasis han de estar subordinados a la fluidez del diálogo al que el verso sirve" (n.p.).

61. Although she had starred as Doña Inés in the miniseries *Don Juan* (1997), Silvia Abascal (Finea) had much more recurring roles in sitcoms like *Hostal Royal Manzanares* (1996–1998), *Aquí no hay quien viva* (2003–2006), and *El comisario* (1999–2009). Macarena Gómez (Nise) had only begun to develop a small profile as a character actor in programs like *Hospital central* (2000–2012) and *Raquel busca su sitio* (2000). Almodóvar girl Verónica Forqué (Octavia), was also a very famous comic actress, known for films like *Bajarse al moro* (1989) and *¿Por qué lo llaman*

Chapter 3

*amor cuando quieren decir sexo?* (1993), and a short-lived sitcom *La vida de Rita* (2003), in which she played the title role. Paco León (the dance instructor) was rising to fame as a comedy actor thanks to his starring role in the sitcom *Aída* (2005–2014) that had debuted a year before the film.

62. Transcription taken directly from a viewing of the episode on site at the TVE headquarters in Prado del Rey, Pozuelo de Alarcón, Madrid.

63. It is appropriate to note here that the program was still called *Primera fila* until 1965.

64. *La viuda valenciana* (1973) was not the first to demonstrate an evolution of the introductory presentation of a Lope adaptation, as *El bastardo Mudarra* (1971) included a narration that directly expressed the mechanisms used by director Antonio Abad in his approach to the episode.

65. Prado del Rey is the area of Madrid in which TVE headquarters are located.

66. The fiscal authorities in question are none other than Spain's *Hacienda*.

67. The episode does not maintain the strict adherence to the textual witnesses of Lope's original that the 1973 episode of *Estudio 1* does, nor does it take the story in a completely different direction to facilitate the inclusion of more *risqué* elements like in 1983. It keeps the majority of Lope's original verse and storyline but enhances dramatic effect by moving some scenes around and adding lines when necessary. For example, I.19 is moved to immediately after v. 800 (I.14; 00:12:23–00:14:50). Urbán cannot immediately spot Camilo (since it's a carnival-like party and the men are wearing masks), so he starts with [added verses] "Una dama principal más hermosa que la luna os ofrece dicha tal que jamás mujer alguna a varón dio por igual." He says this to the wrong man first, then to Camilo, to whom he also says that a woman is waiting for him at her palace. Dialogue then realigns with Lope's text at v. 941 (00:14:52).

68. It would be a full year before the show released another episode, *Urtain* (2011). It continued to broadcast episodes sporadically until 2016, but, to date, it has only managed to successfully air four.

69. *Volver* (2006) is a drama about how three generations of women band together to fight against the sexually abusive men in their family and bond with one another despite their differences.

70. By the end of the calendar year, it only managed the forty-second place for revenue generation for the year with a total of 349.047,98€ earned from only 61.714 spectators as its audience (*Boletín informativo* 2006, 147). *La dama boba* (2006) made 16,140,464€ less than *Alatriste* (2006), which raked in an astounding 16.489.511,68€ and boasted a total of 3.130.710 during the same year (*Boletín informativo* 2006, 147).

*Chapter 4*

# The Phoenix Regenerated (1935–2018)

Lope de Vega himself has been transformed into a character and featured as a protagonist in a variety of Spanish film and television productions. Although these appearances of a dramatized Lope have at times been sporadic, *biopics* and fictional portrayals of the dramaturg's life have slowly been garnering a more stable position in Spanish popular culture. An analysis of these productions shows that there is significantly more interest in the author himself than his remarkable literary production. As such, increasingly more financial and creative resources have been dedicated to keeping the historical figure of Lope de Vega in the collective imagination over the course of the last decade, though these modern avatars often underscore vastly different facets of his personality and major events in his life.

   The *biopic* is a somewhat novel popular culture artifact and studies surrounding this type of biographical narrative are very recent additions to cultural scholarship. As opposed to other types of biographical pieces, such as written (auto)biographies or documentaries, biographical pictures, abbreviated as *biopics* or *bio/pics*, are not meant to be true-to-life recreations of a subject's life and times. They are, conversely, highly dramatized portrayals of figures who are considered important mythical constructs of a culture or nation that combine and interweave presumed historical "fact" with rumors and assumptions about the subject, in addition to completely fictional inventions that screenwriters insert to create a marketable story. From a historiographical standpoint, these productions are extremely problematic. As Murray Pomerance (2016) has observed, "the biopic continually challenges the student to examine what it shows of its subject against the measuring standard of a 'reality' constructed by media and sold as a product to a willing audience" (26). Therein lies a dilemma for historiographical-oriented scholars who wish to include biopics in their study of a given historical figure; in these types of productions, the subject is transformed into a character and the events of their lives are structured into a narrative. As such, I will refer to any and all film and television manifestations of Lope de Vega as a character placed within a narrative of his life and times as a biopic.

Historical figures like Lope are necessarily characterized in ways that screenwriters and directors consider appropriate for their target audiences. The stories of their lives are most often told in such a way so as to provide a moralistic motif to their mere existence. Pomerance (2016) has duly observed that these morals serve a pedagogical purpose for viewers, arguing that "by learning of the life of a notable personage we can transfer some moral power to ourselves, thus improving the nature of our own existence" (27). William Epstein (2016), on the other hand, considers the pedagogical value of biopics to be their potential to reveal intricate details of a society's popular culture and collective morals and standards for admirable behavior.[1] In other words, biopics tend to exalt a certain historical figure and/or his or her circumstances in order to depict an idealized version of a certain culture, often misleading audiences to believe in—as Benedict Anderson (1991) states—"a nation that never was" (299). It is precisely at this juncture that Lope biopics deviate from more mainstream productions of the genre, an aspect that makes them particularly appealing for this study.

As evidenced by the fact that the major motion picture *Lope* (2010) was renamed *The Outlaw* for distribution in English-speaking countries, Lope de Vega is an atypical subject for Spanish biopics. While it is certainly true that all Lope biopics take place during Spain's so-called "Golden Age," his presence as the focal point of these productions—wittingly or not—brings a series of societal contradictions and hypocrisies to the forefront of the film's message that challenge modern conceptions of the times in which he lived. If one compares this to other recent Spanish biopics that mainly reaffirm the assumptions about the sociocultural climate of the times they depict, such as *Juana la loca* (2001), *Isabel* (2011–2014), *El rey* (2014), and *Carlos: Rey emperador* (2015–2016), we can appreciate just how unusual it is for Spain to dedicate so much screen time to a figure like Lope. First of all, almost all of the other twenty-first-century biopics revolve around monarchs, not more obscure cultural icons like a seventeenth-century playwright. Moreover, in comparison to the other subjects, Lope is depicted as much more of a "counter hero" type as opposed to triumphant representations of national heroes.[2]

I use the phrase "counter hero" as opposed to anti-hero because of Michael Gose's (2006) clarification that the counter hero is a protagonist who "has the strengths of a traditional hero, but uses those strengths towards different ends [and] challenges the status quo by personifying values that undercut the values of the dominant culture" in a work (167). Anti-heroes, on the other hand, tend to have the same objectives as traditional heroes but often are forced to break social conventions in order to uphold the overall values of that dominant culture (Brombert, 2001, 4). Golden Age counter heroes have been frequent protagonists in Spanish films like the adaptation of Arturo Pérez-Reverte's *Captián Alatriste* (2006) and the television series *Águila Roja* (2009–2016), which could possibly explain why the figure of Lope, from whose legacy a counter hero is easily formed, has found such a place in modern popular culture that he had never managed to secure previously. Curiously, however, although Lope does appear as a character in Pérez-Reverte's source text, he is entirely absent from the film adaptation, so this film will not be considered here. I will only be including films and television shows in which Lope is presented as a character in our study not only to grasp an understanding of Lope's place in today's popular culture but also as a means to examine Spain's attitudes about its own past during distinct times in the country's recent history.

For the aforementioned reasons, our examination into Lope's personage in modern Spanish popular culture concludes with an analysis of all available Lope biopics that have been released in Spain since *Estudio 1*'s "El mejor mozo de España" (1970) in order to identify any place that Lope's life and times have in modern Spanish popular culture and any possible role he has played in molding a current sense of national identity beyond his literature. In doing so, I hope to establish an understanding of Lope's importance—or lack thereof—to Spanish audiences over the past four decades to complement our examination into how his literature has been treated during the same time periods. A consideration of how the author is treated as a character reveals a great deal into how Spanish popular culture molds its vision of the past according to current trends because, as I will comment upon below, there are many different portrayals of the same historical figure. The fact that the dramaturg is so flexible, malleable, and adaptable to a wide array of different times and sociocultural attitudes is due, primarily, to the many elements that combine to form "the Lope myth."

## THE LOPE MYTH

As Alexander Samson and Jonathan Thacker (2008) explain, Lope's *comedias* lack "the power and philosophical reach" of some of his contemporary rivals—namely William Shakespeare—who are renowned internationally for their artistic genius and have been recreated for a wide array of audiences around the world (1). Therefore, what is left to Spain's popular culture, according to their findings, is a figure whose "exceptional productivity and eventful life" have transformed the dramatist into little more than "a flawed character possessed of a unique genius," or, as they refer to it, "the Lope

myth" (1). Many scholars have called attention to the duality of Lope's character that has transformed him into this mythological figure of Spain's history.
Essentially, academia—along with popular culture—has remembered Lope
as both admirable for his literary prowess, yet reproachable for his amoral
conduct (almost always regarding his love life). Members of both popular and
academic cultures have tended to overlook an important truth about Lope's
life and works: there is not just one, but multiple dualities, dichotomies, contradictions, and paradoxes that surround his legacy. For instance, in life he
was simultaneously a commoner, but educated to the level of a noble; a writer
by vocation, but also out of bare necessity (he was financially burdened to the
point that he had to sell plays to make ends meet); narcissistic (he constantly
wrote about himself and his own experiences), yet willing to display what
proper society would consider his flaws and shortcomings to his broad audience; a headstrong proponent of true love, but also a shameless womanizer;
a "celibate" priest who fathered illegitimate children during his priesthood; a
proponent of justice under an established order that frequently sought to outlaw him; a massive success (he and his works were beloved and profitable)
and a miserable failure (he never achieved his lifelong goal of being accepted
into the nobility or of attaining an official position at Court, like royal chronicler, an occupation he coveted above all others).

Another factor that is often overlooked about the "Lope myth" is that it
existed long before the death of Lope de Vega. In fact, it has been argued that
the dramaturg himself played a major role in its creation. Antonio Sánchez
Jiménez (2006) provides possibly the most comprehensive study of Lope's
self-portraits as he highlights how Lope blurs the lines between fiction and
reality by inviting readers to interpret the omnipresent poetic "yo" as a direct
self-representation.[3] Nevertheless, Sánchez Jiménez warns against readers
taking these idyllic self-portraits too literally, because we must understand
the "diverse invitations to read his poetry as a biography, because they are
extremely numerous, just like the many calls to attention about the fictional-
ity of that biography" (12). Therein lies the primary difficult in understanding
the historical Lope; he was, after all, a writer of fiction whose self-portrayals
were often infused by an elevated degree of fiction.

Lope utilized such literary devices to guide readers to interpret certain
aspects of his life and characteristics of his personality in ways that he
would want to be regarded and remembered. He paints himself as a hopeless romantic in his Moorish romances (Sánchez Jiménez, 2006, 25–35),
as a young courtly gentleman whose emotions range from desperately
enamored to inspired to repentant in his pastoral prose (especially in *La
Arcadia*) (37–40; 47), as "so truly Spanish" in his *Rimas* (46), and even
as both soldier and poet in his later works like *La Dorotea* (47; 80).[4] Public recognition for his military involvement increasingly preoccupied the

playwright, especially since his most hostile contemporary critics often called this facet of his self-fashioned autobiography into question. The resulting defensive strategy became manifest in his poetry, in which he constantly insists that he had served in the Armada Invencible during the disastrous attempted invasion of England in 1588 (2008, 272). Although there has been some scholarly debate on the veracity of these claims, the general academic consensus today is that he was involved in the conflict in some way. Popular culture has enthusiastically followed suit with scholarly opinion, making sure to depict him as a veteran soldier in almost all of his modern representations.

Studies have also shown that Lope had an active role in developing his own reputation as a galivanting womanizer. It has never been a secret that Lope de Vega enjoyed the company of women and that he found it difficult to remain faithful to any of the ones who crossed his path in his lifetime; he often included elements of his love life in his oeuvre, poorly concealing the identities of his lovers—as well as his own—under a thin veil of artistic license by basing characters on them that were less than clandestine.[5] As Hugo Rennert (1968) observes,

> beyond an occasional attempt to puzzle the reader, Lope made no effort to conceal his *amours* from the cultured public, to which they must have been well known. Indeed, he seems during his whole life to have courted rather than shunned the notoriety with which his name was thus constantly associated, and to have derived no less satisfaction from his conquests than from his achievements in the domain of letters. (263)

Essentially, Lope de Vega was keen on highlighting the ambivalent binaries of his lifestyle in his works. He seemed to relish the thought of being considered both poet and soldier, devoted romantic and seducer. Although these facets of his personality are present throughout his works, they pertain principally to an era that Joan Oleza (2003), and Sanchez Jiménez (2018), following in Juan Manuel Roza's (1990) footsteps, categorize as Lope's epoch of "youth" (*juventud*) (73). This period of the author's life, as suggested by the label, corresponds to his younger years and is characterized by more daring and whimsical behavior. The era is distinguished from the final years of Lope's life, which is often called his "elderly" epoch (*senectud*) (73).[6] This second era can be considered a time in which, as accounted for in some of Lope's final letters to the Duke of Sessa, Lope was obsessed with his own death and the legacy he would leave behind.[7] Within these documents, Oleza (2003) has observed that Lope's self-portrayal shifts to that of a repentant sinner (604). Although the modern biopics about Lope de Vega tend to portray only one of these two eras of the author's life (that of *juventud*), they are both necessary in order to understand the facet of the "flawed character" that forms one side of the "Lope myth."

The remaining half of the myth, that of the "genius," was a reputation that the playwright himself also had a hand in creating. The playwright was so prone to self-aggrandizement regarding his innate intellectual superiority and speedy composition skills that scholars today have difficulties calculating how many *comedias* and poems he wrote during his lifetime. Regarding his natural aptitude, he asserts in his *New Art of Writing Plays* (*Arte nuevo de hacer comedias en este tiempo*) (1609) that he had read all of the classical precepts on theater composition by the time he was 10 years old, arguing that his trademark brand of *comedias* was not the product of his ignorance, but rather his desire to compose plays that would attract audiences (vv. 17–20).[8] Drawing on his own experience, Lope argued that seventeenth-century Spanish tastes were not sophisticated enough to appreciate the exquisite art of classical dramatic construction.

The dramatist would again discuss his extraordinary literary talents in the dedication to his son in the 1620 edition of *El verdadero amante*, in which the playwright claims to have written the drama at 12 years of age. The idea that Lope was a literary child prodigy would be echoed again almost immediately after his death when his first biographer and most loyal disciple, Juan Pérez de Montalbán, wrote the following lines about Lope's natural proclivity to reading and writing in his *Fama póstuma* (1636):

> At only two Aprils of age, already in the liveliness of his eyes, already in the charm of his mischievousness, and already in the physiognomy of his features, his presence showed what was later to be of his actions. He went to school and it is well known that he exceeded all others in his zeal for studying his first letters, and since he was not old enough to form words, he repeated his lessons with gestures instead of with his tongue. At five years of old he could read Spanish (*romance*) and Latin, and such was his inclination to verses that even though he did not know how to write, he enjoyed his meals with elders because they would write for him what he dictated. (f.1v)[9]

Whether or not these claims are true, what is certain is that Lope and his followers wanted his legacy to include the idea that he had been an exceptionally gifted child.[10] Doing so, it could be argued, was an attempt at legitimizing his status in Madrid's literary circles. Perhaps he had not been born into a situation that allowed him to roam freely among the intellectual elite, but his innate gifts compensated this accidental misfortune.

In addition to the idea that he had been endowed with a unique gift for literature, Lope also had no qualms about boasting his enormous literary production. In the prologue to his play *El peregrino en su patria* (1604), Lope himself claims to have written 219 *comedias*, and later raises the number to 429 in a 1618 edition. In the *Arte nuevo* he states "but, what can I do if I have written, / counting one that I have just finished this week, / four-hundred eighty three *comedias*?" ["pero, ¿qué puedo hacer si tengo escritas, / con una que he acabado esta semana, / cuatrocientas y ochenta y tres comedias?"] (vv. 367–369) In the prologue to *El verdadero amante* (1620), the number is raised to 900, then to 927 a year later in the prologue to *Parte XV*.[11] In *La filomena* (1621) he reduces the number back down to an even 900, a number which grows significantly by the time he wrote the prologue to *Parte XX* (1625), in which he claims to have written 1,070 plays. The closing lines of *La moza de cántaro*—date unknown but proposed by S. Griswold Morley and Courtney Bruerton (1936) to be from around 1625 (220)—tell audiences that he had written 1,500.[12] Lope would go on to repeat this claim in his posthumously published autobiographical work *Égloga a Claudio* (1637). When taken at face value, the dates of publication and the quantity of plays he claims to have written suggest that, at least in some years, he must have composed more than one play per week.

Though such an accelerated publication rate may seem impossible, many of his contemporaries corroborate his claims by mentioning the high number of *comedias* composed in their own works or in the ones they printed for him. For example, Lisboan printer Perreira wrote in a preface to Lope's *Parte II* (1612) that 500 of his plays had already been performed by the date of publication. Meanwhile, Cervantes comments in the prologue to his *Ocho comedias y ocho entremeses* (1615) that "immediately the freak of nature came in, the great Lope de Vega, and he ascended to the comic monarchy, he overwhelmed and put all the phonies under his jurisdiction, he filled the world with his own well-composed *comedias*; the ones he's written exceed ten thousand sheets of paper" (Prologue, n.p.).[13] As Morley and Bruerton (1936) calculate, at the standard length of 12 "sheets" (*pliegos*) per play, Cervantes's estimation equals a total of 833 completed dramas (218).[14]

Clearly, both friends and foes highly praised his theatrical career. It is well known, for example, that Lope achieved great financial success through the sales of his plays while he was alive and that his formula for creating comedies initiated a school of followers that included canonical playwrights like Calderón de la Barca.[15] Furthermore, the mythical nickname Phoenix of Wits was coined during his lifetime by contemporaries.[16] The analogies of Lope with Greek mythology would continue to form a part of his legacy even once his life had ended. Juan Pérez de Montalbán (1936), for example, compared Lope with several Greco-Roman deities in his *Fama pósthuma*, in which he wrote that his beloved mentor was a

wonder of the orb, glory of the nation, luster of the fatherland, oracle of the tongue, center of fame, cause of envy, guardian of fortunes, phoenix of the centuries, prince of verses, Orpheus of the sciences, Apollo of the muses, Horace of poets, Virgil of epics, Homer of heroes, Pindar of lyricists, Sophocles of tragedy, and Terence of comics. (ff. 1$^r$-1$^v$)

Clearly, Montalbán's elevation of Lope as a national figure comparable to the likes of Greek gods and classical poets and dramatists was the first posthumously published vehicle of the "Lope myth" that had begun during the author's lifetime and continues to perpetuate the complicated web of uncertainties and contradictions that have come to characterize the figure of Lope de Vega over the subsequent centuries.

Though the multifaceted and contradictory quality of the "Lope myth" makes him an interesting figure to depict on big and small screens, it is my belief that it is precisely this indeterminable element of the author's life that has allowed him to appear—albeit sporadically—in popular culture as a national symbol of Spain far beyond his contemporary Spanish peers. As Michael Bruner (2005) posits, "national identity is a politically consequential fiction based on a selective remembering and forgetting" which allows different ideological currents to shape national identity by cherry-picking the historical myths and narratives they find convenient (316). In the case of Lope in Spain, I believe that this is precisely what popular culture has attempted to do with the author, selectively remembering and forgetting certain aspects of his malleable myth to create a space for him in the popular culture of the time. As I will indicate in the following sections, filmmakers and television producers have been eager to portray, in varying degrees, the legendary playwright's virtues and iniquities.

Lope de Vega has not made regular appearances on Spanish screens; in fact, the author has only been featured ten times in the history of Spanish film and television combined. The following is a list of all of the films and television episodes released in Spain (until now) that feature the life and times of Lope de Vega:

1. *La musa y el fénix*, Dir. David Constantin, 1935[17]
2. "La geografía apasionada de Lope de Vega," (*La víspera de nuestro tiempo*, 1969)[18]
3. "El mejor mozo de España" (*Estudio 1*, 1970)
4. "Lope de Vega" (*Paisaje con figuras*, 1984)
5. *Lope*, Dir. Andrucha Waddington, 2010
6. "Tiempo de gloria" (*El ministerio del tiempo*, 2015)
7. *Cervantes contra Lope*, Dir. Manuel Huerga, 2016.
8. "Tiempo de hidalgos" (*El ministerio del tiempo*, 2016)
9. "Tiempo de esplendor" (*El ministerio del tiempo*, 2017)
10. *Lope enamorado*, Dir. Rodolfo Montero de Palacio, 2018

Despite the limited number of titles on this list, the fact that Lope de Vega has been revived as a character on screens at all is significant, given that Cervantes is the only of his contemporaries to have been given this distinction, and Lope's manifestations as a character outnumber that of his rival by over four times. All of these representations of the dramatist accentuate many of the various facets of the "Lope myth" as a means of injecting the memory of this obscure figure into the collective national consciousness. Their choice of which aspects to depict often demonstrates symptoms of "strategic patriotic memory" to spotlight some portions of his legacy while minimizing—or omitting—certain others to please the audiences of their respective times.[19] Although I concur with Esther Fernández (2018) that the "presence of Lope de Vega on Spanish television does not seem to show any artistic progression," I will argue that aspects of his characterization have been greatly highlighted and/or exaggerated by the ideological currents that permeated the popular culture of the moment (12).

Accordingly, certain aspects of Lope's contradictory and dynamic personality are highlighted more than others depending on the impression that television and film executives hoped to present to their audiences. A thorough study of all of Lope's biopics reveals that, in varying degrees, they all include one or more of the following personality traits:

1. Lope, the patriot;
2. Lope, the womanizer;
3. Lope, the hopeless romantic;
4. Lope, the literary genius;
5. Lope, the audacious, and
6. Lope, our contemporary.[20]

The remaining portions of this chapter examine how these aspects of Lope de Vega's life and personality are portrayed in the productions listed above so as to determine if there is indeed a detectable artistic or ideological progression present in his modern manifestations.

## Lope, the Patriot

As demonstrated by the tributes made to Lope de Vega by his contemporaries in Pérez de Montalbán's *Fama póstuma*, Lope was considered an example of Spanish patriotism even during his lifetime. This element of his legacy seems to have only intensified in the centuries following his death, as evidenced as early as 1881 by Mesonero Romanos, who referred to Lope's "unique, exclusive, and national character" (viii) and later more explicitly by Ricardo Arco y Garay's reflection in his 1941 publication titled *La sociedad española en la obra dramática de Lope de Vega*, in which he states that "Lope's love for Spain was intense, like that of a mother to her first-born child" (55).[21] According to Arco y Garay (1941), this profound love of country was the result of the fact that the dramatist had seen and experienced so much of it throughout his travels around the Iberian Peninsula, during which Lope "collected and stored the best national observations" (55) that allowed him to perfect a genuinely national style. This trademark gave him the power to "increase the love for national glories in the hearts of his countrymen" (56).[22] Although it is well known that Lope was born in Madrid and lived in exile in Valencia for a time, his knowledge of the various regions of his country as suggested by Arco y Garay (1947) has been contested by scholars like Juan Millé y Jiménez (1928) and Rudolph Schevill (1941), who doubt that Lope would have experienced such a wide panorama of the Peninsula first-hand due to their deductions that he never participated in the "Attack on England" (*Jornada de Inglaterra*) as part of the Spanish Armada (*Armada Invencible*) in 1588.[23] The assertion that Lope had traveled extensively through the kingdom is corroborated, however, by more recent studies, such as Sánchez Jiménez's (2008), that reiterates that Lope would have at least seen and/or resided in Madrid, Valencia, Sevilla, and Lisbon—which was annexed to Spain for a time during Lope's lifetime—as well as La Coruña and the Bay of Biscay upon his return from England following the disaster of 1588 (269–272).

Such extensive voyages throughout the Spanish territory likely explain Lope's profound understanding of its diverse population. Veronica Ryjik (2011) considers that this personal connection with his compatriots is precisely what allowed him to be popular among such a plural and multicultural audience that spanned the entire country (8). Lope, she argues, was able to use his dramas as a culturally unifying device for the people by highlighting the importance of the characteristics that all Spaniards of the time had in common and using them often as themes in his writing; for example, she lists the "institution of Castilian as the *lingua franca*, the religious uniformity, the extension of Castilian laws and political institutions to other parts of the monarchy and the military conflicts with other states, cultures, and regions" (9). As such, Lope's patriotism has always been an integral factor in his literary and personal legacy and has contributed greatly to the elevation of his status to that of a national treasure.

During Francoism, Spanish national myths were naturally presented somewhat differently than at other moments in Spain's recent history because of the regime's ideological orientation.[24] This perhaps explains why the 1969 episode of *La víspera de nuestro tiempo*—one of only two specials dedicated to the playwright during the dictatorship—focused so much on Lope's travels around the entire country. This ideological affinity has long been considered a motivation for Francoists' supposed admiration of Lope, which allows us to better understand why the historical figure of the dramaturg has so frequently been considered a propagandistic symbol of the regime, despite—as has been seen via the analysis of Lope's adapted works—the historical inaccuracy of this assumption. Moreover, this stereotype explains why Lope's patriotism is brought to the forefront so explicitly in his only on-screen manifestation as a character broadcasted during the dictatorship. To avoid the possibility that Lope's love of country would go unnoticed by audiences, the last 10 minutes of *Estudio 1*'s "El mejor mozo de España" (1970) include a moment in which Lope defends his profound patriotism to a critic who accuses him of being anti-Spanish. As soft, melodic music plays in the background, the camera zooms in for a facial close-up of a pensive-looking Lope, who stares deeply into space as he declares, "I like Spain. I love this land from North to South. I would die of sorrow without her. I carry her people in my guts and, you listen here, young man, what pains you is that I am Spanish through and through" (01:06:10). Clearly, screenwriters had hoped that audiences would finish the episode with a reflection on how Lope's patriotism was his most important virtue, and that this personality trait outweighed any of his negative characteristics. While he speaks, the camera pans to close-ups of the figures of Cervantes and Quevedo, who were casually sharing a drink with Lope at a tavern before the interruption, showing them to be clearly moved by what their rival author is proclaiming, despite any remaining animosity that they may be feeling following the feuds that had erupted among the authors earlier in the episode.

When Lope finishes speaking, a close-up of a member of Góngora's entourage shows him clearly humbled, looking at the ground before challenging Lope, telling him that his patriotism is not noticeable by the plays he writes because he doesn't speak that way via his characters on stage. Lope defends himself, delivering a message clearly intended for the Spanish audience of the time, saying, "What auditorium would tolerate such a monotonous serenade? No, boy, listen to Lope. Look at what's noble about him and judge him afterwards" (01:06:44–01:07:00). Again, the screenwriters' insistence that Lope's virtues eclipse his flaws, thus justifying both his status as a national role model and the creation of the episode in question. Moreover, the conversation is strategically placed at the end of the episode so as to encourage audiences to overlook the more controversial and scandalous aspects of Lope's legacy that have been shown previously during the show since his love of Spain and other noble attributes redeem him overall. It would appear as though the producers of the episode were employing a technique that is common in portrayals of historical figures that they wish to elevate to the level of national hero and icon.

As R. Barton Palmer (2016) has observed, "the biopic can embrace troubling contradictions or conflicts, often refusing easy or crowd-pleasing understandings" of the production's subjects, as long as they offer material that compensates for his or her typically human shortcomings within a specific ideological climate (298).[25] In doing so, "El mejor mozo de España" does not turn a blind eye to Lope's well-known scandalous reputation, yet it clarifies to audiences that these defects in his character do not disqualify him from being considered a national treasure. After all, the program makes it clear that even his flaws are typically Spanish. The character of his wife, Micaela de Luján, informs audiences of this fact in an argument with her husband in which she asks him, "But why can't you be in the middle ground? And tell me, what is the middle ground in Spain if it is not having one legitimate wife and another illegitimate one?" (00:36:55) It is also worth noting here a striking hypocritical contradiction in Francoist society that was touched upon in chapter 2: despite the high moral standards touted by the regime, womanizing—even prostitution—were considered necessary societal evils and, although not encouraged, were widely tolerated.[26]

As I have discussed in chapter 3, Spain's sociopolitical climate was rather turbulent well into the 1980s following the death of the dictator. Consequently, the very concept of what it meant to be Spanish varied depending on social class, age, political affiliation, and especially region, given that the end of the dictatorship brought about a resurgence in regional patriotism (including, but not restricted to, the Catalan, Basque, and Galician historical nationalisms) versus a sense of cultural cohesion. According to Walther Bemecker and Sören Brinkmann (2004), even the most fundamental qualities of Spanishness had to be reconsidered as the "traditionalist and Catholic vision of Spain, fundamentally associated with the Castilian language and culture, with all its authority and pretensions of validity, was lost with the end of the Francoist dictatorship" (96). As Ryjik (2011) posits, this was most likely a direct rebellion against the "notion of a 'united, grand, and free Spain,' disseminated by the regime's propaganda that brought forth a reconsideration and subsequent questioning of the concept of a Spanish nation" (7).[27] These assumptions are, nonetheless, quite debatable. First of all, in order for Spanish popular culture to actively counteract a saturation of medieval and early modern thought, such a phenomenon must have actually existed. Second of all, the figure of Lope de Vega must have been a predominant symbol and icon of the regime that members of society would have attempted to dismantle after the dictatorship. Again, there is little to no evidence to support this supposition.

Bemecker and Brinkmann (2004), Ryjik (2011), and Bayless (2015)—among others—call attention to the fact that, whether factually true or not, a part of Spanish popular culture during the *Transición* certainly conceived of the figure of Lope de Vega as a threat to modernity. It is certainly true that, at least by some, the dramaturg was the epitome of the adjective "Spanish," even shortly after the fall of the regime. Never was this image of Lope expressed more explicitly over a mass media outlet than in the introduction to the 1984 episode of *Paisaje con figuras* in which host Antonio Gala declares:

> If I had to define Lope de Vega with just one adjective, I probably wouldn't doubt it: Spanish. That is his profession. That is his wisdom. That is his ideal. That is his art. Spanishness is, for him, a model and paradigm for everything else. Even our defects. Even our virtues. All of his characters, no matter where they might have been born, even the Virgin Mary, are nothing if not Spanish. Even God himself is one of his characters, of course, a Catholic and Spanish protagonist. And if the present is too sad and not enough for him, he consoles himself by looking to the past. A past that is, inarguably, Spanish as well. (00:00:01–00:02:03)

Gala's remarks seem to demonstrate an attempt at reconciliation between the historical figure whose beliefs and ideology were unfortunately associated with an unhappy recent past and the Spanish people, who could still admire and identify with the author. Essentially, Gala's introduction serves as a plea to participants of Spanish popular culture not to forfeit one of the nation's most treasured literary figures simple because of a negative connotation unjustly given to him by recent historical events.

Ironically, with the exception of his fleeting reference to "defects," Gala does not engage in a direct, explicit characterization of the historical Lope. To a certain degree, it seems as though the host is re-introducing Spain to a forgotten icon, one he prefers to remember not as a sensationalist "myth," but as a human being, representative of all Spaniards, complete with his imperfections. Essentially, the episode shifts the focus away from the scandals around which his television persona had revolved 14 years earlier. Recognizing the multifaceted nature of Lope's persona, Gala encourages a reconsideration of the events in the dramatist's life that might cause him to be forsaken entirely by the new popular culture. The rest of the episode, as I will explore below, seems aimed toward this same objective. Lope is depicted as a humble, dying old man who revisits his past and dialogues with the women he left damaged in the wake of his turbulent love life while visiting the important places that witnessed key events in his lifetime.

*Paisaje con figuras* notably offers audiences one of the only modern manifestation of Lope de Vega in which he is presented as a defeated, repentant, and melancholic figure, the only other being the most recent manifestation of Lope as a character in *Lope enamorado*. Curiously, it is also the only one to show him approaching death and dying. As opposed to "El mejor mozo de España" (1970), the latter two advocate for Lope's memory to center around his overall humanity, manifested in his literary legacy, instead of his interestingly scandalous biography. Moreover, any nod to Lope's pride in his womanizing tendencies would not be advisable during either of these moments, as popular culture was making great strides in leaving this type of protagonist in the past.[28] It would appear, however, that participants in the popular culture of the time were not ready for such an acceptance of Lope in their collective imagination, as he would not appear again on Spanish screens for another 26 years. Thus, if there was indeed a dictatorial stigma of Lope de Vega that Gala was attempting to remove from the collective Spanish imagination, his efforts were in vain. Conversely, one cannot overlook the dynamic changes in public tastes that could have simply rendered the figure of a repentant author tedious and out of tune with the types of protagonists that were popular in 1980s Spanish popular culture.

The 1980s was a time in which Spanish popular culture was much less preoccupied with the country's past and set its sights more on the country's present, often times to criticize societal dysfunction. To combat the invasion of foreign series, detective dramas such as *La huella del crimen* (1985) and *Brigada central* (1989), along with sitcoms such as *Platos rotos* (1985) and *Escalera interior, escalera exterior* (1986), had become TVE's primary focus. As opposed to the idyllic programming of decades past, these new shows sought to offer audiences a taste of social realism that was responsive to the contemporary Spanish experience. Meanwhile, Spanish cinema was infiltrated by the progressive, new-age styles of directors who desired to provide a voice in popular culture to marginalized members of society such as juvenile delinquents, homosexuals, and single women (Borau, 2003, 561–565).[29] Given that biopics of important figures of Spanish history were noticeably scarce on television and film during this period, I find it difficult to attribute Lope's hiatus from Spanish screens to a direct association with Francoism. It seems much more plausible that tastes had simply evolved.

Nevertheless, when Lope does return as a character in 2010's *Lope*, his patriotism is manifested a bit differently than in the first two biopics discussed above. No longer would the historical figure need to give lengthy monologues about his love for his country nor have a modern author discuss his "Spanishness" so extensively because his patriotism would be divulged by and included as part of the narrative that he participated as a soldier in Spain's armed forces. This aspect of the author's life was likely omitted from the earlier productions due to doubts of the historical veracity of this claim, as I have discussed above. Curiously, this debate is hinted at again in episode 1.2 of *The Ministry of Time* when Amelia asserts that Lope's participation as a soldier in the Armada Invencible is up for debate because no one knows for sure whether or not this is true. Irene answers her smugly, "dear, you're forgetting where you are" (00:07:10). Likewise, *Lope* bases its opening on the premise that the author did indeed set sail with the Armada not just once for the *Jornada de Inglaterra*, but also previously during the Conquest of the Azores Islands in 1583.[30]

*Lope* begins with an opening sequence of the titular protagonist sprawled out on the ground, exhausted and possibly injured, as Spanish troops march around him. Meanwhile, we hear a voice-over narration by the titular character in which, in a letter to his mother, he reveals that he is returning to Madrid after the incident. He narrates, "Dear mother, after some days of rest in Lisbon I am finally back in Madrid. I return happy and full of pride after seeing how our flag was raised above the Azores Islands after the glorious victory of our military against their mercenaries at the service of France" (00:02:09). The patriotic overtones could not be clearer: his devotion to the country and opposition to Spain's most historical antagonists, Portugal and France, inspired immense pride in him upon his country's victory. The film goes beyond merely explaining his patriotism with eloquent self-praising rhetoric and visually represents his sacrifice while describing his pride in having served in the military campaign. In addition to the fact that Lope's patriotism is presented in a more graphic, realistic manner in this film than in any of his other on-screen manifestations, the placement of this sequence at the very beginning of the movie is significant in that it continues to perpetuate the idea of the author as a faithful Spanish subject willing to fight for his country's honor.

The conceptualization of Lope as a patriotic soldier would continue to be an integral part of his presence in Spanish popular culture throughout the remainder of his appearances on the screen until 2017. The entire premise of his first appearance in *The Ministry of Time* (episode 1.2 "Time of Glory," 2015) is that at 26 years of age he has enlisted as a soldier in the *Armada Invencible* and runs the risk of getting killed before he ever has the chance of writing some of his most canonical works.[31] However, in stark contrast to all of the previous emphases on Lope's patriotism in his popular culture appearances, this episode presents his bellicose attitude and tumultuous past jocosely, even to the extent of using it as a means by which to ridicule the character. For example, during the scene in which Adrián discovers Lope and Amelia in bed together, the former briefly knocks the author unconscious as he opens the door. Lope stands up clumsily soon thereafter and threatens Adrián by saying to him, "I'm warning you, do not do anything crazy. You see, you are before a man who is familiar with prison and its hardships, who knows how to handle a sword, who has fought, injured, and killed in battle for Spain" (00:44:28). Ironically, given the context and tone, these lines ridicule Lope's military past, which is so often praised in other biopics.

Lope's empty threat is, in turn, entirely ignored by Adrián, who comically continues to scold Amelia for sleeping with a person from the past as it would be a disaster if she were to become pregnant from someone outside of her time. Moreover, his patriotism had already been called into question twice earlier in the episode. First, when Salvador is explaining the mission to the team, he informs them that Lope had enlisted in the armada not out of patriotism, but because it was the "condition given by the wife's family so that they would be married" (00:07:21). Second, when Lope first begins making sexual advances on Amelia and recounts the story of why he was late to enlist in the Armada, humorous dramatic irony is created when his voice-over narration contradicts the action being shown on screen. As Lope describes a terrible storm that prevented him from departing for Lisbon on time, we see him engaged in a sexual encounter with a young woman. As viewers are already clued into the assumption that he only enlisted to avoid legal trouble earlier in the episode, his self-proclaimed eagerness to "defend the country" comes off as a ploy to get Amelia into bed.

Given that Lope's patriotic attitude does not constitute a major part of his characterization in the following two episodes of the show in which he appears, it seems that the *Ministry of Time*, obligated to acknowledge this vital part of the "Lope myth," decided to use his patriotism as a means by which to highlight one of the recurring messages of the episode: the morality and societal attitudes of Spain's Golden Age were paradoxical and often hypocritical, far from the utopic ideal like modern consumers of popular culture—especially its more conservative members—have a tendency to believe. By making Lope out to be a false patriot and, therefore, a hypocrite, the writers of the episode introduce a criticism of Spanish culture they see as deeply rooted, which is summed up by Adrián toward the end of the episode, in which he scoffs, "this is Spain, you see? A lot of talking about honor, but if there is money to be made . . ." (00:53:10). In other words, they see a parallel between modern and archaic Spanish culture in that people's eloquent proclamations are often said in order to create a good impression of oneself but are later directly contradicted by their actions. Such a portrayal of a Spanish myth is interesting in the sense that it confronts, deconstructs, and dismantles both the myth of the author and that of the time in which he lived by disabusing their viewers of what Gérard Bouchard (2013) has deemed the "millenarian cycle," that attempts to utilize national myths in the formation societal goals by presenting "an original golden age, then a trauma followed by a return to the golden age" (277). It is well known that, decades earlier, Franco had fashioned his regime as precisely a reconquest of Spain's imperial glory days. By portraying Lope within—and as a product of—his corresponding time period, the episode manages to completely shatter the first stage of the millenarian cycle and demonstrates to audiences that the "original golden age" was hardly an ideal to which modern Spaniards should aspire.

One aspect of the author's supposed military experience that is present in all of the twenty-first-century biopics is the characterization of Lope as a skilled swordsman.[32] In fact, the very first time that Lope appears in *The Ministry of Time* (1.2), he is engaged in an argument with a jealous boyfriend that quickly escalates into a swordfight. A few scenes later, when Amelia is being harassed and manhandled by two ruffians outside the tavern, Lope comes to her rescue by simultaneously fending off both aggressors with his impressive swordplay. In these two situations, the character development of the patriotic soldier is not done, as in other instances, in a comical fashion; rather, Lope de Vega's physical strength and flawless accuracy with the weapon portray him as a force to be reckoned with. This is not surprising, considering that Lope's supposed history of fighting was part of what caused show creators to want to include him as the focal point of the second show. In an interview with creator Javier Olivares, Simon Breden (2018) directly questioned this decision, asking, "Why was Lope de Vega the first Golden Age author to appear in the series instead of Cervantes or Calderón?" Olivares's answer was equally as straightforward: "because he participated in the Spanish Armada . . . and survived" (Breden 88). His combat skills are likewise shown in the film *Lope*. At 00:36:42, Lope arrives home to find that his office has been ransacked. While he looks at the mess that was made, he is attacked from behind by two hitmen sent by debt collectors but reacts quickly enough to avoid injury. He then counterattacks with such force that his assailants flee in fear for their lives. They only manage for Lope to pay them off with a jewel when one of them returns with a gun, an obvious indication that they were no match for his swordsmanship. Later in the film, Lope publicly insults Jerónimo Velálzquez during a performance of one of his plays and his arrest is ordered. Nevertheless, he avoids being taken prisoner by fighting off the *Alguacil* with a sword he takes from an actor standing on the stage. In addition to adding an element of action to both productions, the precise choreography of the abovementioned swordfights depicts the dramatist as a serious, experienced fighter who is not afraid to attack when necessary.

As I have shown here, each of the biopics of Lope de Vega underscores the extreme patriotism of the "Lope myth" in unique ways. Despite the instances in which his eloquent praise of Spain is used ironically to demonstrate hypocrisy, the majority of these examples causes Lope to seem like a valiant, exemplary, and loyal Spanish subject, at least in public. The next characteristic in our analysis, also found in every biopic, does quite the contrary.

## Lope, the Womanizer and/or Hopeless Romantic

This section deals with two sides of the same coin that Fernández (2018) analyzes as one single trait of Lope's life, which she refers to as attention given to his "vida amorosa" (21). Although it is true that screenwriters and directors of Lope's biographical films and television episodes often position his romantic escapades as the focal point of their biopics, it is also certain that the programs tend to place more emphasis on either his questionable sexual morality or his devoted, yet uncontrollable, affection for multiple women simultaneously. Again, the sociopolitical and ideological undercurrents in Spain during the time of their production tend to influence which of these is accentuated. This dichotomy of Lope's personality is not new to his on-screen manifestations because, as I will explore below, both popular and academic cultures have wrestled with the issue of how to explain his relationships with the multiple women in his life.[33] The choice of which facet they choose to highlight on screen, however, drastically molds his characterization in completely different ways. As such, our analysis of the facets of Lope de Vega's love life is divided into two categories: Lope as the promiscuous womanizer and Lope as a hopeless, misunderstood romantic figure. Of course, there are many instances in his filmic and television appearances in which these two elements of his life intersect, but by dissecting the matter into two separate categories, we will be able to better analyze (a.) how each program coded its vision of the man's romances for its intended viewership and (b.) how the depictions of Lope evolve according to the time period in which they are introduced, if at all.

Although it is well known that Lope de Vega was involved with a number of women during his lifetime, the exact number and their identities is, naturally, hard to pinpoint. Historians and literary scholars alike seem to disagree on the identities and timelines of the dramatist's earliest love interests. For example, Rennert (1968), basing his conclusions on the autobiographical character of Fernando in Lope's *La Dorotea* (1632), deduces that the author's infatuation with Elena Osorio must have begun when he was 17 years old, upon returning to Madrid from his university studies in Alcalá de Henares (11–12). Meanwhile, Entrambasaguas (1935) posits that Lope began a two-year romantic relationship with 15-year-old María de Aragón—with whom he allegedly had his first child in 1581—shortly after he turned 17 (8). The scholar bases his conclusion on a baptismal record he discovered at the Parish of San Ginés in Madrid which listed the birth of a child on January 2, 1581, to parents Lope de Vega and doña María de Aragón. He describes María as "bourgeois, rich, and from a family that is close to the Palace. Her parents, Jaques or Jácome of Ambers, Flemmish, and María of Aragon, are court bakers, at the service of the Empress Doña María, widow of Maximillian II" (10). Moreover, he believes that she was the real-life counterpart of the character Marfisa in *La Dorotea*. Curiously, none of Lope's modern biographers, with the exception of Frank Magill, Christina Moose, and Alison Aves (1999) even mention the possibility that the author had been in any serious relationships or, much less, had a child, before his affair with Elena Osorio upon his return to Spain from the military campaign in the Azores Islands.

Nevertheless, due to the fact that Lope's adult life is much better documented than his adolescence and early adulthood, there does seem to be a significant degree of scholarly consensus regarding his other relationships. His scandalous affair with the married daughter of theater manager Jerónimo Velázquez was, much to his liking, the major piece of society gossip in the Madrid of the 1580s.[34] Once his rift with her had exploded into a hearing that resulted in his eight-year exile from Madrid and a two-year exile from Castile, he allegedly abducted Isabel de Urbina and married her by proxy in 1588.[35] Isabel would die at the court of the Duke of Alba in 1595 and, a year later, Lope's exile would have ended and he would again face legal trouble for concubinage with Antonia de Trillo in Madrid. He married his second wife, Juana de Guardo, in 1598, but the marriage was tainted by Lope balancing a second household in Toledo with Micaela de Luján. The matrimony was further plagued by Lope's very public affair with actress Jerónima de Burgos.[36] The fact that he suffered what Dixon (2008) refers to as a "spiritual crisis" (251) following Juana's death in 1613 that led him to seek solace in his religion and be ordained a priest in 1614 did not stop him from pursuing his lustful desires. He was involved in an affair with actress Lucía de Salcedo before devoting himself to his last known lover, Marta de Nevares, in 1616. In addition to his known wives and partners, others have been alluded to or mentioned in historical documents dating from Lope's lifetime. For example, Rennert (1968) cites a letter written by the author to the Duke of Sessa in September of 1611 in which he openly confesses to cheating on his first wife, Isabel de Urbina, in "the least honest way that I could" while in Lisbon in 1588.

The creators of Lope's biopics in the twentieth and twenty-first centuries obviously took a great deal of inspiration from scholarly biographies of the dramatist when preparing their productions in order to portray him as the promiscuous womanizer that history remembers him as. While constraints for time and content meant that none of them could reasonably include all of his romantic conquests, most of them focus on only one or a few of his most scandalous affairs. In case his oscillation between two women in "El mejor mozo de España" didn't quite characterize him enough or his reputation was not solidified in the minds of the 1970s viewers, hints of his licentious conduct are revealed by the program's dialogues. When a friend of his questions him about his treatment of women and whether or not he is capable of loving any of them, his answer speaks volumes:

> I love all of them and none of them, doctor. One is loved for being beautiful, because she is charming when she speaks. The other for bring cross-eyed but funny. One for being tall, another for being short. One for being tough, the other for being sweet. Because they are women and the world would lack meaning without them. Loving them is easy, but every man chases after one women

and sometimes he never catches her. And his reason to live is that chase of an ideal. . . . Lope would die if he didn't chase. (00:20:28)

This quote from Lope's 1970 avatar demonstrates that his constant pursuit of different women for their distinct attributes reveals to us that, while passionate, the author was susceptible to a multitude of women, thus leading his attention to frequently stray. His friend in the conversation, referred to simply as "Doctor," reaffirms this personality trait by responding that "it's your personality. . . . Have a thousand women and write a thousand *comedias* . . . you're a magnificent monster!" (00:03:55)[37]

His turbulent lifestyle is further complicated by the arrival of Lucía de Salcedo, who gets into a physical altercation with Micaela de Luján in the town square over their infatuation with Lope. Although the program does not follow the correct timeline of Lope's life (Juana de Guardo, his legitimate wife in the episode, would have been dead before his affair with Lucía began), the chaos that his lifestyle has caused is enough for him to introspectively reevaluate his decisions and devote himself to the priesthood and turn his life around. Realizing and lamenting the error of his ways, he tells his companion Baltasar that he is going to "ganar el cielo" by fixing his mistakes (00:41:30). Although a remorseful Lope is not a common occurrence in these biopics, converting the dramatist into a sort of masculine Mary Magdalene is quite necessary in the case of *Estudio 1*'s "El mejor mozo de España," as it is the only way to realign the historical figure's reputation with the ideology of the time. Naturally, there is no mention of the lovers that he had or the children he had fathered after taking holy orders.

The representation of a repentant Lope is also in keeping with other discussions of the author in the popular culture of the time. For instance, P. Vila San-Juan's article in a 1964 edition of *La Vanguardia* called "An Old Poet, Very Modern" vaguely mentions the "random, complicated, and mistaken life" that Lope lived (11).[38] He goes on to explain a bit further, stating that Lope was constantly "illicitly tied up in scandalous adventures" (11). The journalist later continues by affirming that the Golden Age dramatist was not always such a negative representative of Spain, given that he managed to turn his life around to such a degree that he was even ordained a priest, thus justifying how the works written by him were penned "for Spain's greatest honor" (11). In a further attempt to sanctify the legacy of the author, Gabriel Llompart would also publish an article that portrayed Lope as a devout and enthusiastic "nativity scene enthusiast" based on artifacts found during the restoration of his home for use as a museum in a 1965 issue of *La Vanguardia*. Although Lope's religious vocation would naturally cease to become a driving force behind his characterization in later biopics, it would be referred to in passing in later productions.

The 1984 episode of *Paisaje con figuras* that was dedicated to Lope de Vega would minimalize the religious conviction he felt about his treatment of the women in his life and would instead emphasize the severe personal consequences that his lifestyle had caused. This episode presents the largest range of the women in Lope's life, beginning with the voice of the elusive María de Aragón (this is the only biopic in which she is even mentioned, much less given a speaking part) and ending with those of Lucía de Salcedo and Marta de Nevares. He becomes defensive at times, such as when María de Aragón scolds him for abandoning her and for never feeling guilty for doing so in the 60 years that have passed since they last saw one another. He reminds her that he wrote a series of *jaculatorias* to Christ to atone for his sins against her, including one in which he proclaimed "dear Jesus, there is nothing I regret more than not regretting that I have offended you, nor is there anything that consoles me more than not regretting as I would like to" (00:07:11).[39] A common thread in all of the dialogues is the dissatisfaction the women feel with his answers, like María does. When he tells Micaela "even in death I love and adore you," she responds with a bitter tone that she believes "you probably say that to all your women. . . . I understand that you are too much Lope for just one woman" (00:17:09). By the end of the episode, the encounters have clearly taken a toll on him. Despite his many achievements, which are highlighted by close-ups on modern statues bearing his likeness and traveling shots across shelves filled with collections of editions of his works, he appears to be somewhat defeated. We see an old man, melancholy in a big house, who looks exhausted, as if he knows he's soon to die alone, a stark contrast to the frequent company he has always enjoyed. He lays in bed in his clerical habit and closes his eyes before the credits roll.

The opinion of Lope de Vega as an unrepentant, shameless womanizer would come back with a vengeance in the 1990s, as evidenced by Gregorio Morán's 1997 article in *La Vanguardia*, in which he has no qualms about referring to the dramatist as a "corruptor of minors, arrogant pimp, sacrilegious priest, swindler, thief, drunk, hooligan, confidant, sexual impulsive, cheater, despicable lackey, flatterer, fake as a wooden nickel" (21). Although he does praise Lope's poetic and other artistic talents, he does not hesitate to attack his alleged hypocrisy by stating that Lope was a "believer with strong faith, always as long as sex with a woman wasn't in the way; I'm not saying woman, I'm specifically talking about sex with a woman" (21). Clearly, there is no longer a need to try to exalt Lope's piety in an attempt to justify his conduct. If anything, Lope's uncontained sexuality would become a selling-point in his twenty-first-century manifestations up until *Lope enamorado* (2018). Such is the case in the first scene following the opening narration in *Lope*, in which the author is confronted by a man who accuses him of sleeping with his wife. Lope sheepishly denies it—in such a way so as to lead viewers to believe that he is lying—and he is punched in the face. Later, while discussing the possibility of enlisting in the Armada Invencible, Lope tells his brother that he refuses to go immediately back to war because he needs to smell the air of the court, cheekily adding that the women seem even more beautiful there now than when he left.

*Lope*'s film crew took full advantage of the titular character's hypersexual reputation to introduce erotic elements into the production. After receiving news that his play will be performed on stage, Elena goes to congratulate him, and their conversation turns physical. She has him sit on a chair, takes his shirt off, and begins kissing him. She asks him to undress her before straddling him and initiating a sexual encounter. Although he is shown repenting of the incident to his confessor, any illusion of him as a devout follower of his faith is quickly shattered because he begins flirting with Isabel de Urbina while serving his penance.

Similarly to the scene in *Lope* in which he is confronted by a suspicious husband, the first glimpse shown of the author in his debut episode of *The Ministry of Time* is of him in a conflict with a man whose girlfriend he was kissing right in front of him. The shameless dramatist pedantically responds to his accuser by reciting an insulting poem, thus ridiculing his adversary's cultural ignorance (00:20:55).[40] Although his brazen attitude is, again, reminiscent of his demeanor in *Lope*, the screenwriters of the episode take strides to exaggerate the author's reputation as a hypersexual deviant by having him seduce Amelia. While she converses with Julián and Lope over a glass of wine, the latter grabs at her, makes suggestive comments, and talks in sensual, seductive tones. A similar tactic is used to eroticize the historical figure in *Cervantes contra Lope* (2016); his first on-screen appearance shows him in bed nude completing a sexual encounter (00:04:25). After he is dressed, the woman confronts him with rumors she's heard that he has another "friend," an accusation he quickly dismisses. The fact that he is shown as an older man in this manifestation reiterates a common theme in many of his other revivals: religion or not, the essence of Lope's personality does not change or mellow with age. This idea had already been stressed explicitly by María de Aragón in her dialogue with him in *Paisaje con figuras* and repeated in his second appearance of *The Ministry of Time* (2.3) when a mature Lope tells Amelia in the year 1604 "I have already told you that I am not the man I used to be . . . but if you want that man to return, all you have to do is ask" (00:54:40). It would appear as though the screenwriters of the show wished to present a more mature character, but whose vices continued to form an integral part of his lifestyle. The concept of a lifelong womanizer is emphasized even further in his third, and final, appearance on *The Ministry of Time* (3.5), when we see Lope giving advice to the actors during a rehearsal of one of his plays in 1605 and he pays particular attention to an actress, looking at her suggestively and ignoring the man who wishes to ask him a question about his delivery. A very similar situation occurs during two scenes in *Cervantes contra Lope*. In the first, Lope pauses a conversation with Cervantes about how to improve the latter's *comedias* to go chase a woman who is looking at him from the balcony of the *corral*, and in the second, Lope begins making advances on the modern journalist who is interviewing him.[41]

As these examples have shown, the directors and screenwriters of his filmic and televised manifestations have always felt the need to emphasize, embellish, and centralize the conceptualization of Lope de Vega as a hyper-sexual philanderer in their depictions, whether or not this means sacrificing historical accuracy or omitting other aspects of his personality. It is also significant to note what elements of Lope's life are not present in these films. For example, he is rarely shown interacting with his numerous children, although they are referenced at times—the last line of text shown before the credits of *Lope* show is "he fathered fourteen children and died at 73 years of age" (01:39:58)—and three of them are even shown briefly as infants in "El mejor mozo de España." By not showing any paternal concern for his offspring, the lasting effect is that, as far as his personal life is concerned, he was little more than a promiscuous womanizer whose selfish desires were devoid of any preoccupation with the consequences he could inflict on others. By sexualizing Lope, production crews create an entertaining spectacle that, considering the adage "sex sells," attracts audiences. It is even tempting to wonder if seeing one of Spain's national treasures as an aloof, adventurous "bad boy" is a source of pride for the current generation. At any rate, Lope is not always shown as a callous Don Juan type; several efforts have been made to portray him as a hopeless romantic.

Although our study of the course of Lope de Vega's biopics reveals a predominant trend in depicting the playwright as a superficial, hypersexual predator, there are also many instances in which directors and producers have attempted to display a more profound, emotional dimension to the figure. Most frequently, this type of character development arises from the unrequited love story between Lope and the woman many consider to have been his first—and possibly only—true love, Elena Osorio. Beyond being one of Lope's most scandalous and exciting love affairs, it is also one of the best documented by historians and Golden Age scholars. It is well known today, as it was during the dramatist's lifetime, that Lope was—as Rennert (1968) asserts—"completely and so desperately in love with her" (50).[42] It has never been a mystery that the beloved *Filis* character in Lope's pastoral ballads is the poetic pseudonym for Elena, as indicated by a handwritten note in the margin of a 1604 edition of the *Romancero general*[43] and it is also widely accepted that the often treacherous *Zaida* character of the Moorish romances is yet another of her poetic manifestations.[44] Moreover, it has also been proposed by Rennert (1968) that she is the sought-after Dorotea in the eponymous novel (in the form of a prosaic dialogue) (48).

Nevertheless, the most dramatic event of their turbulent relationship is undoubtedly the best documented, as it resulted in criminal action litigation against Lope for libel against her and her family, which culminated in the dramatist's banishment from Madrid and the Kingdom of Castile. According to the legal record, included in Tomillo and Pérez Pastor's (1901) study on the *Proceso de Lope de Vega por libelos contra unos cómicos* (12–45), the Velázquez family was suing Lope for distributing and encouraging the circulation of

> some defamatory libels in the form of satires, some in Latin and others in Spanish,[45] were given to people so that they would be published, and since they have been published at this Court, to his great misfortune, to him and to his children and women, a crime was committed. He requested to proceed against them and for them to be condemned to the punishments they had incurred. (12)

Although the record states that the satires principally attack Damián Velázquez, Jerónimo's brother and Elena's uncle, the fact that it also contained unflattering commentary about Jerónimo, his wife Inés, his daughter Elena, and his niece Ana, all described as "very honorable married women who had and continue to have such reputations" (13-14), was an aggravating factor in the case. Moreover, as Pérez Pastor highlights, the satires contained damning accusations that the Velázquez brothers, aided by Jerónimo's wife Inés, prostituted Elena to potential investors whose funds they were interested in securing (139). The Velázquez family sent a witness to the proceedings, Rodrigo de Saavedra, who testified that he was able to discern Lope's authorship from the "broken Latin that truly sounded like the language and speech patterns of Lope de Vega, a poet at this Court" (14). Lope confessed to the crime and, although he initially appealed the 10-year banishment, served his sentence in exile.

The motives behind Lope's composition of the malicious satires are no mystery to scholars. According to Rennert, Elena became an eligible widow upon her husband's death in 1595 (49). As they were already in a passionate relationship before her spouse's passing, it would seem as though Lope would be an obvious choice for Elena's second nuptials. Nonetheless, she would cast Lope aside for a wealthier man, Francisco Perrenot de Granvela.[46] The rejection would deeply scar the author on an emotional level. Sánchez Jiménez (2006) describes how the sorrow he felt after the incident is reflected in his poetry, which entered into a second stage of literary maturity at this point, by affirming that the "Phoenix frequently laments that his adversary's opulence had kept the lady from preferring the poor Moor-poet: Lope's Moors accuse their lovers of being greedy and superficial, just like Gazul does in Lope's famous romance" (26). Curiously, even those biopics that attempt to bestow a deeper emotional dimension on Lope omit this episode of his life. It is to be inferred, therefore, that industry executives have constantly considered the image of an emotionally wounded Lope unattractive.

A fleeting allusion to the debacle between Lope and Elena is included in *Paisaje con figuras*. During an exchange with Elena's voice, Lope expresses his anger about a love affair she once had that her father had arranged before adding "your father was a ruffian," to which she responds, "and you were arrogant" (00:09:50). The episode is careful, however, not to avoid portraying Lope as a loving, romantic character when it comes to his most famous and turbulent partner. When her voice first comes into his head, he exclaims "how often I have thought of you, and I have missed you" (00:08:30). The creators of the show clearly meant to underscore the degree of passion that defined the love affair by showing, just as Dixon (2008) observes, that the romantic adventure would plague the playwright until the end of his life (251). The off-screen narration provided by Lope's character then continues by reminding her of the affection and "uncontainable passion" that they shared.

As brief as their encounter might have been in this episode, Lope de Vega's affair with Elena Osorio and eventual legal battle with her family would take center stage in *Lope* (2010). The biopic tells the story of their first meeting at her father's house. Although their physical relationship is certainly stressed, the screenwriters and director were very careful also to show the emotional connection the two shared. After all, according to an interview that director Andrucha Waddington gave to *Filmogramas* on June 26, 2009, one of the objectives of the movie was to highlight the "adventures and loves so incredible, so emotional and passionate" of the author's early adulthood (n.p.). Her character, although first annoyed by the playwright's insistence on seeing her father to petition a performance of his latest work, is later smitten with the poet when he spontaneously recites a poem for her. From that point on, Elena begins receiving romantic poems in the mail from him. It is evident that she is impressed with him by the way she runs her fingers over his name. We are shown many close-up sequences of Lope sitting at a table writing while a voice-over reads the sonnets he is supposedly writing for Elena.

Several visual and verbal cues are given in these moments to reinforce his characterization as a thoughtful, doting lover. His character is often shown smiling, almost blushing, as he writes many of these love letters, a sign that his infatuation with the young lady is more than mere physical attraction. The plot of the movie thickens when Lope's character discovers that she is married (a fact that the historical Lope almost certainly knew when he met the real Elena), but instead of being angry that his lover has deceived him, wounded his pride, or is committed to another man, his anguish comes from the idea that when her cuckolded husband returns, they'll only be allowed to see each other sporadically and always in secret. Their relationship does indeed continue, but Lope's attentions are soon stolen away by the young Isabel de Urbina. Lope is seen writing love letters and poems to her, but when he is confronted by Elena, his defensive response causes it to seem as though he's only involved with her in retaliation for the fact that Elena is married. The viewer can appreciate how this frustrates Lope, as he is aware that their relationship will not last and can go nowhere as long as they remain in Madrid, which he expresses by reminding her that "if we have children they won't have my last name" (01:02:55). He urges her to run away with him and the argument escalates when she refuses. His frustration culminates in him revealing that he knows that her father entices investors by offering them a chance to sleep with her, the screenwriters evidently being inspired by the allegations made against Lope in the libel case.[47] His desire to flee with her and his vehement passion regarding the situation portrays what scholars have suggested: that his romantic feelings for Elena were genuine and intense.

There are additional examples of how the biopics depict Lope as a helpless romantic that do not involve Elena Osorio. Despite the comments that are made by and about him, Lope's avatar in "El mejor mozo de España" is shown to be compassionate with the women in his life in such a way that suggests that, while he might not be faithful to them, he does love them. When Juana is upset with him, he comforts her and begs her not to leave him. Although it is evident that some of what he says is clearly an attempt to return to her good graces following a mistake he has made, he is shown as sincere when declaring his love for her, especially during his close-up sequence in which he recites his famous sonnet, "To be discouraged, to dare, to be furious" (00:23:30).[48] This scene is reminiscent to the penultimate scene in *Lope*, in which the dramatist discovers that, thanks to Elena's intercession, he is not to be sent to the gallows but banished.[49] The same sonnet is read by voice-over as Lope looks around and sees Elena smiling fondly at him. Immediately following the last glance that the two share, the film cuts to the final scene in which Lope and Isabel de Urbina ride off together toward the sunset. The resulting message transmitted to viewers is quite similar in both cases: it is not that he is interested solely in physical interactions; he just happens to be capable of feeling the same degree of attraction and affection toward more than one person at a time.[50]

Lope's avatar in *Paisaje con figuras* reiterates this misunderstood amorous plurality on a number of occasions by making comments to the women like "I loved you all. Who can understand me?" (00:22:04) Unlike in the other biopics, Lope's avatar in this episode is given the opportunity to explain himself more thoroughly. As Fernández observes, part of the objective of this show was to question and destabilize "the 'Don Juan-esque' myth that is so easily imposed on our dramaturg, so as to see inside the low points of his life and the complexity of his sentimental relationships" (23). Whether or not Gala intentionally put in place such a contrast to audiences' expectations of Lope's character, the critic is certainly correct in analyzing the effect that his technique causes in modern viewers. In the episode, he reflects on his life while talking to Micaela and says "at each moment of my life I have passionately done what I passionately desired" (00:23:12). Based on his tone and on the context provided by the dialogues up until this point, it is likely that the dramatist is by no means trying to excuse himself by blaming his fickle nature. In the context of this episode, it appears as though Lope is commenting on the changing tides of one's wishes and desires in life, a concept he reiterates moments later when speaking to Juana and states "yes, Juana, I was happy with all of you . . . but perhaps happiness is a *comedia* that cannot last" (00:26:06). In other words, Lope seems to be affirming that, while he loved them all dearly at one point or another, one's feelings in life, along with every other situation or mentality, are subject to change. Underscoring the volatile nature of mankind at this point of Spanish history could be construed as an encouragement for a cathartic reconciliation among members of the divided post-Francoist society.

It is significant, but not surprising, that one of the most recurring avatars of Lope de Vega, the one presented in three episodes of *The Ministry of Time*, is the biggest exception to the trend of displaying the dramatist as a hopeless romantic. Víctor Clavijo, the actor who brings Lope to life in the series, spoke about what he considers to be the most attractive feature of the dramatist's personality to the series' followers on the fourth episode of a follow-up web series called *La puerta del tiempo* in which the actors are interviewed out of character. His answer certainly helps to explain the characterization of the author as he asserts that "people have always enjoyed seeing a *fucker*, which is the novelty here, that's really what he was, even though it's not talked about" (00:10:09).[51] Essentially, he tells us that today's audiences in Spain would not respond well to a hopeless romantic characterization of Lope, given that they prefer something more scandalous and shocking. Apparently, this requires eliminating almost all of Lope's biography from the show. Breden (2018) also cites this quote and interprets it as a reminder that "being a literary figure does not equate to being a good person" (78). With the exception of scattered references to his plays and poetry, almost none of the documented events of Lope de Vega's life are found in any of the three episodes in which his character appears. Clavijo's comments seem to align perfectly with show creator Javier Olivares's who prepared the show attempting to avoid history being presented "like something boring that talks about the past as if it were dead and it's very much alive" (Breden, 2018, 89). Olivares's desire to make history more exciting for the viewers of the series explains why he characterized the dramatist, as he admits, "so as to show the private side of

Lope, a heartless seductor" (88). It is interesting, nonetheless, that the show's creators felt the need to fabricate new scandals for the episodes, given that his biography is littered with plenty of material from which to draw inspiration.

Apart from shedding light on what aspects of the "Lope myth" are most marketable to the current generation, these comments about the playwright also demonstrate how diminished Lope's presence is in popular culture and how little is known about him outside of academic circles. Lope's sexual escapades were never, as has been previously established, particularly private, and his reputation as a ruffian has often been the only piece of information about him to be discussed or portrayed on mass media outlets. The show does acknowledge the difference between an academic perspective versus a modern popular opinion of the author by juxtaposing Amelia, an eighteenth-century scholar, against Julián, a twenty-first-century paramedic. When asked what they knew about Lope in 1.2, Julián is only able to respond uncomfortably "ehh . . . that he was a writer" (00:06:08), while Amelia confidently adds to his answer with "Lope de Vega was one of the most important authors in the history of Spain" (00:06:37). It is interesting to note how a man who was once a central topic of Madrid's gossip circles and rumor mills is now barely known by the Spanish people and how producers today who wish to follow his example of giving "pleasure to the common man" in today's society must do so by leaving such a big part of him out of it.[52] We must ask ourselves, then, if Lope exists in the collective Spanish consciousness in name alone, what about him makes him a desirable subject to be brought to life in these productions?

Comments like that of Spanish film critic Angel Antonio Pérez Gómez (2010)—who declared after viewing *Lope* that "not to be less than the English, we now have our *Shakespeare in Love*" (103)—allow us to understand that, at least for some Spaniards today, Lope stands as a check on Anglo-Saxon cultural hegemony in the Western popular culture tradition.[53] This argument is further reinforced by *The Ministry of Time* 3.5, which features a pair of English thieves who travel to the past to steal Lope's and Cervantes's works and incorporate them into England's literary tradition. The Englishmen constantly berate the Spanish characters and even cheat in a card game that I consider symbolic of the episode's message: England is considered superior to Spain in the Western cultural tradition because of their ruthless dishonesty and willingness to steal and cheat. When they are confronted, they become hostile and attack the "bloody Spaniards!" (00:51:11) Though brief, the implication is quite profound: the untrustworthy Anglo-Saxons feel so threatened by the honorable Spanish that they are compelled to slander their rivals in order to conceal their own dishonest conduct and justify their unwarranted international acclaim. It is worth noting here that the episode was created and filmed at a time in which the producers of *The Ministry of*

*Time* had recently initiated litigation against a North American television series, *Timeless* (2016–2018), for plagiarizing *The Ministry of Time*. Shortly before the episode aired, the case settled outside of court and did not require the American series to halt production.[54]

Essentially, the intriguing figure of Lope de Vega continues to exist as a myth of which new generations simply need reminding. Popular culture does so occasionally because his presence is considered important to Spain's cultural patrimony. In spite of which of his life's events are adapted to film and/or television, he is Spain's point of access into the modern trend of elevating celebrated intellectuals, particularly those of the literary intelligentsia, into national icons and symbols of national pride. For this reason, it is easy to understand why producers of his biopics have always been sure to accentuate his poetic and dramatic proclivity in their depictions of the author.

## Lope, the Literary Genius

While it is true that—for better or for worse—Lope's personal life has made him an enduring national figure, the creators of his biopics have certainly not overlooked the aspect of the "Lope myth" that made him a cultural phenomenon even during his own time: that of his literary—especially theatrical—prowess. His contemporaries and modern biographers alike have attributed his vast bibliography to his natural gifts that permitted him to produce literature virtually effortlessly. According to Dixon (2009), based solely on the number of his plays that have come down to us in the twenty-first century, the author must have written at least one play per month (259). Morley and Bruerton (1940) have also calculated that around 1618 Lope would have been producing *comedias* at a staggering rate of one per week (218).[55] In any case, admirers of Lope de Vega's theater will likely always have difficulty trying to calculate exactly how productive he was and what could possibly have enabled him to write so much during his lifetime. Despite his reputation as exceedingly arrogant regarding several aspects of his life, the historical Lope seems to have maintained a more casual attitude toward his contributions to Spanish theater.

Lope's *Arte nuevo* (1609) is often considered today as a manifesto by which the dramatist instructed would-be dramaturgs on how to revolutionize the theater with his innovative method of composing plays. Nevertheless, as Jonathan Thacker (2017) acknowledges, the work is "rather a practical man-of-the-theater's guide to (and apologia for) what has been shown to work in the Spanish *corral* in front of a mixed audience at the turn of the seventeenth century" (110). Moreover, as Rennert (1968) notes, the tone of the *Arte nuevo* is significant to understanding the author's true attitude toward writing plays, highlighting that the "careless and sometimes halting" versification leads him to believe that "Lope evidently did not take the matter very seriously" (179). Rennert's interpretation of Lope's composition of the *Arte nuevo* is corroborated by the playwright's numerous attempts at success in other literary styles and genres, specifically historical prose. Despite having written some well-received works in prose, it is well known that Lope also unsuccessfully campaigned for the position of Royal Chronicler.[56] It is no surprise that, as Dixon (2009) remarks, Lope would have preferred to be remembered as Spain's most important writer of prose, due to the fact that "writing plays for money, for the *corrales*, was a lowly-esteemed occupation, scorned by nobles and intellectuals" (259). As I will explore below, Lope would not have wanted to be associated by anything that was considered trivial by the upper classes.

His nonchalant attitude toward the theater has been one of the facets of the literary genius component of the "Lope myth" that has been ignored in many of the biopics about him. The only example of such an instance occurs in "El mejor mozo de España" (1970). The episode is full of references to Lope's reception within the literary circles of seventeenth-century Madrid. We see him and his followers taunted and aggressively provoked by envious rivals, casually discussing literature and future projects with the likes of Quevedo, Cervantes, and Góngora (although the disagreements between Lope and the latter do boil over into a series of insults), and negotiating with Inquisitorial censors about the content of his drama. Nevertheless, during a discussion about his love life, friend and confidant Baltasar suggests, "but, Lope, your true love is the theater," to which the dramatists scoffs and replies, "theater? No, Baltasar, stop joking. No, I write it because I know how to" (00:41:05). Although this is an isolated occurrence in which we see Lope dismissing his theatrical activity as something of little importance, there is also a subtle reference to his desires to be a successful prose writer in *Cervantes contra Lope*, when the former alludes to Lope's desires to be a novelist when he explains to the interviewer that "Lope has envied by *Quijote* since day one" (00:04:25). Evidently, the screenwriters of these biopics do not often find it suitable to portray a playwright who does not wholeheartedly enjoy or believe in his work. Perhaps they have feared damaging national pride by broadcasting the accidental nature of the playwright's career.

Therefore, in direct opposition to what the historical Lope seems to have felt about writing plays, it is much more common for the creators of the biopics to portray Lope as an inspired and deeply philosophical writer of successful dramas and spontaneous poet. Such is the case in the film *Lope*. When Lope's character walks into Madrid's *corral de comedias* for the first time, there is a 360-degree traveling close-up of Lope looking up and smiling, clearly showing his fascination for the performative arts. His poetic proclivity is highlighted almost immediately thereafter, when he is hired by Jerónimo Velázquez as a copier for some of the plays he has purchased.

Upon realizing that Lope took the liberty to make changes to Cervantes's *Numancia* (ca. 1585) instead of copying it, he becomes angry and Lope defends himself, saying "I was only trying to give life to the play. I wanted the play to resemble life more, for the characters to be like us, for them to suffer and laugh" (00:25:55). Apparently having interpreted the *Arte nuevo* as a deeply reflective manual by Lope, the screenwriters use concepts from it to put the justification in the character of the author's mouth. He continues to argue with Velázquez, introducing an obvious reference to Lope's concept of *tragicomedy*, saying "Don Jerónimo, in life laughter and tears are mixed" (00:26:15). His emotional connection to the plays he writes is again stressed later in the film, when he explains to Elena Osorio that the characters he creates are so realistic because of his desire and ability to empathize with them. He tells her, "when I write for a Portuguese audience, I try to feel what a Portuguese person feels" (01:02:05). Despite what the historical Lope might have opined about the theater or his role in molding it, his character in *Lope* is certainly depicted as an idealized profound soul with a strong emotional connection to his work.

*The Ministry of Time* also romanticizes Lope's relationship with and vision of the theater in his first appearance in 1.2. Upon meeting Amelia, he drifts into a reflection of his love for writing plays and tells her "theater is . . . it's the true mirror of the world. It makes dreams come true for every man, be he rich or poor. It makes whoever only has a miserable life experience unimaginable adventures" (00:47:03). Breden (2018) uses the same quote from the fictional Lope to argue that both historical figure and character coincide in their views on the theater, referencing specifically the *Arte nuevo* (79–80). I find these lines from the television series, however, to be in direct opposition to the attitude the author demonstrates toward the kind of theater he produced. It is true, as Breden suggests, that Lope did express the utmost esteem for theater, but only in its classical sense,[57] but as he clearly states in the introduction to the work, "what pains me in this part is having written *comedias* without art" (vv. 15–16),[58] he does not consider the types of plays he writes to be composed in this fashion. He was aware that his style was sensationalistic, aimed at an uncultured audience, and that it lacked "el arte" of epochs past. As for the sort of theater that Lope did respect, he maintains that it has no place in the popular Spanish culture of the seventeenth century, arguing that audiences would not appreciate it or pay to see it and that "whoever writes them with art now dies without fame and fortune" (vv. 29–30).[59] Possibly being unfamiliar with the sarcasm found in Lope's recorded observations of the theater of his time, or simply preferring to ignore it so as to create a more congenial character, those responsible for the characterization of the Phoenix in both *Lope* and, especially, *The Ministry of Time,* present a rather sensationalized avatar of the playwright.

Regardless of the historical Lope's opinions of his theater, what was made clear in the seventeenth century and is often represented in the biopics is his unrivaled way to entertain an audience. Lope's Spanishness, one must remember, has often been a central part of his characterization in these productions. Here it is convenient to mention that the screenwriters and directors extended this concept to show how the playwright used his knowledge of the Spanish people as part of his successful formula. In "El mejor mozo de España," the Spanishness of Lope's plays is highlighted on a number of occasions. The most explicit example of this is when the group of novice playwrights are shown discussing their taste in literature and one of them praises Góngora and his cultured style, which he remarks echoes a more European spirit, such as that of France and England.[60] The show makes an unapologetic patriotic point by making it clear that Spanish theatergoers much prefer their own national brand of *comedias*.

Although *The Ministry of Time* is quick to highlight Lope's wit in his first appearance in 1.2, his dominance over the theatrical realm is not explicitly brought to the forefront until 3.5, in which he is shown as having a keener understanding of the Spanish people and their sense of humor than even the highest ranking political official, namely, the Duke of Lerma.[61] When Lerma learns that the comic relief in Lope's newest play *El valido corrompido* is at his expense, he confronts the playwright about it.[62] The following exchange ensues:

DUKE: My dear Lope, this is Spain. People are not prepared for that kind of play.
LOPE: Well . . . satires . . . relieve people so that they can continue to carry the heavy burden of their existence.
DUKE: I do not want people to laugh at me!
LOPE: Your excellency, laughing at the powerful is the poor man's retaliation. That is how order is maintained. (00:45:26)

In one of perhaps the most accurate characterizations found in all of the biopics, this dialogue demonstrates that Lope not only knew how to entertain his audiences, but he understood how his plays can be beneficial to maintaining the proper social order. Lope's profound understanding of the tastes of the Spanish audience is again made evident in *Cervantes contra Lope*. In the special, we see Cervantes's frustration at not managing to get his play *La confusa* (ca. 1685) performed on stage. The famous novelist, admitting that Lope's plays are much better received than his own, seeks his advice during a time in which the two authors are still on friendly terms. Lope informs the struggling dramatist that his problems stem from not paying attention to public tastes, preferring to write plays more suited to past audiences than present ones. If he wants to be successful, Lope continues, recalling some of the precepts from his *Arte nuevo*, Cervantes should modernize his style and be more creative. As his counterpart in *Lope* had argued years earlier, "times change. Why put shackles on the imagination?" (00:26:45)

In addition to his love for the art of writing dramas and how well-acquainted Lope was with the demands of the Spanish public, the biopics often underscore his astounding ability to quickly—at times spontaneously—create or recall verses, poems, and plays. The first of such incidents is the scene in "El mejor mozo de España," in which Lope consoles Juana by reciting his "Desmayarse, atreverse, estar furioso" sonnet. Although the episode does not specify in any way whether Lope's character is creating the poem extemporaneously or recalling it from memory, the objective of the moment is to impress viewers with the fact that he always has a poem at the tip of the tongue.

Similar illusions are created in the film *Lope*, first when he is attempting to charm Elena Osorio and he suddenly begins reciting Sonnet CV from his *rimas*: "Eyes of the greatest grace and beauty" (00:55:58).[63] Given the young age of the poet at this moment of the biopic and the fact that this particular sonnet was not published until later into Lope's adulthood, it is safe to assume that the character is creating it extemporaneously. His proclivity to spontaneous, unprepared verse production is exhibited again later in the film. The Marqués de las Navas accuses Lope of having prepared the verses the night before and Isabel challenges Lope to invent a sonnet on the spot to disprove the noble's presumption and demonstrate that he is indeed capable of composing sonnets on demand. Proving his originality and poetic prowess, Lope's character flawlessly delivers a metaliterary sonnet about how to compose sonnets (his "Violante orders me to make a sonnet").[64] Since the verses were most likely not composed spontaneously during a poetic duel, we have here another perfect example of how the movie attempts to emphasize the literary genius aspect of the "Lope myth."

The film also highlights the speed at which he could compose an entire drama, showing him completing an entire *comedia* from beginning to end in a period of 48 hours. Although such a rate seems, as Alba Carmona (2017) suggests, to be yet another exaggeration of his genius by the screenwriters (48), Dixon (2009) counters her argument by reminding us that "there is evidence for his claim that some were written in twenty-four hours" (259). Nevertheless, it is certain that the film wanted to exemplify the virtual superhuman ability to compose plays quickly that Lope has been famous for over the past four centuries. Such quick production of rhymes and verses is also playfully presented in *The Ministry of Time* 1.2 when he recites spontaneous poetic-sounding phrases, such as "your eyes are corals" to a woman with whom he is making love and she, seemingly aroused by the poetry more than the man himself, insists that he continue during the encounter, pausing her movements as he pauses his recitation (00:30:30–00:31:16). The episode thus illustrates that his literary genius was part of his appeal during his own time and, in doing so, suggests that this helps to explain his ongoing popularity in our time.

Another aspect of Lope's literary genius that is almost always highlighted in the biopics is how adored he is by his contemporary audiences. "El mejor mozo de España" suggests that Lope's positive reception is the result of the fact that his inspiration is often found in moments from everyday life, which makes his plays relatable. When a young friend observes how the author handles the dramatic situation with his lover Juana, Lope asks him "Can you imagine how I am able to write even one *comedia* in the middle of all this chaos?" to which the admirer responds while laughing, "if it weren't for the chaos you wouldn't even write one verse" (00:47:25–00:47:29). Yet again, screenwriters were forced to deviate from the historical records of Lope de Vega's life in order to inject the "Lope myth" with meaning: audiences likely were unaware of the events that inspired the Golden Age author's theatrical texts, so some original interventions not taken from the historical record from screenwriters were required in order to accentuate this facet of the myth.

The episode goes on to highlight the method behind Lope's madness when he is further criticized by a young playwright-aspirant who, out of frustration for not understanding Lope's success, alleges that all Lope knows how to write about are deceits, love-triangles, cross-dressing women, and other trivial matters. He ends his monologue by asking, "Does nothing else happen in Spain? Don't people die, don't we lose lands? Where is the reality of our times in his plays?" (00:43:55–00:44:00) This particular rebuke of Lope's superficial approach to the problems of the seventeenth century is significant for the episode's time, given that it refutes the idea that the Golden Age was an illustrious period, an objective that, as I have reverted to several times throughout this study, many scholars insist was a central aspect of Franco's cultural indoctrination. Again, the evidence challenges these assumptions and calls into question their credibility.

The episode does not immediately address the criticism, but postpones the answer until the very end. Góngora leaves after bidding farewell to the author with a disparaging "you are the master of the superficial, Lope" (01:12:55). Once the performance of the play has started, Góngora appears back at the tavern with Cervantes. He calls the latter's attention to the fact that they are drinking alone, to which Cervantes laughs and tells him that the taverns are always empty when a Lope play is being performed. Góngora angrily looks into the camera and shouts "Lope, Lope, Lope . . . always the same!" (01:13:05) In other words, his envious rivals may criticize him, but his audience loves him. The film *Lope* also shows how audiences enthusiastically receive his work with cries of "Long live Lope!" at the conclusion of a performance of one of his plays. Also, when the version of Cervantes's *Numancia* that Lope has improved debuts, the crowd and the actors in the company respond with overwhelming approval, smiling, cheering, and creating a commotion. This scene does not simply show how crowds received works that Lope wrote or simply touched (it is not revealed how much the character changed of the original), but—given that there is no historical record that Lope interfered at all with the composition of the *Numancia*—it also displays the superiority of Lope's theater to that of Spain's most famous writer of all time, Cervantes.

The preeminence over the author of the *Quijote* is also seen as part of Lope's unbridled literary brilliance in both *Cervantes contra Lope* and *El ministerio del tiempo*. In the first, Lope is depicted as being a passive, wrongfully accused victim of an obsessively envious Cervantes, whose unfounded accusations against the playwright seem to be the result of his frustration at not having achieved the same financial success as his rival. Cervantes's inferior position to Lope in the theater is reiterated twice in *El ministerio del tiempo*. The first instance occurs in 2.3 when Cervantes, angry that Lope is recruiting actors from his company questions their motives for abandoning him in favor of the Phoenix. An actress answers his query with a sincere "Lope is Lope. No offense, but who has heard of Miguel de Cervantes?" (00:25:35) The second situation occurs during both characters' final appearances in the series. In episode 3.5, Cervantes is allowed to present his work to another pillar of European literature, William Shakespeare, while the latter is in Spain accompanying the king to the signing of the peace treaty in 1605.[65] Despite having been given this great honor in lieu of Lope, his insecurities get the best of him and the two end up in a comical "swordfight" (using candlesticks as swords as they were both unarmed at the time) at the end of the episode over whose works will be remembered most throughout history.

With the exception of *Paisaje con figuras*, all of the biopics about Lope de Vega's life have included components praising his literary legend in very similar ways. These depictions have left popular culture with the impression that Lope de Vega was a profoundly emotionally invested, expert entertainer who was sensitive to the comedic demands of the Spanish public. Not only could he produce a large volume of text at an extremely accelerated pace, but he could do so without sacrificing the poetic quality of his verses or the thematic content that his audiences had come to expect in his dramas, as seen by his contemporary public's enthusiastic response to the performances of his works. Moreover, he might even have been a better writer than the reigning monarch of Spanish letters, Miguel de Cervantes. It is only natural that, boasting such impressive accolades, they would also choose to portray a resulting haughtiness in his characterization, as I will explore in the next section.

## Lope, the Audacious

Not surprisingly, a historical figure with such an adoring fan base would certainly not have held a modest opinion of himself. The biopics often underscore the unflattering facet of Lope's legacy that he was uncontrollably arrogant, especially in dealing with other literary celebrities. Televised and filmic representations of Lope de Vega highlight that he was often able to channel the same poetic talents that permitted him such an astounding literary career into a quick and scathing wit with which to attack his adversaries. As I have already discussed a number of times in my study, many of the biopics spotlight his strained relationship with literary rivals and contemporary critics. His rivalry with the author of the *Quijote*, for instance, has been the most embellished by his recent appearances on film and television, as is evidenced by the fact that it is the subject of an entire made-for-TV film, *Cervantes contra Lope*. The conflict between the two authors is also brought to light in episodes 2.3 and 3.5 of *The Ministry of Time*. Moreover, we see Lope in arguments with many unnamed authors and archenemy Góngora in "El mejor mozo de España." What remains of his dramatic and poetic production certainly proves that he had serious, often aggressive disagreements with other Golden Age authors, much more so with Góngora than with Cervantes.[66] Naturally, Cervantes's more prominent position in the collective Spanish imagination makes him a much more attractive target for screenwriters and directors of Lope's biopics. Also worthy of mention is the attention given to Lope's friendship with possibly the most controversial author of Spain's Golden Age, the relentlessly brutal satirist Francisco de Quevedo. Quevedo is seen coming to Lope's defense in "El mejor mozo de España" and laughing at Lope's attacks on Cervantes in *Cervantes contra Lope*, in which we also see him comically draw his sword, as if ready to attack the latter (when he is not around) in defense of his friend. By portraying such an affinity with Quevedo, Lope becomes associated with the side of the Golden Age literary wars that is known for brazen, contentious, and shamelessly vulgar attacks against intellectuals such as Cervantes and Góngora. Nevertheless, Lope is almost always portrayed as being on the receiving, defensive end of the other side's criticisms, using his wit alone to deflect their attacks. Although not afraid to defend himself, the fictitious Lope is rarely seen as the instigator of these conflicts.

There are, however, many instances in which Lope is depicted as having an audacious, even rude, attitude when dealing with those who do not belong to the literary intelligentsia. For example, Lope is confronted by the *alguacil* in "El mejor mozo de España" after being framed for stealing a trout from a market. The misogynistic, *machista* dramatist, capable of speaking so eloquently to the women, critics, and literary colleagues throughout the episode, speaks to the authority in a demeaning, ridiculing tone, laughing and taking the situation very lightly. He shows no reverence to the *alguacil* nor does he seem to fear any potential legal consequences. When asked "and the trout?" he scoffingly retorts "sir, by that name I only know of a very skinny actress," to which the crowd explodes with laughter (00:32:12).

The film *Lope* also shows the author as having a bold personality when the author derisively responds to the man who accused him of sleeping with his wife and never shying away from insisting on having his plays performed or that his alterations to other authors' texts should be kept. Moreover, the film shows an extreme of Lope's gall and fearless use of rhetoric in retaliation for Jerónimo Velazquez's broken promises and mistreatment of daughter Elena. At the end of the debut of his play *El Nuevo Mundo descubierto por Cristóbal Colón* (1614), in the presence of a large audience composed of members of the highest aristocracy and nobility and amid the cries of "Viva Lope," the titular protagonist stands to receive his ovation, but interrupts the crowd by announcing "I want to read some verses dedicated to Don Jerónimo Velázquez and his honorable daughter Doña Elena de Osorio" and proceeds to divulge her father's practice of prostituting her by continuing with a sonnet that contains the verse "a lady sells herself to whoever wants her" (01:13:45).[67] Lope's audacious characterization in *The Ministry of Time* and *Cervantes contra Lope* continues to closely resemble that of his earlier biopics. For example, when Lope is caught in the middle of a sex act by his partner's father toward the beginning of 1.2, he jocosely taunts the man as he prepares to leave the room, saying comically "jumping to conclusions would be premature, no . . . this isn't what it looks like, I swear" (00:30:33).[68] The father is, of course, infuriated by the blatant disrespect and disregard for the gravity of the situation, shouting after him, "to top it all off you speak to me in rhyme!" (00:30:37).[69]

The depiction of Lope's insolence, as can be inferred by the previous examples of his irreverent behavior, is the product of insufferable arrogance, which is often put on display in many of his on-screen manifestations. Cervantes's avatar in *Cervantes contra Lope* explicitly states such an opinion of Lope in his interview by saying "I admire Lope's genius. I admire his constant and virtuous diligence. But that doesn't mean he isn't a proud and arrogant man" (00:09:52). The portrayal of Lope throughout the program does lead viewers to share Cervantes's opinion, as his character is seen gloating about the brilliance of his play *El testimonio vengado* (1604) to the novelist while they both witness a performance of the drama at a *corral*. The program later shows to what level of cruelty his arrogance can extend during the session of the Academia de Madrid in which Lope presents and reads aloud his *Arte nuevo* and asks Cervantes to lend him his pair of eyeglasses. When he puts them on to read, he ridicules his rival in front of the Academia by saying smugly, "curious spectacles, I hadn't noticed. They look rather like two poorly cooked fried eggs. Doesn't the author of the *Quijote* have enough money to get some new ones?" (01:03:35). Although it would seem as though the roles are somewhat reversed in this scene and that Lope is bullying his rival unprovoked, viewers are aware that his arrogant attack is indeed a retaliation against an insulting sonnet that Lope has blamed Cervantes for.

*The Ministry of Time* also includes several incidents of Lope's arrogance that are reminiscent to those included in *Lope* and *Cervantes contra Lope*. For example, Lope initially refuses to attend to Alonso in episode 2.3 and only changes his mind when the later refers to him as the acclaimed "fénix de los ingenios." Alonso attempts to persuade Lope not to sell his *comedias* to a pair of English buyers during the same conversation, arguing that he, along with the people of Madrid, are anxious for another one of his plays. Lope responds complacently, saying "you all aren't the only ones. I don't mean to brag, but my work has started to provoke admiration overseas" (00:38:41). As is the case in *Cervantes contra Lope*, the latter directs his arrogance at Cervantes in their following appearance in *The Ministry of Time 3.5*. This time, Lope seeks out Cervantes to ridicule him for being appointed to write a chronicle for the king about the signing of the peace treaty whereas he was preparing a *comedia* that would commemorate the occasion. He continues his provocation by encouraging Cervantes to attend the play, then exits the room smiling. The viewer sees him standing outside the door in anticipation until Cervantes's agonizing scream is heard off camera. He walks away from the door with a smug look of satisfaction and chuckling to himself.

Although the specific scenes shown in the biopics are complete inventions and dramatic embellishments of events referred to in historical documents on behalf of the screenwriters, they are useful in characterizing Lope's avatars with a trait that has long been attributed to the author: his insurmountable delusions of grandeur. As far as the historical Lope was concerned, his social inferiority complex—the result of having been born into a modest household of artisan parents—was a common one during his time. As Rennert reminds us, Lope's preoccupation with being considered noble was "a universal weakness among Spaniards" during the seventeenth century and that "everybody sought to pose as a *hidalgo* and—as a natural corollary—to avoid work" (1–2). Many scholars, including Profeti (2000), inform us that Lope was no exception to this rule, given that he would feign "a nobility that he has no claim to" (227). Unfortunately for the dramatist, none of his contemporaries took his claims of noble descent very seriously and he was never afforded any official military orders.[70] Nevertheless, Lope sought claims of noble heritage from his maternal lineage, claiming to be a descendent of Bernardo del Carpio.[71]

The historical Lope even went so far as to usurp the crest of Bernardo del Carpio's noble family and affix a portrait of himself to it that would be printed in *La arcadia* (1592–1594). The portrait, according to Sánchez Jiménez, is significant in understanding Lope's self-fashioning of an ideal self because it depicts a young Lope dressed in courtly garb above the Latin inscription: *Quid humilitate, Invidia?*[72] Sánchez Jiménez (2006) understands that the phrase "corresponds to one of the Phoenix's favorite self-representations: that of a brilliant poet harassed by the envy of his contemporaries" (37). The self-elevation did not go unnoticed in the seventeenth century and sparked one of Góngora's most vicious attacks against the playwright. Góngora, an authentic noble by birth, had developed a bitter contempt for Lope's uncultured style, poor reputation, and proximity to members of the plebeian social class. He took special offense to Lope's use of a noble crest in *La Arcadia* (1605), penning a sonnet about the matter titled "To the *Arcadia* by Lope de Vega Carpio," which reads: "For the sake of your village, little Lope, please erase the nineteen towers from your coat of arms because, even though they're all made from wind, I doubt you have enough wind for that many towers" (vv. 1–4).[73]

Sánchez Jiménez (2018) recognizes how brutal Góngora's sonnet is and how effectively it attacks Lope by arguing that

> the poet from Cordova reveals and destroys Lope's self-fashioning strategy with this scathing sonnet. Góngora first declares that the Phoenix should "erase" his crest because it is false, made "from wind." Additionally, the informal appellative "little Lope" brings the Phoenix down from his imaginary position as a noble Carpio to that of a common child of an embroiderer, an occupation of little prestige held by Lope's father. (39)

The creators of the film *Lope* also took notice of the playwright's unsubstantiated ostentation and included it in their biopic. Early in the film, the fictitious Lope's mother passes away and the author, wishing to give her the proper burial he feels she deserves, has the usurped noble crest imprinted on her casket. To complete the illusion, he hires some friends of his who are actors to attend the service disguised as nobles. Despite the anachronism—Lope's mother likely died in 1589, years before the action of the movie takes place—the scene effectively characterizes a Lope who will stop at nothing to achieve his goals, be they romantic, professional, personal, or social. The rest of Lope's on-screen representations omit this particular scene from their portrayals of his life and times, but they do not hesitate to indirectly hint at his noble pretensions in other ways. With *Paisaje con figuras* being another notable exception, Lope is always shown dressed in a way that would not correspond to his actual social class. He is always shown dressed in elegant garments that are evocative of noble attire.

## Lope, Our Contemporary

In addition to the characterization techniques employed by the screenwriters and directors to create the various avatars of Lope de Vega as I have been discussing in this chapter, they all seem to have the common objective of finding a place for the playwright in the modern world. Again, as evidenced by the 1965 article "An Old Poet, Very Modern," this appears to have been a preoccupation in popular culture for several decades. The challenge is understandable. What is the appropriate way to represent in contemporary times a historical figure whose lifestyle was so antithetical to his own seventeenth-century culture? Although the objective may be common to all of the biopics, their approaches to answering this question differ greatly.

For example, "El mejor mozo de España" is formatted in such a way that viewers see Lope de Vega in his own time, surrounded by characters who pertain to the same time, and no interference from the future is detected at all (as is the case in most of the subsequent productions). However, the characters make various references to Lope's lasting theatrical importance and literary impact in Spain by referencing how he will be remembered in the country's chronicles, thus foreshadowing his permanent place in the Hispanic literary cannon by highlighting his overwhelmingly positive contemporary reception. Additionally, his views on his own Spanishness and profound connection with the Spanish people suggest an enduring cultural identity that transcends the centuries between the historical Lope and his 1970s representation.

Lope's place in the modern collective imagination of Spain is made more explicit in *Paisaje con figuras*, in which his avatar walks the streets and passes by monuments of himself in 1980s Madrid. As the creator of the show and narrator of the episode Antonio Gala reveals in his 1985 memoirs of the show, also titled *Paisaje con figuras*, he placed Lope in the contemporary setting in order to create a bond between the twentieth-century spectators and the seventeenth-century playwright. He affirms that, with this program, "we are going to prove that, at the end of the day, where those characters were, we were. And they are today where we are" (18). The same strategy was employed by the producers of *La víspera de nuestro tiempo*, who created a similar effect with the voice overs of Lope's poetry superimposed over some of the most important places in the playwright's life. According to Fernández (2018), such a bond between past and present was intended to encourage television audiences to reevaluate their preconceived notions of Spanish history (22). Whether or not such an introspective reflection was achieved may never be known, but the episode certainly manages to convey the idea that, given the great deal of societal advancements over the centuries, not everything has changed. This conceptualization of history opens the possibility for modern audiences to relate to the historical figure of Lope on a more profound level.

Lope's twenty-first-century adaptations bring the idea of making Lope de Vega relatable to a more realistic plane. By showing aspects of his life not often represented in other biopics about him, such as the family tension between Lope and his siblings, and his relationship with his mother and the constant drive to make her proud, the historical figure is further humanized in the film *Lope*. Moreover, the way in which the more scandalous elements of his biography are portrayed on screen suggest that they were not necessarily the result of his sexually compulsive urges; rather, we see a young, ambitious man get carried away in a situation that is, in many ways, beyond his control. It is true, for example, that his love affair with Elena is depicted as a ploy by which to get his play performed at first, but it later spirals into a passionate romance that, in different circumstances or in a different time, may not have been problematic. These screenwriters and directors find a place for Lope in modern culture that demystifies the historical figure by spotlighting his natural, human attributes.

The creators of *The Ministry of Time* and *Cervantes contra Lope* take a radically different route to placing Lope de Vega in modern popular culture than any of the previous biopics by having the seventeenth-century playwright interact with modern characters such as governmental authorities and journalists. His relatability to the people of today is highlighted at the beginning of his first appearance in *The Ministry of Time* 1.2 when Julián learns that Lope was accused of abducting his first wife Isabel de Urbina, to which he exclaims, "he kidnapped her?! Ha . . . Lope was something else!" (00:07:45) The notion that Spain's classical authors and their lives could be as entertaining as anyone today is cemented by Salvador's response to Julián: "Pretty much, you see what you miss out on by not reading our classics?" (00:07:49) Additionally, the episode goes on to show how Lope's seductive methods not only worked on the women of his own time but also on Amelia who is from the nineteenth century. The intended message behind this exchange is, in my opinion, that Lope is such a transgenerational figure that he could easily coexist in any time period. This interpretation of the scene is supported later in the episode when Adrián refuses to accept Amelia's defense of the playwright because he belonged to a different time, to which he asserts, "a jerk is a jerk in the twenty-first century and in the sixteenth" (00:45:15). The episode intends to demonstrate that Lope's life, in many ways, was not different to ours today because, perhaps, modern people have not evolved and progressed as much as we like to believe we have.

The remaining two episodes in which Lope has a crucial role highlight some striking parallels between the seventeenth and twenty-first centuries, such as those duly noted by Breden (2018): "the relationship between art and power, the need to employ art to be critical; at the same time, it shows the pressures that a power without imagination exerts, represented here by an inflexible Lerma" (88). Thus, the ghost of Lope de Vega is invoked as a representative of the Golden Age so as to demonstrate how the present mirrors the past and, in addition to exposing what Breden identifies as "the open wounds" from Spain's history (88), challenge the notion that, as the character Angustias states in 1.2, "it's been said: any time in the past was better" (00:04:25).[74]

The producers of his twentieth- and twenty-first-century appearances as a character on screen thus often use the author as a representative of early modern Spanish people and cultures so as to highlight the societal hypocrisy and corruption that characterized the age and challenges the conceptualization of the Golden Age as an idyllic time period after which modern Spanish society should model itself. Nevertheless, the turbulent nature of his life and the appeal of his scandals in contemporary popular culture are elements of his biography that, at times, can lend themselves well to the television and film culture of a particular moment. Whether it is by exalting him as a flawed character who is still deserving of the distinction of national symbol or by utilizing him as an example of a complicated historical period that has been misconstrued as utopic, what is clear is that the diverse range of characterizations made possible by the flexible "Lope myth" have perpetuated the shadow of the Phoenix into the digital age.

## NOTES

1. Epstein (2016) gives the specific example of Loretta Lynn's biopic *Coal Miner's Daughter* (1980) that elevates the stigmatized southern Appalachian culture as an example of the epitome of simple, albeit fundamental, American values and customs, a technique, he posits, that promotes a "strategic patriotic memory" (11–15).

2. This should not be confused with the anti-hero of the *picaresque* tradition as defined by Gustavo Alfaro (25).

3. Felipe Pedraza Jiménez (2009, 58–61) and Robert Jammes (1987, 70–72) also comment upon the self-representation of the author in Lope de Vega's works.

4. Sánchez Jiménez (2006) recognizes that many of these caricatures could simply be the result of the author relying on stereotypical characters from the genres in which Lope wrote. However, he also highlights many instances, such as the death of his daughter, in which biographical events are depicted in his poetry (*Lope pintado* 48–50).

5. See Sánchez Jiménez (20-74), Rennert (1967, 21, 69, and 77), and Dixon (2009, 251–253).

6. The divide between these two moments of Lope's creative life are examined especially closely in Francisco Javier Ávila's "La Dorotea: arte y estrategia de senectud, entre la serenidad y la desesperación" (1995), Sánchez Jiménez's *Lope: El verso*

*y la vida* (2018), and María José Martínez Lopez's *El entremés: radiografía de un género* (1997).

7. Many of these letters are preserved and edited in the Real Academia Española's collection of the *Epistolario de Lope de Vega* (1989). Oleza (2003) provides a thorough analysis of the letters and offers insight into how these demonstrate Lope's obsession with his public image and legacy (604).

8. The verses in question read: "No porque ignorase los preceptos, / gracias a Dios, que ya, Tirón gramático, / pasé los libros que trataban de esto / antes que hubiese visto al sol diez veces" (vv. 17–20).

9. The complete title of the volume is *Fama póstuma a la vida y muerte del Doctor Frey Lope Félix de Vega Carpio y elogios panegíricos a la inmortalidad de su nombre escritos por los más esclarecidos ingenios, solicitados por el Doctor Juan Pérez de Montalbán.*

10. Scholars over the past three centuries, from Mesonero Romanos (1951, xiv), to Rennert (1967, 19), to Profeti (2000, 793), to Dixon (2006, 259), to Alba (2017, 127) have cautioned against taking Montalbán's biographical details about Lope at face value, especially those of his childhood, as the 40-year age difference between mentor and mentee would have made it impossible for Montalbán to know any of this information first-hand.

11. In this calculation he also includes his *auto-sacramentales*, leaving number of *comedias* in this quantity indecipherable.

12. See also Morley and Bruerton's (1940) authoritative study on the chronology of Lope de Vega's comedies.

13. Original: "entró luego el monstruo de naturaleza, el gran Lope de Vega, y alzóse con la monarquía cómica, avasalló y puso debajo de su jurisdicción a todos los farsantes, llenó el mundo de comedias propias y bien razonadas que pasan que diez mil pliegos los que tiene escritos." The complete title of the volume is *Ocho comedias y ocho entremeses nuevos, nunca representados.*

14. Tirso de Molina mentions that Lope had written 900 plays in his *La fingida arcadia* (1621). Pellicer de Salas went on to repeat Lope's claim of 1,500 in his *El fénix y su historia natural* (1630), a number also cited by Montalbán in his *Para todos* (1632), by Juan Antonio de la Peña in his *Égloga elegiaca* (1635), and Francisco de Peralta in his *Oración funeral* (1635). Montalbán would later inflate the number a final time, to 1,800 in his *Fama pósthuma.* Such unreliable—and often contradictory—claims have complicated the process of determining exactly how prolific of an author Lope was. Maria Grazia Profeti assures us that, while 470 of Lope's plays survive, it is still difficult to establish a precise number of his authentic productions because not all of the texts can certifiably be attributed to him ("Lope de Vega" 793). Nevertheless, Lope constantly reminded his audience of the exorbitant numbers of his composed *comedias*, which has contributed to the "genius" facet of the "Lope myth" that lives on to this day.

15. For more on the "escuela lopista" or, as he calls it, the "ciclo lopesco," see Enrique González Mas's *Historia de la literatura española* (III: 91–103).

16. The nickname in Spanish is *Fénix de los ingenios.*

17. Unfortunately, no copy of this film can be located for viewing. According to José Luis Estarrona, archive manager of the Filmoteca Nacional in Madrid, it

is likely that the negatives were destroyed in August 1945 when flames from an unknown source engulfed the Cinematiraje Riera laboratories in Madrid that housed all of Spain's film negatives and archived originals to that date. As so little is known about the film and I was unable to view any part of it, it must be omitted from our analysis.

18. The episode of *La víspera de nuestro tiempo* (1967–1969) titled "La geografía apasionada de Lope de Vega," produced in 1968, was broadcasted on January 15, 1969. The episode includes voice-over readings of some of Lope's poetry while contemporary shots of monuments and areas around the Iberian Peninsula that were important to the author are displayed. As Fernández (2018) observes, "esta exposición directa a la obra de Lope, sin apenas contexto narrativo, invitaba al telespectador a disfrutar más que a aleccionarle" (22). In other words, although the episode does not present Lope de Vega as a character nor does it offer a great deal of information about his life, it is unique in that it gives viewers the opportunity to appreciate his poetry without the interference of any of the biographical information that tends to distract modern audiences from enjoying his work. It does not, however, feature the author as a character and the lack of biographical information disqualifies this episode from our study.

19. The concept of "strategic patriotic memory" is described by Epstein (2016) in his introduction to *Imagined Lives, Imagined Communities* as the manner in which historically significant national figures are portrayed as characters in a manner that highlights the events in their lives that contribute to creating a national history that creates an image of the history of a nation with which audiences can relate (1–24).

20. Fernández (2018) characterizes the aspects of Lope's personality in a similar fashion, identifying the following four elements of analysis: "(1) su genialidid y copiosa obra dramática; (2) su rivalidad con Cervantes; (3) su vida amorosa; y (4) su contemporaneidad" ("Lope en la televisión" 21).

21. It is curious to consider the historical contexts in which both of these very similar reflexions were stated: nineteenth-century Spanish popular culture, as a reaction to the Napoleonic invasion, had become permeated with the concept of Spanish nationalism in the face of increasing French cultural influence. In 1941, the Francoist dictatorship was promoting nationalistic rhetoric as a means by which to unite the country under his newly instated regime.

22. Joaquín de Entrambasaguas would later echo the idea of Lope traveling to Spain's "regiones más distintas e intersantes," thus leading to "el concepto amplio y pleno que tuvo de su patria" in his 1957 monograph *Estudios sobre Lope de Vega* (10).

23. See Millé y Jiménez (1928), "Lope de Vega en la Armada Invencible" and Schevill (1941), "Lope de Vega and the Year 1588." Lope's time in the armada is also given very close examination in Rennert's (1967) *Life of Lope de Vega* (59–89). Additionally, Rennert makes a passing reference to Lope's brother, who "accompanied Lope in 1588 on the disastrous expedition of the Armada to England, whence he never returned" (3). Lope's siblings are only presented in the 2010 biopic *Lope*, in which his brother encourages him to join the Armada with him.

24. A compilation of studies, titled *Imaginarios y representaciones de España durante el franquismo* (2015) delves into exactly how specific national myths were appropriated by the regime.

25. Barton (2016) applies this concept to Steven Spielberg's biopic *Lincoln* (2012), in which American president Abraham Lincoln's turbulent relationship with his wife is depicted in ways that do not flatter the historical figure, but his flaws are compensated for by his passionate zeal for maintaining national unity and abolishing slavery (281–300).

26. Mirta Núñez Díaz-Balart (2003) offers an in-depth look into this phenomenon in *Mujeres caídas: prostitutas legales y clandestinas en el franquismo*. See also Guereña (2003, 399–444).

27. Bayliss (2015) also comments upon the changing attitudes toward the concept of "Spanishness" and the role of Lope de Vega in the transitional period between dictatorship and democracy by reminding us that "más que nunca durante las décadas inmediatamente después de la muerte de Franco, cuando la 'españolidad' experimentó cambios drásticos que implicaban un despojo de los iconos y símbolos (como Lope de Vega) propagados durante la dictadura" (717).

28. As we have mentioned previously, Spain's popular culture during the early 1980s was shifting toward a more inclusive aesthetic that treated women and minorities with a higher degree of respect. A proud philanderer figure would not have been well-received by audiences. Similarly, in 2018, due to an influx of cases involving women being abused—and even murdered—by men, it was a wise decision to show a more repentant, respectful Lope when it came to the treatment of his lovers.

29. It is convenient here to remember that Eloy de la Iglesia, Pilar Miró, and Pedro Almodóvar's new-age style of films were massively popular during this time.

30. For more on the attacks on and conquest of the Azores in 1583, see Timothy Walton's *The Spanish Treasure Fleets* (2015, 80–85) and Francisco García Fitz and João Gouveia Monteiro's *War in the Iberian Peninsula: 700–1600* (2018, ch. 7). Victor Dixon also references Lope's role in the expedition in his contribution to the *Cambridge History of Spanish Literature* called "Lope Félix de Vega Carpio" (2006, 251).

31. For a full synopsis and interpretation of Lope de Vega's appearances in the series, see Simon Breden's (2018) article "La presencia de Lope de Vega en *El Ministerio del Tiempo*."

32. It should also be noted, however, that the character of Lope in "El mejor mozo de España" also carries a sword throughout the entire episode. Although the program does include a swordfight between two playwrights, neither one is Lope.

33. The difficulty of studying this aspect of the author's bibliography is also expressed by Victor Dixon (2009) when he reiterates that "Lope de Vega's life, throughout most of its seventy-two years, was notoriously turbulent and riddled with contradictions" (12).

34. According to Rennert (1968), textual evidence from *La Dorotea* suggests that the relationship between Lope de Vega and Elena Osorio would have lasted around five years (12–13).

35. See Sánchez Jiménez (2008, 270), Dixon (2008, 251), Rennert (1968, 57–58), and Pedraza Jiménez (2009, 33).

36. Although Jerónima de Burgos appears as Lope's lover in both *Lope* and *Cervantes contra Lope*, her presence in his life is hardly mentioned by the playwright's most modern biographers. She is central to Rennert's (1968) biography of the author, who goes so far as to claim that Lope's conduct was, in part, to blame for the influence that spending so much time around actors, given their lowly social status and "unenviable repute" (170).

37. Using Cervantes's term "monstruo" to describe Lope's conquests provokes an easy association: Lope's romantic conquests were as extensive as his literary production.

38. The title of the article in Spanish is "Un poeta viejo, modernísimo."

39. These verses are the first of *Cien jaculatorias a Cristo nuestro señor*, compiled and edited by Cayetano Rosell for the volume *Colección escogida de obras no dramáticas de Fray Lope Félix de Vega Carpio* (1856), published by the Biblioteca de Autores Españoles.

40. The verses Lope recites in this sequence, "por qué una reina querría someterse / a un monstruo contrahecho pudiendo tener a un rey yaciendo en su lecho," as Amelia identifies, is a loose translation of the thirty-fifth stanza of Canto 28 of Ludovico Ariosto's epic poem *Orlando furioso* (c. 1516), in which the final four verses of the stanza read "—A uno sgrignuto mostro e contrafatto / Dunque (disse) costei si sottomette, / Che'l maggior re del mondo ha per marito, / Più bello e più cortese? oh, che appetito!—" (65).

41. The program *Cervantes contra Lope* is a mockumentary in which both featured historical figures are "interviewed" by modern journalists while dramatized scenes of their lives in Madrid are intertwined.

42. The situation has been described by his biographers as one that would "abrasarle las entrañas durante muchos años" (Pérez Pastor, 1901, 210) due to him being "ciegamente enamorado" (82). Furthermore, Dixon (2008) concurs with these scholars by informing us that the relationship with Elena "was marked by a passion that would haunt him forever after" (251).

43. See Rennert (1968, 47).

44. See Rennert (1968, 48) and Sánchez Jiménez (2006, 26) for more in-depth descriptions of the Zaida personage, complete with textual evidence to support these claims.

45. The term used is not *español*, but rather *romance*.

46. According to Pérez Pastor (1901), Perrenot de Granvela's appeal went beyond his monetary wealth. He was also the great nephew of Cardenal Antonio Perrenot de Granvela, giving considerable sociopolitical influence to those who shared his last name (129–131). See also Sánchez Jiménez (2006, 25) and Rennert (1968, 51).

47. In the following scene he reiterates his sentiments by telling Elena, in front of her father, "no soy yo el que te convierte en una puta . . . sino él" (01:07:25).

48. The original title of the poem is "Desmayarse, atreverse, estar furioso." The sonnet comes from Lope's *Rimas humanas* (1602), published under Lope's pseudonym Tomé de Burguillos. The *rimas*, according to Antonio Carreño (2014) in his introduction to *El castigo sin venganza*, recount the author's entire love life (until that

point) in the Petrarchan style and resulted in Lope's love life becoming the main topic of gossip in the Spanish court of the time (70).

49. Although this scene does not remain completely faithful to Lope's recorded biographies, it does, again, draw from the libel case against him. Pérez Pastor (1901) mentions the possibility that Elena Osorio aided Lope in getting his sentence reduced, possibly in hopes of marrying him at a later date (211).

50. Leonor Watling, who plays Isabel de Urbina in *Lope*, noticed a similar undertone to the movie while she was filming it, remarking that although the protagonist "por momentos parece un ser amoral o inconsistente, no encuentra nada extraño en amar a dos mujeres a la vez (y no estar loco)."

51. Although the interview, including the answer cited here, was in Spanish, Clavijo used the English term *fucker*.

52. Lope's famous line in Spanish is *darle gusto al vulgo*.

53. This claim is, of course, given more veracity by the release of the film titled *Lope enamorado* in the following decade.

54. The case is examined in the article titled "El litigio por plagio" from a 2017 edition of *El País* (May 26, 2017).

55. It should be noted that these figures were calculated by taking Lope and Montalbán's numbers at face value, which they admit is likely not reliable, as Lope would have happily exaggerated the truth and his disciple had a record of embellishing his hero's positive attributes and achievements (225).

56. See Rennert (1968, 197), Samson and Thacker (2008, 101), Ryjik (2011, 39), Profeti (2000, 112) Sánchez Jiménez (2006, 72), and Dixon (2008, 254).

57. See especially the *Arte nuevo* (vv. 119–27).

58. Original: "lo que a mí me daña en esta parte / es haber [las comedias] escrito sin arte."

59. Original: "quien con arte agora las escribe / muere sin fama y galardón."

60. The character is making a clear reference to *culteranismo* (sometimes pejoratively referred to as *gongorismo* for the Spanish poet most associated with this convention), defined by the *Dictionary of the Literature of the Iberian Península* as a type of poetry "categorized by a highly Latinized syntax and a wealth of classical allusions," (Bleiberg et al., 1993, 479) of which Lope de Vega was a famous opponent. Though controversial in Spain, the style was popular in England and France.

61. Francisco Gómez de Sandovál (1552–1625), the Duke of Lerma was the first of the Hapsburg *validos* (most valuable, or favorites). He wielded unmatched political power during the reign of Felipe III and was a vehemently hated figure during the Golden Age. History remembers him as a principal cause for the decline of the Spanish Empire because his foreign policy centered around hostile attacks against England and the Low Countries that effectively bankrupted the monarchy.

62. No record of a play with this title is recorded anywhere in the bibliographies of Spanish Golden Age plays. It is most likely an original invention for the episode.

63. Original: "Ojos de mayor gracia y hermosura."

64. The original title is taken from the first line of the poem, "Un soneto me manda hacer Violante." The sonnet is taken from Lope's play *La niña de plata*, first published in his *Parte IX de comedias* (ca. 1657). The first line of the poem is modified

in the film to "un soneto queréis en este instante" (00:53:13) in order to avoid the reference to the character Violante.

65. As Paul Franssen indicates, there have been two additional fictitious meetings between Cervantes and Shakespeare: once in Anthony Burgess's story "A Meeting in Valladolid" (1989) and again in a Spanish film titled *Miguel y William* (2007). Despite the intriguing possibilities of a face-to-face encounter between these two authors, he also makes it clear that it is highly unlikely, if not impossible, that they ever met in real life (217–19). Jon Benson agrees, signaling that "there is no evidence that Shakespeare ever met Cervantes" (24).

66. See Sánchez-Jiménez (2006, 10–21) for a synthesis of the insulting poetic exchanges between Lope and Góngora, as well as Begoña López Bueno's *El poeta soledad: Góngora (1609–1615)* for an analysis of the personal attacks made between the two poets through a controversial series of letters (264–270).

67. According to Pedraza Jiménez (2009), the satirical sonnet is a *suelto* that, the critical editor of Lope's rimas notices, "parece una reflexión desapasionada sobre el asunto de Elena Osorio" (330).

68. The original lines uttered in Spanish in the episode are "sacar conclusiones sería prematuro, no . . . no es lo que parece, lo juro."

69. Original: "¡encima me habláis en rima!"

70. He was, however, as Sánchez Jiménez (2006) indicates, awarded the distinction of Orden de San Juan de Jerusalén by Pope Urban VIII, which allowed him to "anteponer a su nombre el título de 'frey' y ostentar en su pecho la cruz de San Juan," but this was not nearly as prestigious an honor as others in Spain and by no means guaranteed noble status (40).

71. See Entrambasaguas (1935, 9), Profeti (2000, 113), and Sánchez Jiménez (2006, 40).

72. The Latin text roughly translates to "What humility, Invidia?" Invidia is the Roman equivalent to the Greek mythological figure of Nemesis, the goddess of ill will, discord, and envy. Ovid has been credited as being the first author to personify her in his *Metamorphoses* (vv. 2,760–796).

73. Original: "Por tu villa, Lopillo, que me borres / las diez y nueve torres del escudo, / porque, aunque todas son de viento, dudo / que tengas viento para tantas torres."

74. This interpretation of the episode is reinforced by Ernesto's retort to this statement: "eso no es verdad, te lo aseguro" (00:04:40).

# Conclusions

## *The Shadow of the Phoenix*

Many myths surrounding Lope de Vega's life and works have been examined, reconsidered, and challenged in the present volume. The belief that either Lope or his dramas were used intentionally as ideological vehicles for any particular government or regime has been revisited and problematized. In doing so, this volume presents the case that, contrary to popular belief, Lope de Vega has had a much stronger presence in Spanish popular culture following Francisco Franco's death in 1975 than he ever did during the dictatorship. Furthermore, the findings presented here suggest that any possible ideological manipulation of the texts in the adaptation is much more evident in the current Democratic Era than during Franco's regime. Although it may come as a surprise to many scholars and critics, this study does not reveal a trajectory of Lope being used as a pawn in Franco's mass indoctrination systems that disappeared after his regime officially concluded in 1978. On the contrary, it is much more apparent that film and television producers from the dictatorship attempted to treat Lope and his works as untouchable classics that they manipulated as minimally as possible, only to discover that the dramatist existed in the collective Spanish imagination in name alone as a myth that must be fortified with meaningful discourse in order to receive a positive reception from audiences. Thus, it is possible to trace an evolution from sacred national classic to moldable myth that begins during the early days of Franco's dictatorship and still continues to develop to this day.

In chapter 1, two adaptations of a supposed Lope de Vega drama that were prohibited by Franco's censors in the late 1940s and early 1950s have been critically examined for the first time, providing perhaps the most definitive piece of evidence that having Lope's name on the cover was not enough to save screenplays from chopping block. Thus, it is impossible to continue to assume that the regime encouraged, fostered, or gave any preferences to works by this author. As the analysis continued to an examination of the films and television programs that were given production permissions by the censorship to create and distribute Lope adaptations, it became clear that only minimal manipulation of the source texts was present in the finished products during the Francoist dictatorship, dismantling yet another common assertion that his dramas were used by the regime as an ideological vehicle or propaganda machine. Once Francisco Franco died and the remnants of his bureaucratic systems officially dissolved, the adaptors of Lope de Vega's works, as demonstrated in chapter 3, began to make artistic decisions that distorted the source texts to a much larger degree than their dictatorial counterparts. The resulting films and television episodes can be interpreted in such a way that suggests ideological motives were behind the adaptive mechanisms employed. Simply put, all evidence indicates that Lope's texts were manipulated, perhaps for sociocultural reasons, by democratic producers much more than they ever were by their Francoist counterparts.

While these findings do not substantiate the claims that Spanish governments have had an active role in promoting the productions of Lope biopics or adaptations of his works, a review of the films and television episodes and the reactions to them suggests that measures were taken by their creators to make them as responsive to their respective popular culture trends as possible. In almost every situation, further evidence is presented to support John Street's (2013) assertion that "political thoughts and actions cannot be treated as somehow separate or discrete from popular culture. . . . The connection between politics and popular emerges in the way we choose our pleasures and judge our political masters, in the way the aesthetic blends into the ethical" (4). In the case of the programs studied in the preceding chapters, we could broaden these observations to argue that, as exemplified by the treatment of Lope de Vega in popular culture, it is also true that the ethical often blends reciprocally into the aesthetic.

Such determinations are not, of course, original to this study. The concept of art and life mutually imitating one another has been central to studies in Western humanities since Aristotle elaborated on Plato's theories of art, life, and nature as expressed in his *Poetics* (ca. 335 BCE). We need not, however, look to the classical theater of antiquity to find examples of how theatrical productions have been used to fuse ethics with aesthetics. As discussed in chapter 2, Lope's *Fuenteovejuna* is just one example of a play that has been revived at pivotal moments in history both in Spain and abroad so as to disseminate its sociopolitical subtext throughout the imagination of the masses. Examples of historical theater's potential political charge abound in much more recent circumstances, including some from here in the United States.[1] Unfortunately for Spain's Phoenix, however, his works have, thus far, always been remained in the shadow of another, more internationally renowned dramaturg: William Shakespeare.

## THE SHADOW OF THE BARD

Apart from Spain's drive to compete on an international level with its cinematic production, film executives also wanted Lope, one of the country's greatest literary heroes, to finally garner the national and international respect that had always been denied him. The comparison of Lope and the English Bard has always been a point of contempt for Spain's literary scholars, who have always recognized the brilliant, unrivaled profundity of Shakespeare's dramas, but argue that Lope's genius outweighs that of his English counterpart because of his prolificacy, a fact that is often overlooked both inside and outside of Spain. Spanish audiences have apparently always needed the most convincing in this regard. A recurring thread in all of the Lope adaptations, from the earliest to the most recent, is an attempt to assure audiences that Spain's seventeenth-century playwright was equal to England's. As Shakespeare adaptations became increasingly prevalent in British and American cinemas and television programs, Spain's inferiority complex with Anglo-Saxon culture seems to have reached a boiling point. The attempt at making Spain's audiences appreciate the Phoenix as much as they did the Bard is one of aspects of all of these adaptations that transcend all time periods, governments, and media.

Though the promotional materials for the earliest film adaptations do not specifically mention Shakespeare, the Spanish press expressed a preoccupation with other Western countries taking advantage of film to disseminate their literary traditions and overshadowing Spain's as early as 1942. J.L. Gómez Tello (1943) expressed his fear that another country would steal Spain's best literary works and adapt them to the big screen before Spain, urging the readers of *Primer plano* to imagine "how outrageous it would be for another cinema that wasn't Spanish to attempt to film a movie about the Catholic Monarchs" (3). The remedy, in his opinion, was to look to Spain's rich theatrical tradition, specifically those works by Lope de Vega, in which he saw the "national mysticism that we should demand of the national cinema" (3). Miguel Herrero García (1943) echoed this preoccupation a year later when he recognized the pragmatics of adapting Lope's brand of *comedia* to film, considering it as Spain's only hope to impose its cultural superiority upon the Western world. Referring directly to the innovations present in Lope's theater, he declared that "the day that Spain makes its own technical engineering techniques in cinematography, its triumph will be incomparable. The movement is its own conquest from three centuries ago. Photographing that movement is today's conquest" (11). When the first Lope adaptation, *Fuenteovejuna* (1947) was officially announced in 1946, the promotional posters were all labeled with the slogan, "Lope de Vega's immortal play will be the greatest triumph of Spanish cinema."

As time passed and film and television evolved into the grand enterprises they were destined to become, Lope continued to be in Shakespeare's shadow in Spanish popular culture. The importance of Spain's literary giant was stressed on many occasions. For example, a promotional spot in *Teleradio* for *Estudio 1*'s "El caballero de Olmedo" (1968), emphasized that "this play by Lope, one of the most important ones, not just for Spanish theater, but for universal theater" and attempted to shed light on Spain's important contributions to the Western literary canon (53). When the show adapted *Peribáñez* two years later, the producers were careful to more explicitly instruct Spanish audiences about Lope's theatrical prowess by juxtaposing him directly against Shakespeare, naming his rival for the first time on Spanish television or film in direct comparison to Lope. The episode's off-screen opening narration makes the point quite clearly:

> In some time periods, including our own, Lope has been considered as a type of skillful, mechanical, and practical poet, stripping him of his authentic grandiosity out of a comparison for example with Shakespeare. We know today that although the swan of Avon surpasses him in psychological depth and dramatic complexity, Lope does not lag behind in poetic quality; in fact, he has an advantage in his theatrical construction. Therefore, we could say, paraphrasing the witches' greeting to Banquo, "Hail Lope, lesser than Shakespeare and greater." (00:01:43–00:02:16)[2]

The episode's introduction continued with the tradition of including brief narrations that explained the complexity of Lope's plots in order to promote an appreciation with audiences regarding their literary value that had been commonplace in his televised adaptations since the mid-1960s.[3] Only in this case, however, was the author's genius brought to the forefront to defend his theater from "unfair" comparisons to Shakespeare.

The 1983 episode of *Las pícaras* that recreated *La viuda valenciana* promoted the episode by again attempting to convince potential viewers of Lope's worth in comparison to Shakespeare, acknowledging his plays' shortcomings, but highlighting their redeeming qualities. A review by M.A. (1983) in an edition of *TeleRadio* informs its readers that

> [Lope] was not the writer of a play: he tackled everything, especially theater; if the bases of Spanish theatrical renovation are due to him, he did not leave behind, in any way, a well-rounded, completed oeuvre: *Fuenteovejuna, Peribáñez, El mejor alcale, el rey* and *El caballero de Olmedo*, the best ones

suffer from superficiality, the lack the dramatic tension that the English genius, for example, Shakespeare, put into *Hamlet, Macbeth,* etcetera, in order to convert these plays into mirrors of universal passions that have been valid for centuries. (27)

In other words, Lope's plots may pale in comparison to his English counter-part's for a modern audience, but the article assures readers that his wide vari-ety of themes and the role he had in renovating and improving a genuinely Spanish theater make his plays extremely valuable pieces of Spain's literary patrimony that deserve to be preserved and presented to the day's television viewers.

No television executives or filmmakers took greater offence to Lope hav-ing been cast into Shakespeare's shadow than director Pilar Miró, who reiter-ated her frustration with the Spanish author's obscurity on many occasions during the promotion of her adaptation of *El perro del hortelano* (1996). Diego Galán (2004) recalls a conversation he had with Miró in which she told him "The English do all of Shakespeare in their cinema, the French do their Cyrano with all of his verses. . . . Why wouldn't we do the same with our clas-sics?" (n.p.) She voiced her lamentations again to *El País* journalist Luis Mar-tínez (1996), telling him that it was regrettable that "a certain Shakespeare had a certain gift for weaving passions, ambitions, and other all-too-human functions; Lope, however, when it comes to cinema, there is only one shred of evidence: how thick the layers of dust can be" (n.p.). Miguel García Posada (1997), another journalist for *El País*, came to Miró's defense for creating a film that the press considered an irresponsible economic endeavor, echoing the director's sentiments by writing, "as great as Shakespeare might be, and he is, there is no apparent reason why the English-speaking cinema has man-aged to make such brilliant pieces with his texts and, at the same time, Span-ish cinema has refused to the same; even if it doesn't have Shakespeare and his blank verse, it has Calderón, of whose enormous greatness we are not all aware, and it also has various memorable titles by Lope" (n.p.). Unfortunately for Miró and Lope, Spain's attitudes have not shifted much regarding Lope's works and its popular culture is not as interested in his many memorable titles as García Posada encouraged them to be.

There is no doubt that the struggles of Lope's characters are not nearly as universally relatable as those of his English rival. As politicians, literary scholars, film and television executives, and other participants in popular culture have reminded us for over a century, Lope's characters and plots are perhaps too responsive to the reality of Spaniards in the seventeenth century. Although adaptations of them serve as interesting historical artifacts, their themes and motives reflect a societal design that, notwithstanding some of the obvious parallels with today's sociopolitical conflicts, does not directly resonate with modern audiences. I daresay the cultural rivalry between Spain and England has been more of a motivation for Spanish film and television producers to create Lope adaptations than any political or ideological incentive. I also venture to guess that the permanent fixture of Anglo-American popular culture in worldwide film and television also possibly explains why Spanish studios have ceased to invest in Lope adaptations in recent years. The uphill battle against institutions such as Hollywood and Shakespeare appears to have been lost and attempts to inject Lope's works into film and television have not been lucrative.

Perhaps it is unfair to expect Lope's dramas to have the same international reach as other playwrights. As I have reiterated many times throughout this volume, the Phoenix's literary works have always contained an essence and character that is very particular to Spain whereas authors like Shakespeare did not infuse their writings with such an elevated degree of a national flavor. Furthermore, the English-speaking world's dominance over film and television in the modern era makes literature originally penned in English much more appealing targets for adaptation and revival. For this reason, much further study into the matter is necessary to draw more definitive conclusions.

## BEYOND THE PHOENIX

This study should by no means be considered conclusive regarding the dialogue among scholars about how Spain's Golden Age continues to exist in popular and academic imaginations to this day. After all, there are film and television adaptations of works by other canonical seventeenth-century playwrights such as Calderón and Tirso that have been largely ignored by audiences and scholars alike.[4] A thorough study of those productions would be mutually beneficial to this study in that a comparative analysis of the treatment of works by different authors during various moments in recent history would broaden the conclusions presented in these chapters.

Purificació Mascarell's (2014) study on the adaptation techniques employed in the contemporary theater by the Compañía Nacional de Teatro Clásico provides us with a thorough analysis of how the institution has taken strides to make classical authors' plays attractive to today's theatergoers. Performance studies scholars could likely collect a plethora of data on how the same Lope originals can be presented and performed similarly and differently on three distinct media by using Mascarell's examination as a point of departure. Likewise, Shakespeare specialists can enhance their vast compendium of scholarship on film and television adaptations by comparing and contrasting the adaptation styles of the productions studied in these chapters with those of Shakespeare's works released around the same time.

Some of Lope's original plays have been adapted in Latin America and have yet to receive the same attention by critics as adaptations from Spain, such as the free adaptation of *La viuda valenciana*, titled *La viuda celosa* (Mexico, 1945) and *Fuenteovejuna* (Cuba, 1963). Additionally, a Mexican adaptation of Tirso's *El condenado por desconfiado* was released in 1952. Calderón's *La dama duende* was brought to Argentina's cinema screens in 1945, and his *El casado casa quiere* was adapted by Mexican filmmaker Gilberto Martínez Solares in 1947. Despite Juan de Mata Moncho Aguirre's preliminary study of these adaptations in his unedited dissertation titled *Las adaptaciones de obras del teatro español en el cine y el influjo de éste en los dramaturgos* (2000), these films have not been given any substantial degree of critical attention by today's scholars. Due to the differences in sociopolitical systems, time periods, and audience demographics, more thorough examinations of these adaptations are imperative to understanding how different interpretive communities mold the ways in which the source texts are presented in a wide variety of contexts.

Beyond Spanish Golden Age studies, an analysis of adaptations of literary works from other periods and genres could also shed a great deal of light on many of the issues presented in this monograph. The works of Benito Pérez Galdós, just to provide one example, had an extremely healthy presence on Spanish screens before and during the Francoist dictatorship, but have largely been ignored by film and television producers in the democratic era. In addition to the major motion picture adaptations of his novels and short stories, namely *Marianela* (1940), *Adulterio* (1943), *Doña perfecta* (1950), *La loca de la casa* (1950), *Nazarín* (1958), *Fortunata y Jacinta* (1969), *Tristana* (1969), *Marianela* (1972), *Doña perfecta* (1977), and *Tormento* (1974), Galdós's works were also adapted several times to television. *Estudio 1* adapted titles such as *La loca de la casa* (1967), *El abuelo* (1969), and *Misericordia* (1977). *Cuentos y leyendas* also aired an adaptation of his novel *Miau* in 1972. Though his film adaptations have been paid some attention by scholars in recent years, the televised manifestations of his works have continued to fly under the radar of Hispanic adaptation scholars.[5] Given that many of his titles were adapted on more than one occasion during different stages of the regime, an analysis of these productions would likely allow for an enhancement or reconsideration some of the conclusions drawn in this study, specifically regarding those from chapter 2 that deal with the role of cinema during the dictatorship. Likewise, a comparison of the 1974 film adaptation of Leopoldo Alas Clarín's masterpiece *La Regenta* (1884) with the 1995 television miniseries of the same title would also be an ideal addition to this field of research.[6]

# THE FUTURE OF THE PHOENIX

Although Lope de Vega's dramas have yet to successfully transcend international borders in the same way as authors like the English Bard, audiences today continue to consume his works and draw parallels between them and current sociopolitical circumstances. As recently as October 2021, for example, reviewer Antonio Illán Illán wrote his reflections on a stage production of *Peribáñez y el comendador de Ocaña* to ABC Toledo, in which he reiterated that the play is "a very modern classic" due to its accomplishing the "objectives of bringing to life a project in which the viewer can, while enjoying the show, consider some matters about his or her present by contemplating a story from the past" (n.p.). What such commentary reveals to modern participants in Spanish popular culture is that, far from being a relic of a bygone era, Lope de Vega's verses continue to inspire and attract audiences for the same reasons as they did in the Early Modern Era; namely, that lessons from the past can shed light on issues that continue to define our current existence. It is impossible, however, to overlook the fact that Lope's literature thrives only in its original medium, the theater, in the twenty-first century.

It would be a mistake, however, to reduce Lope de Vega to a historical figure whose dramas are only suitable to being recreated in the theater and whose turbulent life is only appropriate for scandalous television and film productions. If the present volume unveils anything about Lope and Spanish popular culture, it is that the latter always finds a way to allow the Phoenix of Wits to resurface as an important, interesting, controversial topic. As new popular culture artifacts arise, the figure of Lope manages to find his place among them. The most recent evidence of this is the fact that Lope de Vega has been included on social media platforms such as Twitter (@ lopedevegac) and Instagram (_lope.de.vega_ and lope_de_vega_2020). As opposed to his dramas or his personal life, the historical figure on these platforms continues to engage in the literary wars of his lifetime with figures such as Miguel de Cervantes (Twitter: @cervantes_sabe, Instagram: miguel .de.cervantes_esc), Francisco de Quevedo (Twitter: @QuebeboVillegas, Instagram: quevedo_2.0), and Luis de Góngora (Twitter: @Gongora_Revixit, Instagram:2.0gongora). Although these parodical manifestations of the historical authors is primarily academic in nature, I believe that the fact that some of these accounts have garnered tens of thousands of followers demonstrates that Spain's literary Golden Age, complete with its most prolific writer, will always have some presence in the collective Spanish imagination.

At any rate, it is true that Lope de Vega's most prominent position in modern society is in academic and not popular culture. Nevertheless, I urge scholars today not to discredit the importance of the presence of Lope's life and times on social media, biopics in modern Spanish popular culture, and/or film and television adaptations, regardless of their immediate degree of success with audiences. As the preceding chapters have demonstrated, the only modicum of success that Lope has had in the twenty-first century has been in his manifestations as the subject of biographical films and television programs, which likely would not have been possible without his re-introduction into the national imagination by means of the adaptations of his dramas in earlier decades. Though his presence in the collective Spanish imagination has waxed and waned to a considerable degree since his death in the seventeenth century, the fact that productions like the made-for-TV movie *Lope enamorado* continue to be released in Spain is nothing but further proof that, at least in some way, Spanish popular culture will always find itself to some degree under the *Shadow of the Phoenix*.

## NOTES

1. On May 21, 2017, for instance, the Public Theater's Free Shakespeare in the Park's New York production of *Julius Caesar* drew a great deal of critical attention from a wide array of commentators for portraying a version of the title role that established a clear parallel to the former US president Donald Trump. In her article titled "*Julius Caesar* Isn't Unique. Americans Love Talking About Politics Through Shakespeare" that was published in *Time* magazine just a few weeks prior to the play's debut, Emma Talkoff sheds light on how this production, like many before it, provoked reinterpretations of the Bard's works "to fit the current political scene" (n.p.).

2. The greeting to which the host is referring is from Shakespeare's *Macbeth* in which the three witches exclaim "Hail!" upon Macbeth and Banquo's entrance, followed by the first witch's prophetic line to the latter, "Lesser than Macbeth and greater" (I.3, v. 66) The Spanish translates to "Más grande que Macbeth serás, si menos."

3. The adaptations of *Los milagros del desprecio* (1967), *Fuenteovejuna* (1967), *El caballero de Olmedo* (1968), *El bastardo Mudarra* (1968), and *Los milagros del desprecio* (1972) include similar introductory narrations, though none pit Lope against Shakespeare as directly as this one.

4. Only recently have scholars begun exploring the adapted works of Calderón. For an in-depth analysis of his television adaptations since the beginning of television in Spain, see Danae Galdo González's thorough investigation into the topic. For a look into the four film adaptations of *El alcalde de Zalamea*, see Agustín Gómez and Nekane Parejo.

5. Galdos's film adaptations have been examined, albeit rather superficially, in Patricia Santoros's *Novel into Film* (1996), Ramón Navarrete's *Galdós en el cine español* (2003), Sally Faulkner's *Literary Adaptations in Spanish Cinema* (2004), Carlos Heredero and Antonio Santamaría's *Biblioteca del cine español: fuentes literarias 1900–2005* (2010), and Sally Faulkner's *A History of Spanish Film: Cinema and Society 1910–2010* (2013).

6. Iván Cavielles Llamas (2012) offers a very complete contemplation of all of the film adaptations of *La Regenta*, including films that do not explicitly claim to be based on the literary source text in "Oviedo Express: adaptación, diálogo intertextual y reescritura de *La Regenta*."

# Bibliography

Abellán, Manuel. 1980. *Censura y creación literaria en españa, 1939–1976*. Barcelona: Ediciones Península.

Albera, François. 2009. *La vanguardia en el cine*. Buenos Aires: Manantial.

Alfaro, Gustavo. 1977. *La estructura de la novela picaresca*. Bogotá: Instituto Caro y Cuervo.

Algora Weber, María Dolores. 1996. *Las relaciones hispano-árabes durante el régimen de Franco: la ruptura del aislamiento internacional, 1946–1950*. Madrid: Ministerio de Asuntos Exteriores.

Álvarez Barrientos, Joaquín. 2003. *El teatro popular y sus representaciones*. Madrid: CSIC.

Álvarez Junco, José. 2016. "Cervantes y la identidad nacional." In *Miguel de Cervantes: de la vida al mito (1616–2016)*, edited by José Álvarez Junco and José Manuel Lucía Megías, 184–199. Madrid: Biblioteca Nacional de España.

Amo, Fermín del. 1949. "Informe emitido sobre el guión de *La Estrella de Sevilla* (1949) por el Departamento de Censura." Archivo General de la Administración, Box No. 36/04572, Case File No. 13110, Folder 5.

Anderegg, Michael. 2010. *Cinematic Shakespeare*. Lanham: Rowman and Littlefield Publishers.

Anderson, Benedict. 1991. *Imagined Communities: Reflections on the Origin and Spread of Nationalism*. London: Verso.

Andioc, René. 1998. "De *La Estrella de Sevilla* a *Sancho Ortiz de las Roelas*." *Criticón* 72 (March): 143–164.

André-Bazzana, Bénédict. *Mitos y mentiras de la transición*, translated by Lourdes Arencibia Rodríguez. Madrid: El Viejo Topo.

Arco y Garay, Ricardo. 1947. *La sociedad española en las obras dramáticas de Lope de Vega*. Madrid: Escelicer.

Arias, Félix, José García Avilés, and Virginia Martín Jiménez. 2018. "La información en Televisión Española durante la Transición democrática." In *Una televisión con dos cadenas: la programación en España (1956–1990)*, edited by Julio Montero Díaz, 335–354. Madrid: Cátedra.

Ariosto, Ludovico. (1516) 2016. *Orlando Furioso*, edited by Emilio Bigi, Cristina Zampese, and Piero Floriani. Milan: BUR Rizzoli. Top of Form.

Armas, Frederick de. 1980. "Italian Canvasses in Lope de Vega's Comedias: The Case of Venus y Adonis." *Crítica Hispánica* 2: 135–142.

Armas, Frederick de. 1994. "Splitting Gemini: Plato, Girard, and *La Estrella de Sevilla*." *Hispanófila* 111 (May): 17–34.

Armas, Frederick de. 1996. *Heavenly Bodies: The Realms of La Estrella de Sevilla*. London: Bucknell University Press.

Ávila, Francisco Javier. 1995. *La Dorotea: arte y estrategia de senectud, entre la serenidad y la desesperación*. Madrid: Universidad Autónoma de Madrid.

Baget Herms, José. "El mal endémico de TVE." *ABC*, October 17, 1975: 134.

Ballesteros, Isolina. 2001. *Cine (ins)urgente: textos fílmicos y contextos culturales de la España posfranquista*. Madrid: Fundamentos.

Balme, Christopher. 2018. *Commedia Dell'arte in Context*. Cambridge: Cambridge University Press.

Barton, Simon. 2009. *A History of Spain*. New York: Palgrave Macmillan.

Batista González, Juan. 2007. *España estratégica: guerra y diplomacia en la historia de España*. Madrid: Sílex.

Bayliss, Robert. 2015. "Lope enamorado: Patrimonio cultural y cine postnacional." *Hispania* 98.4 (September): 714–725.

Beigbeder, Marc. 1941. "*L'Etoile de Seville* de Lope de Vega." *Esprit: Revue Internationale* 9 (April): 425–426.

Bell, Aubrey. 1931. "The Authorship of *La Estrella de Sevilla*." *Modern Language Review* 26: 97–98.

Benson, Jon. 2016. *Death of Shakespeare – Part One*. Annapolis: Nedward.

Berger, Verena. 2009. "El teatro del Siglo de Oro y el cine español: *La dama boba* (2006) de Manuel Iborra." In *Escenarios compartidos: cine y teatro en España en el umbral del siglo XXI*, edited by Verena Berger and Mercè Saumell, 60–74. Berlin: Lit.

Bernecker, Walther, and Sören Brinkmann. 2004. "La difícil identidad de España. Historia y política en el cambio de milenio." *Iberoamericana* 4.15: 85–102.

Bezio, Kristen, and Kimberly Yost, eds. 2018. *Leadership, Popular Culture and Social Change*. Northampton: Edward Elgar Publishing.

Bleiberg, Germán, Maureen Ihrie, and Janet Pérez. 1993. *Dictionary of the Literature of the Iberian Peninsula*. Westport, CT: Greenwood Publishing Group.

Borau, José. 2003. *La pintura en el cine, el cine en la pintura: discursos de ingreso en las RR. AA. de bellas artes de San Luis y de San Fernando, con los de contestación correspondientes*. Madrid: Ocho y Media.

Bouchard, Gérard. 2013. "National Myths: An Overview." In *National Myths: Constructed Pasts, Contested Presents*, edited by Gérard Bouchard, 276–297. London: Routledge.

Boyd, Carolyn. 1997. *Historia Patria: Politics, History, and National Identity in Spain, 1875–1975*. Princeton: Princeton University Press.

Breden, Simon. 2018. "La presencia de Lope de Vega en *El Ministerio del tiempo.*" *Anuario Lope de Vega. Texto, literatura, cultura* 24: 75–93.

Brenneis, Sara, and Gina Herrmann. 2020. *Spain, the Second World War, and the Holocaust: History and Representation*. Toronto: University of Toronto Press.

Brombert, Victor. 2001. *In Praise of Antiheroes: Figures and Themes in Modern European Literature (1830–1980)*. Chicago: University of Chicago Press.

Brownlee, Shannon. 2018. "Fidelity, Medium Specificity, (In)Determinancy." In *The Routledge Companion to Adaptation*, edited by Dennis Cutchins, Katja Krebs, and Eckart Voigts, 157–168. London: Routledge.

Bruner, Michael. 2005. *Strategies of Remembrance: The Rhetorical Dimensions of National Identity Construction*. Columbia: University of South Carolina Press.

Burnett, Mark, and Adrian Streete, eds. 2011. *Filming and Performing Renaissance History*. London: Palgrave Macmillan.

Bustamonte, Enrique. 2013. *Historia de la radio y la televisión en España: una asignatura pendiente de la democracia*. Barcelona: Gedisa.

Calderón, Ylán. 2017. *La transición española*. Madrid: Akal.

Caldevilla Domínguez, David, Vallés Gonzálvez, and Lorenzo Cabezuelo. 2012. *La imagen del franquismo a través de la séptima arte: Cine, Franco y posguerra*. Madrid: Visión Libros.

Cameron, Keith. 1999. *National Identity*. Exeter: Intellect Books.

Cañadas, Iván. 2005. *Public Theater in Golden Age Madrid and Tudor-Stuart London: Class, Gender, and Festive Community*. Aldershot: Ashgate Publishing Company.

Caparrós, Martín. "Los restos de Franco." *The New York Times en español*, August 31, 2018.

Caparrós Lera, José María. 1983. *El cine español bajo el régimen de Franco (1936–1975)*. Barcelona: Universidad de Barcelona.

Caparrós Lera, José María. 1992. *El cine español de la democracia: de la muerte de Franco al "cambio" socialista (1975–1989)*. Barcelona: Anthropos.

Carmona, Alba. 2017. "Ausencias y presencias: la recepción de Lope y Shakespeare a través del cine." *Anuario Lope de Vega: texto, literatura, cultura* 23: 286–317.

Carmona, Alba. 2019. *Las reescrituras fílmicas de la comedia nueva: un siglo en la gran pantalla*. Bern: Peter Lang.

Carreño, Antonio, ed. 1979. *El romancero lírico de Lope de Vega*. Madrid: Gredos.

"Carta a la Junta de Censura y Apreciación de Películas de la Dirección General de Cultura Popular y Espectáculos, Subdirección General de Cinematografía." Box No. 36/05098, Case File No. 64782, Folder 11.

Cavielles Llamas, Iván. 2012. "Oviedo Express: adaptación, diálogo intertextual y reescritura de *La Regenta*." In *Teoría y práctica de la adaptación fílmica*, edited by Barbara Zecchi, 99–117. Madrid: Universidad Complutense.

Cayuela, Anne. 1993. "La prosa de ficción entre 1625 y 1634: Balance de diez años sin licencias para imprimir novelas en los Reinos de Castilla." *Mélanges de la Casa de Velázquez* 29.2: 51–76.

Cazorla Sánchez, Antonio. 2014. *Franco: The Biography of the Myth*. London: Routledge.

Cervantes, Miguel de. 1615. *Ocho comedias y ocho entremeses nuevos, nunca representados*. Madrid: Imprenta de Alonso Martínez.

Charney, Maurice. 2005. *Comedy: A Geographic and Historical Guide*. Westport: Praeger.

*Cine para leer*. 2006. Madrid: Ministerio de Cultura – Instituto de la Cinematografía y de las Artes Audiovisuales.

Claramonte, Andrés de. (c. 1623) 2010. *La estrella de Sevilla*, edited by Alfredo Rodríguez López-Vázquez. Madrid: Cátedra.

Cofiño, Juan. "El Valle de los Caídos y la exhumación de los restos de Franco." *La Nueva España*, August 25, 2018.

Coira, Pepe. 2005. *Antonio Roman: un cineasta de la posguerra*. Madrid: Universidad Complutense.

"Coliseum: 'Fuenteovejuna'." *Arriba*, November 20, 1947. Archivo General de la Administración, Box No. 36/04688, Case File No. 07414, Folder 3.

"Coloquio sobre *El perro del hortelano*." *Versión Española, RTVE*, uploaded July 10, 2014. http://www.rtve.es/alacarta/videos/version-espanola/coloquio-sobre-perro-del-hortelano/2653741/.

"Con Lope y su 'Dama boba' vuelve el teatro de TVE." *Diario16*, September 26, 1980: 31.

Coromina, Irene. 2001. "Sancho IV: el pecado hecho hombre en *La Estrella de Sevilla*." *Bulletin Hispanique* 103.1: 281–306.

Corral, Enrique del. "Crítica de la semana." *ABC*, October 26, 1975: 126.

Corrigan, Timothy. 2017. "Defining Adaptation." In *The Oxford Handbook of Adaptation Studies*, edited by Thomas Leitch, 23–35. Oxford: Oxford University Press.

Coscolla Sanz, Vicente. 2005. *Viaje a través de Marruecos*. Valencia: Carena.

Cruz, José Ignacio. 2012. *Prietas las filas: las falanges juveniles de Franco*. Valencia: Universitat de València.

Cuenca, Luis Alberto de. 2005. "Prólogo." In *Visiones del Quijote desde la crisis española de fin de siglo*, edited by Jesús García Sánchez, 1–22. Madrid: Visor, 2005.

Cutchins, Dennis. 2017. "Bakhtin, Intertextuality, and Adaptation." In *The Oxford Handbook of Adaptation Studies*, edited by Thomas Leitch, 71–86. Oxford: Oxford University Press.

D'Antuono, Nancy. 1970. "The Spanish Golden Age Theater." In *Mantillas in Muscovy: The Spanish Golden Age Theater in Tsarist Russia, 1672–1917*, edited by Jack Weiner, 240–245. Lawrence: University of Kansas Press.

Demattè, Claudia. 2003. "Mélanges et littérature mêlée: De *La Dorotea* de Lope de Vega (1632) au *Para todos* de Juan Pérez de Montalbán (1632)." In *Ouvrages miscellanées e théories de la connaissance à la Renaissance: Actes de journées d'études organisées par l'École nationale des chartes*, edited by Dominique de Courcelles, 185–195. Paris: École de chartes.

Díaz, Lorenzo. 1999. *Informe sobre la televisión en España*. Barcelona: Grupo Zeta.

Díaz-Plaja, Fernando. 1972. *La Epaña franquista en sus documentos*. Barcelona: Plaza & Janes.

Diego, Patricia, Elvira Canós, and Eduardo Rodríguez Merchán. 2018. "Los programas de ficción de producción propia: los inicios y el desarrollo hasta 1975." In *Una televisión con dos cadenas: La programación en España (1956–1990)*, edited by Julio Montero Díaz, 71–98. Madrid: Cátedra.

Diego González, Álvaro. 2015. "La prensa y la dictadura franquista. De la censura al 'Parlamento de papel'." *Repositorio Institucional Universidad de Málaga* (May): 1–22.

Dixon, Victor. 2008. "Translating the Polymetric *Comedia* for Performance (With Special Reference to Lope de Vega's Sonnets)." In *The Comedia in English: Translation and Performance*, edited by Susan Paun de García and Donald R. Larson, 54–66. Woodbridge: Tamesis.

Dixon, Victor. 2009. "Lope Félix de Vega Carpio." In *The Cambridge History of Spanish Literature*, edited by David Gies, 251–264. Cambridge: Cambridge University Press.

Duggin, Susan, and Jason Pudsey. 2006. *Feminist Alliances*, edited by Lynda Burns. Amsterdam: Rodopi.

Duplá Ansuategui, Antonio, and Goñi A. Iriarte. 1990. *El cine y el mundo antiguo*. Bilbao: Servicio editorial de la Universidad del País Vasco.

"El caballero de Olmedo." Directed by Cayetano Luca de Tena, *Estudio 1*, Radiotelevisión Española, October 29, 1968. Archivo Digital RTVE.

"El mejor alcalde, el rey." Directed by Gustavo Pérez Puig, *Estudio 1*, Radiotelevisión Española, May 28, 1970. Archivo Digital RTVE.

*El ministerio del tiempo*. Created by Javier Olivares and Pablo Olivares, Cliffhanger Productions, 2015. RTVE. www.rtve.es/television/ministerio-del-tiempo/.

"El perro del hortelano." Directed by Cayetano Luca de Tena, *Estudio 1*, Radiotelevisión Española, May 7, 1981. Archivo Digital RTVE.

"El perro del hortelano." Directed by Pedro Amalio López, *Estudio 1*, Radiotelevisión Española, February 2, 1966. Archivo Digital RTVE.

"*El perro del hortelano* de Lope de Vega." *ABC*, May 8, 1981: 117.

"El primer desnudo de Cristina Marsillach." *Interviú* 8.365 (May 11–17, 1983): 72.

"El teatro en celuloide: 'Estudio 1.'" *ABC*, January 9, 1981: 77.

"El villano en su rincón." Directed by Juan Guerrero Zamora, *Estudio 1*, Radiotelevisión Española, March 5, 1970. Archivo Digital RTVE.

Emmerson, Richard. 2011. *Key Figures in Medieval Europe: An Encyclopedia*. London: Routledge.

Encarnación, Omar Guillermo. 2008. *Spanish Politics: Democracy After Dictatorship*. Cambridge: Polity.

Entrambasaguas, Joaquín de. 1935. *Un Amor de Lope de Vega desconocido: La "Marfisa" de La Dorotea*. Murcia: Universidad de Murcia.

Entrambasaguas, Joaquín de. 1969. "Los estudios de Menéndez y Pelayo sobre el teatro de Lope de Vega." *Revista de la Universidad de Madrid* XVIII.69: 102–180.

Epstein, William. 2016. "Introduction." In *Invented Lives: The Biopic and American National Identity*, edited by William Epstein and R. Barton Palmer, 1–24. New York: SUNY Press.

España Arjona, Manuel. 2018. "¿Una transposición encubierta o la funcionalidad urgente de un texto cervantino? Los elementos encubiertos de El celoso extremeño de Miguel de Cervantes en la serie televisiva Las pícaras." *eHumanista* 38: 673–688. https://www.ehumanista.ucsb.edu/volumes/38.

"Este no es Lope." *ABC*, February 6, 1966: 94.

"Estreno de *Fuenteovejuna* en el nuevo teatro." *La voz de España*, January 20, 1948. Archivo General de la Administración. Box No. 36/05098, Case File No. 64782, Folder 11.

"Estudio 1 vuelve con Aitana Sánchez-Gijón y Fran Perea." *RTVE.ES*, March 15, 2010. http://www.rtve.es/television/20100315/estudio-1-vuelve-aitana-sanchez -gijon-fran-perea/323762.shtml.

Falmagne, Rachel, and Marjorie Hass. 2002. *Representing Reason: Feminist Theory and Formal Logic*. Lanham: Rowman & Littlefield.

Fernández, Esther. 2012. "El periplo artístico de la escenificación de un clásico: *La moza de cántaro* de Lope de Vega." *Bulletin of the Comediantes* 64.2: 171–194.

Fernández, Esther. 2018. "Lope de Vega en televisión." *Anuario de Lope de Vega* 24: 10–37.

Fernández, Luis Miguel. 2014. *Escritores y televisión durante el Franquismo (1956–1975)*. Salamanca: Universidad de Salamanca.

Fernández Labayen, Miguel. 2007. "La casa de los Martínez." In *Las cosas que hemos visto: 50 años y más de TVE*, edited by Manuel Palacio, 98–115. Madrid: RTVE, 2007.

Feros, Antonio. 2017. *Speaking of Spain: The Evolution of Race and Nation in the Hispanic World*. Cambridge: Harvard University Press.

"Finaliza el rodaje de *Lope enamorado*, TVmovie de RTVE." *Prensa RTVE Online*. http://www.rtve.es/rtve/20180629/finaliza-rodaje-lope-enamorado-tvmovie-rtve -jesus-olmedo-sara-rivero/1757714.shtml.

Font, Domenich. 1976. *Del azul al verde: El cine español durante el franquismo*. Barcelona: Avance.

Foulché-Delbosc, Raymond. 1920. "*La Estrella de Sevilla* edition critique." *Revue Hispanique* 18: 496–677.

Franssen, Paul. 2016. *Shakespeare's Literary Lives: The Author as Character in Fiction and Film*. Cambridge: Cambridge University Press.

Fucilla, Joseph. 1959. "Lope's *Viuda Valenciana* and Its Bandellian Source, *Superbi colli et altri saggi*." *Bulletin of the Comediantes* 10.1: 3–6.

"Fuenteovejuna." Directed by Juan Guerrero Zamora, *El teatro*, Radiotelevisión Española, February 3, 1975. Archivo Digital RTVE.

"Fuenteovejuna." Directed by Roberto Carpio, *Teatro de Siempre*, Radiotelevisión Española, September 29, 1967. Archivo Digital RTVE.

"Fuenteovejuna." *Fotogramas* 3, December 15, 1946. Archivo General de la Administración, Box No. 36/04688, Case File No. 07414, Folder 3.

Fusi, Juan Pablo. 1999. *Un siglo de España. La cultura*. Madrid: Marcial Pons.

Gala, Antonio. 2000. *Paisaje con figuras*. Madrid: Espasa-Calpe.

Galán, Diego. "'*El perro del hortelano*' de Pilar Miró." *El País*, March 26, 2004: n.p. https://elpais.com/diario/2004/03/26/cine/1080255611_850215.html.

Galdo González, Danae. 2020. "La representación de Calderón en la televisión pública española en sus sesenta años de historia (1956–2016)." In *Calderón más allá de España: Traslados y transferencias culturales*, edited by Hanno Ehrlicher and Christian Grünnagel, 77–98. Kassel: Reichenberger.

Gallo, Isabel. "'Estudio 1,' otra vez a escena." *El País*, March 16, 2010: n.p. https:// elpais.com/diario/2010/03/16/radiotv/1268694003_850215.html.

García Delgado, José Luis. 2000. *Franquismo: el juicio de la historia*. Madrid: Alcaná.

García Fitz, Francisco, and João Gouveia Monteiro. 2018. *War in the Iberian Peninsula, 700–1600*. London: Routledge.

García Lorenzo, Luciano. 2000. "Puesta en escena y recepción de *Fuenteovejuna* (1940–1999)." In *Atti del Congresso Internazionale su Lope de Vega*, edited by Gaetano Chiappini, 85–105. Florence: Alinea.

García-Martín, Elena. 2017. *Rural Revisions of Golden Age Drama: Performance of History, Production of Space*. Lewisburg: Bucknell University Press.

García Mascarell, Purificació. 2014. *El Siglo de Oro español en la escena pública contemporánea. La Compañía Nacional de Teatro Clásico (1986–2011)*. Unedited Dissertation. Valencia: Universidad de Valencia.

García Posada, Miguel. "Un perro muy particular." *El País*, February 6, 1997: n.p. https://elpais.com/diario/1997/02/06/cultura/855183606_850215.html.

García Santo-Tomás, Enrique. 2000a. "Diana, Lope, Pilar Miró: horizontes y resistencias de clausura en '*El perro del hortelano*.'" In *Atti del Congresso Internazionale su Lope de Vega*, edited by Gaetano Chiappini, 51–61. Florence: Alinea.

García Santo-Tomás, Enrique. 2000b. *La creación del "Fénix": recepción crítica y formación canónica del teatro de Lope de Vega*. Madrid: Biblioteca Románica Hispánica.

García Velasco, José Luis. "Informe provincial sobre *Fuenteovejuna* (1947)" Archivo General de la Administración, Box No. 36/04688, Case File No. 07414, Folder 3.

Garrido Ardila, Juan Antonio. 2015. "A Concise Introduction to the History of the Spanish Novel." In *A History of the Spanish Novel*, edited by J. A. Garrido Ardila, 1–55. Oxford: Oxford University Press, 2015.

Gasparetti, Antonio. 1939. *Las "novellas" de Matteo Maria Bandello como fuentes del teatro de Lope de Vega*. Salamanca: Cervantes.

Gil, Rafael, dir. *El mejor alcalde, el rey*. 1974; Madrid (RTVE, 2005). DVD.

Gil Gascón, Fátima. 2018. "El cine en la televisión de la época de Franco." In *Una televisión con dos cadenas: La programación en España (1956–1990)*, edited by Julio Montero Díaz, 116–140. Madrid: Cátedra.

Gómez, Agustín and Nekane Parejo. 2020. "Cuatro adaptaciones españolas de *El alcalde de Zalamea* al lenguaje cinematográfico." In *Calderón más allá de España: Traslados y transferencias culturales*, edited by Hanno Ehrlicher and Christian Grünnagel, 177–202. Kassel: Reichenberger.

Gómez Crespo, Paloma. 2004. *Movimientos de población: migraciones y acción humanitaria*. Barcelona: Icaria.

Gómez Tello, José Luis. 1943. "El cine." *Primer plano* 141 (June 27): 3.

González Álvarez, José Luis. "Carta al Director General de Cinematografía y Teatro, 25 de febrero de 1953." Archivo General de la Administración, Box No. 36/04688, Case File No. 07414, Folder 3.

González-Marcos, Máximo. 1982. "El antiabsolutismo de *La Estrella de Sevilla.*" *Hispanófila* 2: 1–24.

González Mas, Ezequiel. 1989. *Historia de la literatura española: 3.* San Juan: Ediciones de la Torre.

Gose, Michael. 2006. *Getting Reel: A Social Science Perspective on Film.* New York: Cambria Press.

Greeley, Robin. 2006. *Surrealism and the Spanish Civil War.* New Haven, CT: Yale University Press.

Green, Martin, and John Swan. 1993. *The Triumph of Pierrot: The commedia dell'arte and the Modern Imagination.* University Park: Pennsylvania State University Press.

Grudzińska, Grażyna. 2009. *Transición en retrospectiva: los casos de Polonia y España.* Warsaw: Instituto de Estudios Ibéricos e Iberoamericanos de la Universidad de Varsovia.

Gubern, Román. 1981. *La censura: función política y ordenamiento jurídico bajo el franquismo (1936–1975).* Barcelona: Península.

Guereña, Jean-Louis. 2003. *La prostitución en la España contemporánea.* Madrid: Marcial Pons.

Guillory, John. 2013. *Cultural Capital: The Problem of Literary Canon Formation.* Chicago: University of Chicago Press.

Guneratne, Anthony. 2008. *Shakespeare, Film Studies, and the Visual Cultures of Modernity.* New York: Palgrave Macmillan.

Herranz Martín, Manuel. 2013. *La recepción de El Quijote en la España franquista (1940–1970): literatura y pensamiento.* Unedited Dissertation, Universidad Autónoma de Madrid.

Herrero García, Miguel. 1943. *Contribución de la literatura a la historia del arte.* Madrid: CSIC.

Hicham, Mulay. 2015. *Diario de un príncipe desterrado: viaje al reverso de Marruecos, el "reino ejemplar".* Barcelona: Península.

Higginbotham, Virginia. 1988. *Spanish Film Under Franco.* Austin: University of Texas Press.

Huerga, Manuel, dir. 2016. *Cervantes contra Lope, Radiotelevisión Española.* Archivo Digital RTVE.

"Iborra presenta en Málaga su versión del clásico de Lope de Vega *La dama boba.*" *El País,* March 13, 2006. https://elpais.com/cultura/2006/03/23/actualidad/1143068405_850215.html.

Illán Illán, Antonio. "Peribáñez de Lope/Vasco en el teatro de Rojas." *ABC Toledo,* October 31, 2021: n.p. https://www.abc.es/espana/castilla-la-mancha/toledo/abci-antonio-illan-illan-peribanez-lopevasco-teatro-rojas-202110311401_noticia.html.

"Informes emitidos sobre el visionado de *Fuenteovejuna* (1947) por el departamento de censura." Archivo General de la Administración, Box No. 36/04688, Case File No. 07414, Folder 3.

"Informes emitidos sobre el visionado de *Fuenteovejuna* (1972) por el departamento de censura." Archivo General de la Administración, Box No. 36/05098, Case File No. 64782, Folder 11.

Ingram, Kevin. 2011. *The Conversos and Moriscos in Late Medieval Spain and Beyond*. Leiden: Brill.

Isasi Angulo, Amando Carlos. 1973. "Carácter conservador del teatro de Lope de Vega." *Nueva Revista de Filología Hispánica* 22.2: 265–279.

Iser, Wolfgang. 1993. *Prospecting: From Reader Response to Literary Anthropology*. Baltimore: Johns Hopkins University Press.

J. M. B. 1983. "Seis pícaras, seis." *TeleRadio* 1319 (April 8–14): 26.

Jameson, Fredric. (1991) 2019. *Postmodernism: Or, the Cultural Logic of Late Capitalism*. London: Verso.

Jammes, Robert. 1987. *La obra poética de don Luis de Góngora y Argote*. Madrid: Castalia.

Jellenik, Glenn. 2017. "On the Origins of Adaptations, as Such: The Birth of a Simple Abstraction." In *The Oxford Handbook of Adaptation Studies*, edited by Thomas Leitch, 36–52. Oxford: Oxford University Press.

Johnson, Harvey. 1945. "A Recent French Adaptation of *La Estrella de Sevilla*." *The Romanic Review* 36: 222–234.

Jurado Marín, Lucas. 2014. *Identidad: represión hacia los homosexuales en el franquismo*. Málaga: La Calle.

Kennedy, Ruth Lee. 1993. "*La Estrella de Sevilla* as a Mirror of the Courtly Scene – And of Its Anonymous Dramatist (Luis Vélez???)." *Bulletin of the Comediantes* 45: 103–143.

Kercher, Dona. 2015. *Latin Hitchcock: How Almodóvar, Amenábar, de la Iglesia, del Toro and Campanella Became Notorious*. New York: Columbia University Press.

Kerr, Lindsay G. 2017. *Luis de Góngora and Lope de Vega: Masters of Parody*. Woodbridge: Boydell & Brewer.

Kohler, Eugène. 1939. "Lope et Bandello." In *Hommage a Ernest Martinenche*, edited by Kenneth Muir, 116–142. Paris: Editions d'Artrey.

"La autocrítica sobre 'la Transición' es una asignatura pendiente." Cartas a la directora. *El País*, August 27, 2018. https://elpais.com/elpais/2018/08/27/opinion/.

"La dama boba." *ABC*, March 20, 1969: 67.

"La dama boba." *ABC*, March 30, 1969: 77.

"La dama boba." Directed by Alberto González Vergel, *Estudio 1*, Radiotelevisión Española, March 25, 1969. Archivo Digital RTVE.

*La dama boba*. 2006. Directed by Manuel Iborra. Madrid: Flamenco Films. DVD.

"La discreta enamorada." Directed by Cayetano Luca de Tena, *Estudio 1*, Radiotelevisión Española, July 20, 1980. RTVE, Archivo Digital RTVE.

"La Estrella de Sevilla." *Primer Plano*, March 11, 1950: 15–21.

"La leyenda del caballero de Olmedo." Directed by Jesús Fernández Santos, *Cuentos y leyendas*, Radiotelevisión Española, October 17, 1975.

"La moza del cántaro." *Estudio 1*, Radiotelevisión Española, January 9, 1981. RTVE, Archivo Digital RTVE.

*La moza de cántaro*. Directed by Florián Rey, Atenea, Chamartín Producciones y Distribuciones, 1954. Archivo Digital de la Filmoteca Española.

"La moza de cántaro en el Gran Vía." 1954. *¡Hola!* 495 (February 25): n.p.

"La musa y el fénix." *ABC*, September 4, 1935: 15.

"La nueva programación de los telediarios." 1976. *Revista española de la opinión pública* 46: 420–428.

"La viuda valenciana." *Estudio 1*, Radiotelevisión Española. April 28, 1975. RTVE. Archivo Digital RTVE.

Lacalle, Charo. 2018. "Memoria histórica y democrácia: La ficción en el periodo socialista." In *Una televisión con dos cadenas: la programación en España (1956–1990)*, edited by Julio Montero Díaz, 611–635. Madrid: Cátedra.

"Las pícaras: Los clásicos españoles en la pequeña pantalla." *La Nueva España*, April 8, 1983. 42.

Llompart, Gabriel. 1965. "Lope de Vega, belenista: una entrañable devoción del 'Fénix de los Ingenios.'" *La Vanguardia*, December 25, 1965: 47.

Llopis, Bienvenido. 2009. *La censura franquista en el cine de papel: Un apasionante recorrido por los carteles, fotos, postales y programas de mano, prohibidos en la España de franco*. Granada: Cacitel.

*Lope*. 2010. Directed by Andrucha Waddington. Madrid: Antenta 3 Films. DVD.

López, Francisca, Elena Cueto Asín, and David George. 2009. *Historias de la pequeña pantalla: Representaciones históricas en la televisión de la España democrática*. Madrid: Iberoamericana.

López Bueno, Begoña. 2011. *El poeta soledad: Góngora 1609–1615*. Zaragoza: Universidad de Zaragoza.

López López, Yolanda. 2017. *El Siglo de Oro en el cine y la ficción televisiva: Dirección artística, referentes culturales y reconstrucción histórica*. Madrid: Asociación Cultural y Científica Iberoamericana.

Lupton, Deborah. 1998. *The Emotional Self: A Sociocultural Exploration*. London: Sage.

M. A. 1983. "La viuda valenciana de Lope de Vega." *TeleRadio* 1321 (April 22–28): 27.

Macdonald, Dwight. 1953. "A Theory of Mass Culture." *Diogenis* 1.3: 1–17.

Maeztu, Ramiro de. 1903. "Ante las fiestas del *Quijote*." *Alma española* 1.6: 2–4.

Maeztu, Ramiro de. (1934) 2017. *Defensa de la hispanidad*. Madrid: Ediciones Rialp.

Magill, Frank N., Christina J. Moose, and Alison Aves. 1999. *Dictionary of World Biography: 4*. London: Fitzroy Dearborne.

Manso Menéndez, León. "Informe Provincial." Archivo General de la Administración, Box No. 36/03472, Case File No. 13807, Folder 1.

Marquina, Rafael. "¿Qué orientación debe darse a la producción cinematográfica nacional?" *La pantalla*, April 14, 1929: n.p.

Marsh, Steven. 2005. *Spanish Popular Film Under Franco: Comedy and the Weakening of the State*. Basingstoke: Palgrave Macmillan.

Martín Jiménez, Virginia. 2018. "Programación y estrategias de programación en la Transición." In *Una televisión con dos cadenas: La programación en España (1956–1990)*, edited by Julio Montero Díaz, 319–334. Madrid: Cátedra.

Martín-Márquez, Susan. 2008. *Disorientations: Spanish Colonialism in Africa and the Performance of Identity*. New Haven: Yale University Press.

Martínez, Luis. "Bertolucci, Pilar Miró y Emma Suárez, en 'Lo+Plus'." *El País*, September 19, 1996: n.p.

Martínez-Carazo, Cristina. 2012. "Cine, literatura y política." In *Teoría y práctica de la adaptación fílmica*, edited by Barbara Zecchi, 137–161. Madrid: Universidad Complutense.

Mata Moncho Aguirre. 2000. *Las adaptaciones de obras del teatro español en el cine y el influjo de éste en los dramaturgos*. Unedited Dissertation. Alicante: Universidad de Alicante.

McKendrick, Melveena. 1974. *Woman and Society in the Spanish Drama of the Golden Age: A Study of the Mujer Varonil*. Cambridge: Cambridge University Press.

Menéndez y Pelayo, Marcelino. (1909) 2017. *Historia de las ideas estéticas en España*. Madrid: Forgotten Books.

Menéndez y Pelayo, Marcelino. (1921) 1949. *Estudios sobre el teatro de Lope de Vega 11*. Santander: CSIC.

Mesonero Romanos, Ramón de. 1951. *Dramáticos contemporáneos a Lope de Vega*. Madrid: Imprenta de los sucesores de Hernando.

Millé y Jiménez, Juan. 1928. "Lope de Vega en la Armada Invencible." In *Estudios de literatura española*, edited by Juan Millé y Jiménez, 103–149. Madrid: Biblioteca de Humanidades.

Mills, Brett. 2008. *Television Sitcom*. London: British Film Institute.

Mir, Conxita. 2013. *Pobreza, marginación, delincuencia y políticas sociales bajo el franquismo*. Lleida: Universidad de Lleida.

Miró, Pilar, dir. 1996. *El perro del hortelano*. Madrid: Creativos Asociados de Radio y Televisión. DVD.

Molina, Tirso de. (c. 1622) 2016. *La fingida arcadia*, edited by Victoriano Roncero López. Madrid: Instituto de Estudios Tirsianos.

Montero, Julio, and María Antonia Paz. 2014. "Lo barroco en la televisión franquista: tipos y temas; actores y escenarios." *Bulletin of Spanish Studies* 91.5: 773–792.

Montero Díaz, Julio, and Teresa Ojer. 2018. "Los programas de ficción de producción extranjera durante la dictadura." In *Una televisión con dos cadenas: La programación en España (1956–1990)*, edited by Julio Montero Díaz, 99–116. Madrid: Cátedra.

Mora, Miguel. 2001. "Se publica la serie *Alatriste* en edición escolar." *El País*, May 24, 2001: n.p. https://elpais.com/diario/2001/05/24/cultura/990655206_850215.html.

Mora Gaspar, Víctor. 2016. *Al margen de la naturaleza: La persecución de la homosexualidad durante el franquismo: Leyes, terapias y condenas*. Barcelona: Debate.

Moradiellos García, Enrique. 2002. *Francisco Franco: Crónica de un caudillo casi olvidado*. Madrid: Biblioteca Nueva.

Moradiellos García, Enrique. 2018. *Franco: Anatomy of a Dictator*. London: Taurus.

Morán, Gregorio. "Las varias cosas que da un Lope." *La Vanguardia*, October 25, 1997: 21.

Moreno-Caballud, Luis. 2018. *Cultures of Anyone: Studies on Cultural Democratiza-tion in the Spanish Neoliberal Crisis.* Liverpool: Liverpool University Press.

Moreno-Luzón, Javier, and Xosé Núñez Seixas. 2017. *Metaphors of Spain: Rep-resentations of Spanish National Identity in the Twentieth Century.* New York: Berghahn.

Morley, S. Griswold, and Courtney Bruerton. 1936. "How Many *Comedias* did Lope de Vega Write?" *Hispania* 19.2: 217–234.

Morley, S. Griswold, and Courtney Bruerton. 1940. *The Chronology of Lope de Vega's Comedies, With a Discussion of Doubtful Attributions, the Whole Based on a Study of His Strophic Versification.* New York: The Modern Language Associa-tion of America.

Muñoz, Diego. "Entrevista a Pilar Miró, cineasta." *La Vanguardia*, November 26, 1996: 47.

North, Janice, Karl Alvestad, and Elena Woodacre. 2018. *Premodern Rulers and Postmodern Viewers: Gender, Sex, and Power in Popular Culture.* New York: Springer.

Nourry, Philippe. 1986. *Juan Carlos: un rey para los republicanos.* Barcelona: Planeta.

*Novísima recopilación de las leyes de España: dividida en XII libros en que se reforma la recopilación publicada por el Señor Don Felipe II en el año 1567 . . . y se incorporan las pragmáticas, cédulas, decretos, órdenes y resoluciones reales, y otras providencias no recopiladas, y expedidas hasta el de 1804, mandada formar por el Señor Don Carlos IV.* 1992. Madrid: Boletin Oficial del Estado.

Núñez Díaz-Balart, Mirta. 2003. *Mujeres caídas: prostitutas legales y clandestinas en el franquismo.* Madrid: Oberón.

O'Callaghan, Joseph F. 2011. *The Gibraltar Crusade: Castile and the Battle for the Strait.* Philadelphia: University of Pennsylvania Press.

Oleza, Joan. 1999. "La traza y los textos. A propósito del autor de La estrella de Sevilla." In *Asociacion Internacional Siglo de Oro Actas V*, edited by Christoph Strosetzki, 42–68. Madrid: Iberoamericana.

Oleza, Joan. 2003. "El Lope de los últimos años y la materia palatina." *Criticón* 67.1: 603–620.

Orizana, Gabriel. 1940. "La literatura española como medio de formar la juventud de la nueva España." *Atenas* 5.101: 110–111.

Palacio, Manuel. 2008. *Historia de la televisión en España: 3.* Barcelona: Gedisa.

Palacio, Manuel. 2012. *La televisión durante la transición española.* Madrid: Cátedra.

Palmer, R. Barton. 2016. "Spielberg's *Lincoln*: Memorializing Emancipation." In *Invented Lives, Imagined Communities: The Biopic and American National Iden-tity*, edited by William H. Epstein and R. Barton Palmer, 281–300. New York: SUNY Press.

Pando, Juan. 2016. "La dama boba." *Fotogramas* 1949 (March): 128.

Payne, Stanley. 2012. *The Spanish Civil War.* Cambridge: Cambridge University Press.

Payne, Stanley. 2018. *Franco: A Personal and Political Biography.* Madison: Uni-versity of Wisconsin Press.

Pedraza Jiménez, Felipe. 2009. *Lope de Vega: pasiones, obra y fortuna del "monstruo de naturaleza."* Madrid: Edaf.

"Películas en rodaje: 'Fuenteovejuna'." *Primer Plano* 338 (April 6, 1947): 51.

Pemán, José María. 1957. *De doce cualidades de la mujer.* Madrid: Alcor.

Pepin, Paulette. 2016. *María de Molina, Queen and Regent: Life and Rule in Castile-León, 1259–1321.* Lanham: Lexington Books.

Pérez de Montalbán, Juan. 1632. *Para todos: Ejemplos morales, humanos y divinos, en que se tratan diversas ciencias, materias y facultades.* Madrid: Imprenta del Reino, a costa de Alonso Pérez, su padre.

Pérez de Montalbán, Juan. 1636. *Fama posthuma a la vida y muerte del Doctor Frey Lope Felix de Vega Carpio y elogios panegiricos a la inmortalidad de su nombre escritos por los mas esclarecidos ingenios, solicitados por el Doctor Iuan Perez de Montaluan.* Madrid: Imprenta del Reyno.

Pérez Fernández, Julián Jesús. 2019. "De Claramonte a Trigueros o de *La Estrella* a *Sancho Ortiz*." *Lemir* 23: 165–186.

Pérez Galdós, Benito. (1905) 2005. "Una carta sobre el *Quijote*." In *Visiones del Quijote desde la crisis española de fin de siglo*, edited by Jesús García Sánchez, 15–19. Madrid: Visor.

Pérez Gómez, Ángel Antonio. 2010. "Lope." In *Cine para leer.* Madrid: Mensajero.

Pérez Pastor, Cristóbal and Atanasio Tomillo. 1901. *Proceso de Lope de Vega por libelos contra unos cómicos.* Madrid: Impreso a expensas del excelentísimo señor Marqués de Jerez de los Caballeros.

"Peribáñez y el comendador de Ocaña." Directed by Ricardo Lucía, *Teatro de siempre*, Radiotelevisión Española, January 26, 1967. Archivo Digital RTVE.

Politzer, Patricia, and Eugenia Weinstein. 2010. *Mujeres: la sexualidad secreta.* Mexico: Grijalbo.

Pomerance, Murray. 2016. "Empty Words: Houdini and Houdini." In *Invented Lives: The Biopic and American National Identity*, edited by William Epstein and R. Barton Palmer, 25–48. New York: SUNY Press.

Pozo Arenas, Santiago. 1984. *La industria del cine en España: legislación y aspectos económicos (1896–1970).* Barcelona: Universidad de Barcelona.

Preston, Paul. 2012. *Juan Carlos: Steering Spain From Dictatorship to Democracy.* London: Harper.

Profeti, Maria Grazia. 2000. "Otro Lope no ha de haber." In *Atti del convegno internazionale su Lope de Vega, 10–13 Febbraio 1999*, edited by Maria Grazia Profeti, 225–237. Florence: Alinea.

Qualia, Charles B. 1993. "The Date of *Sancho Ortiz de las Roelas*." *Hispanic Review* 1.4: 337–338.

Quiroga, Alejandro. 2014. *Making Spaniards: Primo de Rivera and the Nationalization of the Masses 1923–30.* New York: Palgrave Macmillan.

Rennert, Hugo A. 1968. *The Life of Lope de Vega, 1562–1635.* New York: B. Blom.

Rodríguez Díaz, Antonio, and Alfonso J. Maestre. 2015. *España en su cine: Aprendiendo sociología con peliculas españolas.* Madrid: Dykinson.

Rodríguez Merchán, Eduardo. 2014. "Antecedentes, orígenes y evolución de un programa mítico: *Estudio 1* de TVE." *Estudios sobre el Mensaje Periodístico* 20: 267–279.

Rof Carballo, Juan. 1990. "El problema del seductor en Kierkegaard, Proust y Rilke." In *Entre el silencio y la palabra*, edited by Juan Rof Carballo, 45–53. Madrid: Espasa Calpe.

Román, Antonio, dir. 1947. *Fuenteovejuna*. Madrid: Alhambra Films. Madrid, RTVE, 2002. DVD.

Romero Castillo, José. 2015. *Teatro español. Siglos XVIII–XXI*. Madrid: UNED.

Romero Santos, Rubén. 2014. *La pistola y el corazón: conversaciones con Agustín Díaz Yanes*. Madrid: Tecmerin.

Rozas, Juan Manuel. 1990. *Estudios sobre Lope de Vega*. Madrid: Cátedra.

Rueda Laffond, José Carlos, and María del Mar Chicharro Merayo. 2006. *La televisión en España 1956–2006*. Madrid: Fragua.

Ruiz Cano, Marina, and Anne Laure Feuillastre. 2019. *El teatro de protesta: Estrategias y estéticas contestatarias en España*. Paris: L'Harmattan.

Rull, Enrique. 1968. "Creación y fuentes de *La viuda valenciana* de Lope de Vega." *Segismundo* 7: 25–40.

Ryjik, Veronika. 2011. *Lope de Vega en la invención de España: el drama histórico y la formación de la conciencia nacional*. Woodbridge: Tamesis.

Ryjik, Veronika. 2019. *La bella España: el teatro de Lope de Vega en la Rusia soviética y postsoviética*. Madrid: Iberoamericana.

Samson, Alexander, and Jonathan Thacker, editors. 2008. *A Companion to Lope de Vega*. Woodbridge: Tamesis.

Sánchez Jiménez, Antonio. 2006. *Lope pintado por sí mismo: mito e imagen del autor en la poesía de Lope de Vega Carpio*. Woodbridge: Tamesis.

Sánchez Jiménez, Antonio. 2008. "Lope de Vega y la Armada Invencible: biografía y poses del autor." *Anuario de Lope de Vega* 14: 269–289.

Sánchez Jiménez, Antonio. 2018. *Lope: el verso y la vida*. Madrid: Cátedra.

Sánchez Noriega, José Luis. 2000. "Panorama teórico y ensayo de una tipología." In *De la literatura al cine: Teoría y análisis de la adaptación*, edited by José Luis Sánchez Noriega, 45–77. Barcelona: Paidós.

Sánchez Noriega, José Luis. 2005. "Diez reflexiones o convicciones (que no tesis) sobre la adaptación de textos literarios al cine." In *Cine y literatura: Textos literarios y sus versiones cinematográficas*, edited by Antonio Rey Hazas and Juan de la Cruz Martín, 11–19. Madrid: Asociación de Profesores de Lengua "Francisco de Quevedo.

Schevill, Rudolph. 1941. "Lope de Vega and the Year 1588." *Hispanic Review* 9.1: 65–78.

Scungio, Raymond. 1981. *A Study of Lope de Vega's Use of Italian 'Novelle' as Source Material for His Plays*. Ann Arbor: Michigan University Press.

Sieber, Harry. 1994. "Cloaked History: Power and Politics in *La Estrella de Sevilla*." *Gestos* 9.17: 133–145.

Singer, Armand. 1965. *The Don Juan Theme, Versions and Criticism: A Bibliography*. Morgantown: West Virginia University Press.

Sinova, Justino. 2001. *Todo Franco: franquismo y antifranquismo de la A a la Z*. Barcelona: Plaza & Janés.

Stam, Robert. 2012. "Beyond Fidelity: The Dialogics of Adaptation." In *Film and Literature: An Introduction and Reader*, edited by Timothy Corrigan, 74–88. New York: Routledge.

Street, John. 2013. *Politics and Popular Culture*. New York: John Wiley & Sons.

Taylor, Scott. 2008. *Honor and Violence in Golden Age Spain*. New Haven: Yale University Press.

*TeleRadio* 1321 (April 22–28, 1983): 28.

Thacker, Jonathan. 2002. "El duque de Viseo and *La Estrella de Sevilla*." In *Role-Play and the World as Stage in the Comedia*, edited by Jonathan Thacker, 152–176. Liverpool: Liverpool University Press.

Thacker, Jonathan. 2010. "Lope, the Comedian." In *A Companion to Lope de Vega*, edited by Alexander Samson and Jonathan Thacker, 159–171. Woodbridge: Tamesis.

Thacker, Jonathan. 2017. "The *Arte nuevo de hacer comedias* by Lope de Vega." *Bulletin of the Comediantes* 69.1: 163–166.

*The Bible*. 1998. Authorized King James Version. Oxford: Oxford University Press.

Thomas, Henry, trans. 1923. *The Star of Seville*. Oxford: Clarendon Press.

Tong, Rosemarie. 2018. *Feminist Thought: A More Comprehensive Introduction*. Abingdon: Routledge.

Torres, Augusto M. 2004. *Directores españoles malditos*. Madrid: Huerga y Fierro.

Torres, Rosana. "Éxito de la Compañía Nacional de Teatro Clásico en Almagro." *El País*, September 13, 1987: n.p. https://elpais.com/diario/1987/09/13/cultura /558482405_850215.html.

Torres, Rosana. "Pilar Miró: 'Lope se adelanta a su tiempo en los personajes femeninos.'" *El País*, May 3, 1997: n.p. https://elpais.com/diario/1997/05/03/cultura /862610407_850215.html.

Treceño, Jaime. "Esperanza Aguirre: 'La Ley de Memoria Histórica es fratricida y debería de haberla derogado el PP.'" *El Mundo*, July 27, 2016. https://www .elmundo.es/madrid/2016/07/27/5798d995e2704e92298b45ae.html.

Trueba, David. "Aquí es distinto." *El País*, November 30, 2021: n.p. https://elpais .com/opinion/2021-11-30/aqui-es-distinto.html.

Tusell, Javier. 1999. *Historia de España en el siglo XX: 4*. Madrid: Taurus.

"TVE recupera el mítico 'Estudio 1' con 'La viuda valenciana.'" *FórmulaTV*, March 12, 2010: n.p. https://www.formulatv.com/noticias/14432/tve-recupera-el-mitico -estudio-1-con-la-viuda-valenciana/.

"Un *Estudio 1* totalmente español." *ABC*, September 28, 1980: 108.

"Un pícaro subido." *El País*, April 28, 1983: 66.

"Una serie española de telefilmes: *La familia Colón*." 1966. *Teleradio* 472 (January): 11–16.

Valencia-García, Louie Dean. 2018. *Antiauthoritarian Youth Culture in Francoist Spain: Clashing With Fascism*. New York: Bloomsbury.

Valls, Fernando. 1983. *La enseñanza de la literatura en el franquismo (1936–1951)*. Barcelona: Clarasó.

Vega Carpio, Félix Lope de. (c. 1595–1599) 2001. *La viuda valenciana*, edited by Teresa Ferrer Valls. Madrid: Castalia.

Vega Carpio, Félix Lope de. (c. 1599–1603) 1958. "Los milagros del desprecio." In *Obras escogidas*, edited by Federico Sainz de Robles. Madrid: Aguilar.

Vega Carpio, Félix Lope de. (c. 1605–1608) 2006. *Peribáñez y el comendador de Ocaña*, edited by Juan María Marín. Madrid: Cátedra.

Vega Carpio, Félix Lope de. (c. 1606) 2006. *La discreta enamorada*, edited by Francisco Romero. Alicante: Biblioteca Virtual Miguel de Cervantes.

Vega Carpio, Félix Lope de. (1609) 2016. *Arte nuevo de hacer comedias*, edited by Felipe Pedraza Jiménez. Cuenca: Universidad de Castilla-La Mancha.

Vega Carpio, Félix Lope de. (1611) 1970. *El villano en su rincón*, edited by Alonso Zamora Vicente. Madrid: Espasa-Calpe.

Vega Carpio, Félix Lope de. (c. 1612–1614) 1993. *Fuenteovejuna*, edited by Juan María Marín. Madrid: Cátedra.

Vega Carpio, Félix Lope de. (c. 1613) 1998. *El perro del hortelano*, edited by Mauro Armiño. Madrid: Cátedra.

Vega Carpio, Félix Lope de. (1613) 2004. *La dama boba*, edited by Diego Marín. Madrid: Cátedra.

Vega Carpio, Félix Lope de. (c. 1615–1626) 1993. *El caballero de Olmedo*, edited by Francisco Rico. Madrid: Cátedra.

Vega Carpio, Félix Lope de. (c. 1618) 1990. *La moza de cántaro*, edited by José María Díez Borque. Madrid: Espasa-Calpe.

Vega Carpio, Félix Lope de. (c. 1620–1623) 2001. *El mejor alcalde, el rey*, edited by José María Díez Borque. Madrid: Castalia.

Vega Carpio, Félix Lope de. (c. 1634) 2014. *El castigo sin venganza*, edited by Antonio Carreño. Madrid: Cátedra.

Vega Carpio, Félix Lope de. 1990. *Epistolario de Lope de Vega*. Madrid: Tipología de Archivos.

Verdugo, Richard R., and Andrew Milne. 2016. *National Identity: Theory and Research*. Charlotte: Information Age Publishing.

Vicent, Manuel. "Franco todavía." *El País*, November 7, 2021: n.p. https://elpais.com /opinion/2021-11-07/franco-todavia.html.

Vidler, Laura. 2014. *Performance Reconstruction and Spanish Golden Age Drama: Reviving and Revising the Comedia*. New York: Palgrave MacMillian.

Viestenz, William. 2014. *By the Grace of God: Francoist Spain and the Sacred Roots of Political Imagination*. Toronto: University of Toronto Press.

Vila San-Juan, P. "Un poeta viejo, modernísimo." *La Vanguardia*, October 17, 1964: 11.

Villar y Romero, José María. "Monarquía Popular." *ABC Sevilla*, July 5, 1967: 3.

Walton, Timothy R. 2015. *Spanish Treasure Fleets*. Sarasota: Pineapple Press.

Wheeler, Duncan. 2008. "A Modern Day *Fénix*: Lope de Vega's Cinematic Revivals." In *A Companion to Lope de Vega*, edited by Alexander Samson and Jonathan Thacker, 285–299. Woodbridge: Tamesis.

Wheeler, Duncan. 2012. *Golden Age Drama in Contemporary Spain*. Cardiff: University of Wales Press.

Wheeler, Duncan. 2020. *La puesta en escena del teatro áureo: ayer, hoy y mañana*, translated by Mar Diestro-Dópido. Kassel: Reichenberger.

Wickersham Crawford, James Pyle. 1930. "An Early Nineteenth-Century English Version of *La Estrella de Sevilla*." In *Estudios eruditos in memoriam Adolfo Bonilla y San Martín*, 495–505. Madrid: Viuda e Hijos de Jaime Ratés.

Wollstonecraft, Mary. 1891. *A Vindication of the Rights of Women: With Strictures on Political and Moral Subjects*. London: Paternoster.

"Y mañana, 'Las Pícaras.'" *Marca*, April 7, 1983: 2.

Zecchi, Barbara, and Jacqueline Cruz. 2004. "Maternidad y violación: dos caras del control sobre el cuerpo femenino." In *La mujer en la España actual: ¿evolución o involución?*, edited by Jacqueline Cruz and Barbara Zecchi. Barcelona: Icaria.

Ziomek, Henryk. 2014. *History of Spanish Golden Age Drama*. Lexington: University of Kentucky Press.

Zurdo, David, and Ángel Gutiérrez. 2005. *La vida secreta de Franco: el rostro oculto del dictador*. Madrid: Edaf.

# Index

# About the Author

**Philip Allen** is an assistant professor of Spanish at Midwestern State University in Texas, where he provides all levels of instruction of Spanish language and literatures. His current line of research centers around modern adaptations of Golden Age dramas on film and television. In addition to his work on adaptations, he has also published the most recent critical edition of *La más constante mujer* by Juan Pérez de Montalbán.